Praise for *Janesville*

"Moving and magnificently well-researched . . . *Janesville* joins a growing family of books about the evisceration of the working class in the United States. What sets it apart is the sophistication of its storytelling and analysis."
—*The New York Times*

"Goldstein is a gifted storyteller, and *Janesville* is a raw, beautiful story, one that sheds needed light on a country searching for some pathway to the future."
—J.D. Vance, author of *Hillbilly Elegy*

"Anyone tempted to generalize about the American working class ought to meet the people in *Janesville*. The reporting behind this book is extraordinary and the story—a stark, heartbreaking reminder that political ideologies have real consequences—is told with rare sympathy and insight."
—Tracy Kidder, Pulitzer Prize–winning author of *The Soul of a New Machine*

"*Janesville* is haunting in part because it's a success story. . . . One is awed by the dignity and levelheadedness of its protagonists, who seem to represent the best of America. . . . Goldstein is a talented storyteller, and we root for her characters as, moment by moment, they try their hardest."
—*The New Yorker*

"Brilliant, probing, and disturbing. A gripping story of psychological defeat and resilience."
—Bob Woodward, *The Washington Post*

"A superb feat of reportage, *Janesville* combines a heart-rending account of the implications of the closing on GM workers and their families with a sobering analysis of the response of the public and private sectors. The book is a must-read for anyone who wants to understand the economy of the Rust Belt—and its implications for America's once-proud middle class."
—*The Philadelphia Inquirer*

"We've been hearing a lot since the November '16 election about the press missing The Story of a middle class losing ground, hope, and heart. But it turns out that Amy Goldstein, one of our finest reporters, was on it all along. Her vivid portrait of a quintessential American town in distress affirms Eudora Welty's claim that 'one place understood helps us understand all places better.'"

—Diane McWhorter, Pulitzer Prize–winning
author of *Carry Me Home*

"Energetically reported and sympathetically narrated . . . The story of ordinary people, how they cope or don't cope with a largely, though not entirely, unexpected economic disaster."

—*The Wall Street Journal*

"Goldstein gives the reader a gripping account of the GM layoff, the real loss it caused and the victims' heroic resilience in adapting to that loss. By the end of this moving book, I wanted her to write a sequel on what might have been done to prevent the damage in the first place."

—*The Washington Post*

"Reflecting on the state of the white working class, J.D. Vance's *Hillbilly Elegy* focuses on cultural decay and the individual, whereas Amy Goldstein's *Janesville* emphasizes economic collapse and the community. To understand how we have gotten to America's current malaise, both are essential reading."

—Robert D. Putnam, *New York Times* bestselling
author of *Bowling Alone* and *Our Kids*

"Goldstein provides a welcome addition to the conversation on the broken social contract. Janesville is a town like countless others, and this book offers a useful cautionary tale for public officials, sociologists, economists, and engaged citizens alike."

—*The Boston Globe*

"*Janesville* is as relevant to the moment as a breaking news bulletin. It should be required reading for anyone who wants to understand how the

Great Recession and deindustrialization have disrupted social, economic and political life in the American heartland. If you want to know why 2016 happened, read this book."

—E.J. Dionne Jr., *New York Times* bestselling
author of *Why the Right Went Wrong*

"Fair-minded and empathetic . . . While it highlights many moments of resilience and acts of compassion, Amy Goldstein's *Janesville: An American Story* also has a tragic feel. It depicts the noble striving of men and women against overpowering forces—in this case, economic ones."

—*Milwaukee Journal Sentinel*

"Based on three years of probing interviews, Pulitzer Prize–winning *Washington Post* journalist Goldstein makes her literary debut with an engrossing investigation. . . . A simultaneously enlightening and disturbing look at working-class lives in America's heartland."

—*Kirkus Reviews* (starred review)

"Amy Goldstein was in the right place at the right time to help us understand why we no longer 'just get along.' Having immersed herself in Paul Ryan's idyllic hometown after its GM plant closed forever, she illuminates disrupted lives, marriages, and childhoods as the manufacturing and strong unions that built our modern middle class fade—fracturing the community and breeding the political polarization that helped give rise to Donald Trump."

—Sheldon Danziger, president of the Russell Sage
Foundation and coauthor of *America Unequal*

"[Goldstein] shatters a lot of conventional wisdom."

—*Minneapolis Star Tribune*

"Goldstein's exhaustive, evenhanded study of the plight of America's working class through the lens of one emblematic community is deeply humane and deeply disturbing, timely and essential."

—*Library Journal* (starred review)

Janesville

★ An American Story ★

Amy Goldstein

Simon & Schuster Paperbacks

New York   London   Toronto   Sydney   New Delhi

*For Cynthia and Robert Goldstein, who taught
me to love—and look up—words and have never
stopped trying to improve their community*

Simon & Schuster Paperbacks
An Imprint of Simon & Schuster, Inc.
1230 Avenue of the Americas
New York, NY 10020

First Simon & Schuster paperback edition January 2018

SIMON & SCHUSTER PAPERBACKS and colophon are registered trademarks of Simon &
Schuster, Inc.

For information about special discounts for bulk purchases, please contact Simon & Schuster
Special Sales at 1-866-506-1949 or business@simonandschuster.com.

The Simon & Schuster Speakers Bureau can bring authors to your live event. For more
information, or to book an event, contact the Simon & Schuster Speakers Bureau at
1-866-248-3049 or visit our website at www.simonspeakers.com.

Interior design by Ruth Lee-Mui

Printed and bound by CPI Group (UK) Ltd, Croydon, CR0 4YY

10 9 8 7 6 5 4 3 2

Library of Congress Cataloging-in-Publication Data is available.

ISBN 978-1-5011-0223-3
ISBN 978-1-5011-9975-2 (pbk)
ISBN 978-1-5011-0228-8 (ebook)

Contents

Part Two

★ 2009 ★

Part Three

★ 2010 ★

Part Four

* 2011 *

Part Five

* 2012 *

Part Six
* 2013 *

51. Night Drive   266
52. The Ebb and Flow of Work   272
53. Project 16:49   275
54. Glass More than Half Full   277
55. Graduation Weekend   284
    Epilogue   291

    Acknowledgments   299
    Appendix 1—Explanation and Results of the Survey
        of Rock County   303
    Appendix 2—Explanation and Results of the Job-Retraining
        Analysis   311
    Notes and Sources   317
    Index   343

Cast of Characters

The Autoworkers and Their Families

Kristi Beyer – 13-year worker at Lear Corp., a factory that makes seats for General Motors

The Vaughns
Mike – 18-year worker at Lear Corp.; shop chairman for United Auto Workers Local 95
Barb – 15-year worker at Lear Corp.
Dave – General Motors retiree after 35 years at the Janesville Assembly Plant; vice president of UAW Local 95

The Whiteakers
Jerad – 13-year worker at the assembly plant
Tammy – part-time data-entry worker for Home Entry Services
The twins, **Alyssa and Kayzia**
The younger brother, **Noah**

The Wopats

Marv – General Motors retiree after 40 years at the assembly plant; former UAW-GM Employee Assistance Program representative; member of the Rock County Board of Supervisors

Matt – 13-year worker at the assembly plant

Darcy – part-time worker setting up Hallmark displays

The girls, **Brittany, Brooke, and Bria**

The Other Workers

Linda Korban – 44-year worker at the Parker Pen Company

Sue Olmsted – 19-year worker at SSI Technologies, manufacturer of automotive and industrial components

The Politicians

Tim Cullen – former and future Democratic state senator; co-chair of the GM Retention Task Force

Paul Ryan – Republican member of the U.S. House of Representatives, 1st Congressional District of Wisconsin

The Educators

Ann Forbeck – social worker; homeless student liaison for the Janesville School District

Sharon Kennedy – vice president of learning at Blackhawk Technical College

Deri Wahlert – social studies teacher at Parker High School; creator of the Parker Closet

The Business Leaders

Diane Hendricks – chairman of ABC Supply Co., Inc., in Beloit; co-chair of Rock County 5.0 economic development initiative

Mary Willmer – community president of M&I Bank; co-chair of Rock County 5.0

The Community Leaders

Bob Borremans – executive director of the Southwest Wisconsin Workforce Development Board; runs the Rock County Job Center

Stan Milam – former *Janesville Gazette* reporter; host of *The Stan Milam Show* on WCLO 1230 AM radio

Prologue

At 7:07 a.m., the last Tahoe reaches the end of the assembly line. Outside it is still dark, 15 degrees with 33 inches of snow—nearly a December record—piled up and drifting as a stinging wind sweeps across the acres of parking lots.

Inside the Janesville Assembly Plant, the lights are blazing, and the crowd is thick. Workers who are about to walk out of the plant into uncertain futures stand alongside pensioned retirees who have walked back in, their chests tight with incredulity and nostalgia. All these GM'ers have followed the Tahoe as it snakes down the line. They are cheering, hugging, weeping.

The final Tahoe is a beauty. It is a black LTZ, fully loaded with heated seats, aluminum wheels, a nine-speaker Bose audio system, and a sticker price of $57,745 if it were going to be for sale in this economy in which almost no one anymore wants to buy a fancy General Motors SUV.

Five men, including one in a Santa hat, stand in front of the shiny black SUV holding a wide banner, its white spaces crammed with workers' signatures. "Last Vehicle off the Janesville Assembly Line," the banner says, with the date, December 23, 2008. It is destined for the county historical society.

Television crews from as far away as the Netherlands and Japan have come to film this moment, when the oldest plant of the nation's largest automaker turns out its last.

So the closing of the assembly plant, two days before Christmas, is well recorded.

This is the story of what happens next.

★

Janesville, Wisconsin, lies three fourths of the way from Chicago to Madison along Interstate 90's path across America from coast to coast. It is a county seat of 63,000, built along a bend in the Rock River. And at a spot on the banks where the river narrows sits the assembly plant.

General Motors started turning out Chevrolets in Janesville on Valentine's Day of 1923. For eight and a half decades, this factory, like a mighty wizard, ordered the city's rhythms. The radio station synchronized its news broadcasts to the shift change. Grocery prices went up along with GM raises. People timed their trips across town to the daily movements of freight trains hauling in parts and hauling away finished cars, trucks, and SUVs. By the time the plant closed, the United States was in a crushing financial crisis that left a nation strewn with discarded jobs and deteriorated wages. Still, Janesville's people believed that their future would be like their past, that they could shape their own destiny. They had reason for this faith.

Long before General Motors arrived, Janesville was an industrious little city, surrounded by the productive farmland of southern Wisconsin. It was named for a settler, Henry Janes, and its manufacturing history began early. A few years before the Civil War, the Rock River Iron Works was making agricultural implements in a complex of buildings along South Franklin Street. By 1870, a local business directory listed fifteen Janesville carriage manufacturers. Along the river, a textile industry thrived—wool, then cotton. By 1880, 250 workers, most of them young women, were weaving cloth in the Janesville Cotton Mills.

As the twentieth century opened, Janesville was a city of about thirteen thousand—descendants of the original settlers from the East Coast and immigrants over the decades from Ireland, Germany, and Norway. Downtown, Franklin and River Streets were lined with factories. Milwaukee and Main Streets were crowded with shops, offices, and, at one point, a saloon for every 250 residents. Stores stayed open on Saturday nights for farm families to come into town once their week's work was done. The bridge that carried Milwaukee Street over the river was still wooden, but electrified streetcars running north and south from downtown had replaced the old horse-drawn trolley service. Janesville was a railroad hub. Each day, sixty-four passenger trains, plus freight trains, pulled in and out of town. Raw materials arrived for factories, politicians for whistle-stop tours, and vaudeville stars for performances at the Myers Grand Opera House.

In Janesville's long history of making things, two figures stand out. They are homegrown captains of industry, obscure to most Americans but legend to every Janesville schoolkid. They shaped the city's identity along with its economy.

The first was a young telegraphy instructor in town named George S. Parker. In the 1880s, he patented a better fountain pen and formed the Parker Pen Company. Soon, Parker Pen expanded into international markets. Its pens showed up at world leaders' treaty signings, at World's Fairs. Parker Pen imbued the city with an outsized reputation and reach. It put Janesville on the map.

The second was another savvy businessman, Joseph A. Craig, who made General Motors pay attention to Janesville's talent. Near the close of World War I, he maneuvered to bring GM to town, at first to make tractors. Over the years, the assembly plant grew to 4.8 million square feet, the playing area of ten football fields. It had more than seven thousand workers in its heyday and led to thousands of jobs at nearby companies that supplied parts. If Parker Pen put Janesville on the map, GM kept it there. It proved that Janesville could surmount adversity under trying circumstances, seemingly immune to the blows of history. During the Great Depression, it closed—and reopened a year later. During a sitdown strike, a seminal event in U.S. labor history, while autoworkers rioted elsewhere, peace held in Janesville. During World War II, the plant

turned out artillery shells as part of the home front before postwar production resumed, greater than ever. Even as the auto industry's fortunes
in the 1970s started to fade, dooming other plants, Janesville's assembly
line moved on and on.

So when the assembly plant stopped on a frozen December morning of 2008, how could people in town have known that this time would
be different? Nothing in their past had prepared them to recognize that
another comeback would not save them now.

The work that vanished—as many as nine thousand people lost their
jobs in and near this county seat in 2008 and 2009—was among 8.8 million jobs washed away in the United States by what came to be known as
the Great Recession. This was, of course, not the first moment at which
some American communities have hemorrhaged jobs in their defining
industries. The textile mills of Lowell, Massachusetts, began to shut down
or move to the South as early as World War I. Youngstown, Ohio's, Black
Monday of 1977 began to erase an eventual fifty thousand jobs in steel
and related industries. But this mighty recession—the worst economic
time since the 1930s—stole American jobs, not in a single industry, not in
a cluster of ill-fated communities, but up and down the economic ladder,
from the East Coast to the West, in places that had never been part of the
Rust Belt or any other bad economic belt and had never imagined that
they would be so bruised. Places like Janesville.

★

Today, the assembly plant is padlocked behind a chain-link perimeter.
Over the portico of the Art Deco main entrance, its logo is visible still.
The logo is the outline of three gears, a different design in each one. In
the right gear, the GM symbol. In the left, the crest of the United Auto
Workers. Between them, a white field shaped like Wisconsin, with a
candy pink heart near the bottom where Janesville sits. And in black letters across the top: JANESVILLE PEOPLE WORKING TOGETHER. The logo
is starting to rust.

Inside, the plant is dark. Its innards—lathes to welders to five-ton
hoists, all the equipment that a dead auto factory no longer needs—have

been picked over and auctioned off. Outside, the parking lots' concrete acres are empty except for a security guard's lone sedan. Against the sky, smokestacks seem to go on forever, spewing nothing at all.

Out back, nature has reclaimed an expanse where the rows of gleaming SUVs used to be parked before they were shipped away—fields now, with saplings sprouting up. At the back entrance, a small sign is perched atop a guard's gate, missing a few letters: T FOR HE MEMORIES.

Without its assembly plant, Janesville goes on, its surface looking uncannily intact for a place that has been through an economic earthquake. Keeping up appearances, trying to hide the ways that pain is seeping in, is one thing that happens when good jobs go away and middle-class people tumble out of the middle class. Along Racine Street, the route from the Interstate to the center of town, little American flags flutter from every street lamp. Main Street, with its nineteenth-century buildings of red and Milwaukee cream brick, retains its architectural grace. That some of its storefronts are vacant is nothing new; the mall began pulling business away from downtown in the 1970s. A recent Heart of the City Outdoor Art Campaign has splashed large pastel murals on the sides of downtown buildings, each mural commemorating one of Janesville's first decades, from its founding in 1836. The mural on the back of City Hall, illustrating the coming of the railroad through town in the 1850s, has a steam locomotive and a spike-driving man, and, lettered across the bottom, "History. Vision. Grit."

So Janesville goes on, yet it is altered. The change can be glimpsed from the many "For Sale" signs that appeared along residential streets, from the payday loan franchises that opened along the Milton Avenue commercial drag running north from downtown, from the enlarged space now occupied by the Salvation Army Family Center.

And the citizens of Janesville? They set out to reinvent their town and themselves. Over a few years, it became evident that no one outside—not the Democrats nor the Republicans, not the bureaucrats in Madison or in Washington, not the fading unions nor the struggling corporations—had the key to create the middle class anew. The people of Janesville do not give up. And not just the autoworkers. From the leading banker to the social worker devoted to sheltering homeless kids, people take risks for one another, their affection for their town keeping them here.

It is hard. The deserted assembly plant embodies their dilemma: How do you forge a future—how do you even comprehend that you need to let go of the past—when the carcass of a 4.8-million-square-foot cathedral of industry still sits in silence on the river's edge?

Still, people cling to Janesville's can-do spirit. A month before the assembly plant closed, its managers and its United Auto Workers local announced together that the last Tahoe would be donated to the United Way of North Rock County and raffled off for charity. So many tickets, at $20 apiece or six for $100, were sold, so many of them to laid-off workers who didn't have a clue where their next paycheck would come from, that the raffle raised $200,460, pushing the United Way's annual campaign above its goal in the depths of the recession.

The winning ticket went to a GM retiree who had worked at the plant for thirty-seven years and has so cherished the Tahoe that it seldom leaves his garage.

Part One

★ 2008 ★

★ 1 ★

A Ringing Phone

P aul Ryan was standing in his kitchen when the cell phone clipped to his belt began to ring. If the phone were ringing on a different weeknight, Paul would have been in Washington, working late and, likely as not, sleeping on a cot in his office in the marbled Longworth House Office Building across from the U.S. Capitol. But this was a Monday night, and he was not due back in Washington until the next afternoon.

It has been just months shy of a decade since Paul, then all of twenty-eight, was first elected to Congress and began this split existence, shuttling the eight hundred miles between Janesville and Capitol Hill. Throughout this decade, he has clung to the singular comfort of coming home. By this particular Monday, June 2, 2008, he has been home for more than the usual weekend. A dozen days ago, he issued a plan with the august title "A Roadmap for America's Future," a new peak in his climb to become the Republican Party's foremost budget wonk. Then came nearly two weeks' recess over Memorial Day to decompress with Janna and the kids—which is why, on this night of the call, Paul was in the kitchen of their home on Courthouse Hill. It is a stately redbrick house—a Georgian Revival that lies within an entire neighborhood on the National Register of Historic Landmarks and is separated by nothing more than a small patch of woods from the backyard of the house where Paul grew up.

The Janesville to which Paul comes home is recognizable to him as the place where he never bothered to lock his bike as a kid. Where he was elected junior class president and, as a perk, was "Rhett," the king of the "Gone with the Wind"–themed prom. Where, when he stops at the hardware store, he runs into guys who were the boys with whom he played varsity soccer, or their brothers or sisters or parents or kids.

The continuity in the Janesville portion of his life is so pervasive, so ingrained that it has left him ill-equipped to grasp the enormity of the change that a ringing cell phone can bring.

When he unclips the phone from his belt and answers the call, Paul is startled to hear that the voice on the other end belongs to Rick Wagoner, General Motors' chairman and chief executive. Paul may have faith in free markets, but with GM the largest employer in his hometown, as well as the entire 1st Congressional District of Wisconsin, he has made a point of nurturing relationships with the company's top brass. When Rick is in D.C., Paul meets him for breakfast. Nearly every week, he talks with Troy Clarke, president of GM North America. So he certainly is not oblivious to the facts that GM has been faltering since before the recession, gasoline prices just past $4 a gallon are on the brink of an all-time high, and the Janesville Assembly Plant is churning out full-size, gas-guzzling SUVs whose popularity has fallen off a cliff.

Paul is aware of these facts, and yet, lately, as General Motors' fortunes have been falling and falling, his private conversations with Rick and the rest of the brass have yielded no whiff of concern that the assembly plant's future is in peril.

So it is hard for him to absorb what Rick is telling him: Tomorrow, General Motors will announce that it is stopping production in Janesville.

For an instant, Paul is stunned.

Then, suddenly, he is furious. Straight out his kitchen windows, he can see the houses of a couple both working at GM, of a family living on wages from the seat-making factory that is the assembly plant's largest supplier with hundreds of jobs that will surely vanish if the plant goes down.

"You know you'll destroy this town if you do this," Paul yells into his phone. "These are the best workers you've got, and this town has been loyal to you. Why don't you shut down a plant in a big city where it won't have that much of a devastating impact?"

And yet, even as these words, so contrary to his usual genial persona, surge from Paul, another sensation is rushing up alongside his anger: confidence that he can change the CEO's mind. It's simple, he realizes. If the public no longer wants to buy the gas-guzzling SUVs that Janesville is producing, then GM must give the plant's workers another, more popular kind of vehicle to make.

The congressman starts rattling off GM models. "Give us Cavaliers," he tells Rick. "Give us pickups."

After he hangs up, Paul calls his congressional chief of staff—a Janesville guy, like him. First thing in the morning, Paul tells him, they will need to start working the phones to coordinate a response.

Paul has a sleepless night. Lying awake, he thinks about the GM payroll, about the economic shock. He thinks about the guys he grew up with who work down at the plant, or whose parents are still down at the plant. A gut punch.

Still, he is solid in the belief that, by pulling together—no Republicans, no Democrats, just a community fighting for its future—the city will prevail with General Motors.

'Cause we've never had a plant shut down, Paul tells himself. It's Janesville!

*

"Breaking news!" The voice coming over WCLO 1230 AM talk radio is crackling with adrenaline. It is just before 5:30 a.m., and Stan Milam, veteran Janesville journalist and now host of a midday radio show, has been up all night. Yesterday, Stan had sensed the rumors getting thicker, that something big was going to happen when General Motors convened its annual shareholders meeting this morning in Delaware. And if it took staying up all night to break the biggest story of his life, he was going to stay up all night. Hour after hour, he peered at his computer screen in his cramped study until he spotted a teaser about a wire story coming soon that General Motors was closing four North American plants, Janesville among them. He woke up a GM public relations guy and weaseled out of him that a press conference is scheduled for this morning. Stan wasn't going to wait around for any press conference. He raced to the radio station, whizzed by the general manager, ran into the control room, and yelled to the startled board operator, "Give me the mike."

★

First shift begins at 5:48 a.m., after the news bulletin is already out. But talk radio isn't popular that early in the day, so the GM'ers don't seem to have heard by the time they file into the assembly plant. And so the morning begins like any other for Jerad Whiteaker.

By this morning, Jerad has been a GM'er for thirteen years and six days. During this time, he has worked all over the plant—the medium-duty truck line while it lasted and, since then, on the SUV. And the truth is, each of the stations he has worked along the assembly line has bored him. Yet no other jobs in town match $28 an hour, and most of the years, until SUV sales slowed, have come with ten sweet hours a week of time-and-a-half overtime. His father and his father-in-law hated their thirty years at the plant before they retired on good GM pensions, so, as he approaches his own middle age, Jerad figures that, if they could stick it out, he can, too. At least, working first shift, he is home for dinner with Tammy and their three kids. Family is everything.

Jerad clocks in. He is about to head to his spot on the fuel line in final assembly when a strange thing happens. He is handed a flyer, as all 1,250 first-shift workers are being handed, saying that, at 6:30 a.m., the assembly line will be halted, and everyone is to report to the plant's second floor. So, after barely a half hour of injecting gas and oil and transmission fluid into almost finished SUVs, Jerad stops. He becomes part of a mass of workers going up the staircases. In an open area on the second floor, where the truck cab line used to be, an executive from Detroit, Bill Boggs, is standing on a stage with a couple of grim-looking leaders from United Auto Workers Local 95.

Boggs's announcement is terse. The news doesn't take long to deliver.

The Janesville Assembly Plant will cease production by 2010. It has two more years, if that. General Motors will not give Janesville a new product to build.

That is it. Boggs takes no questions.

A few people around Jerad begin to cry. Most are silent. Somber. They all troop back downstairs. The assembly line starts up again.

As Jerad injects the SUVs with their fluids, his main reaction to this news surprises him. Some around him are talking about being worried, but he is feeling relief. The assembly line has never suited him. Within two years, the assembly line will stop. As a GM'er, unemployment benefits and union layoff pay will nearly equal his wages. They will carry his family through, he expects, until he finds work that he enjoys more. Much as he has disliked this job, he does not doubt that it will protect him after it is gone.

★

Three days to go. This morning is Tuesday, and Thursday will be the last day of her second year teaching social studies at Parker High. Deri Wahlert is dressed for work, sitting on the end of her unmade bed. Rob, a Parker science teacher, is in the bathroom with the door open, shaving. Avery, their nine-month-old, is in her arms, taking his bottle. The television in the bedroom is on, tuned to the NBC affiliate in Madison. And all of a sudden, the TV is saying that a major announcement is coming about General Motors.

"Shit. Oh shit," Deri says.

She knows what this means, and she knows something about jobs that end.

Deri grew up in Fort Atkinson, a half hour north of Janesville, and her father worked as a manager at a nearby Friskies pet food plant. When she was in seventh grade, her father got sick with a virus that settled in his spine and paralyzed him from the waist down, forcing him to retire a couple of years later. Having a father in a wheelchair while she was a teen-ager imprinted on Deri a sensitivity to people who are hurting.

So, by reflex, her thoughts are jolted now to who will be hurting at General Motors. She thinks of Rob's best friend, Brad, an engineer at the assembly plant. Brad is Avery's godfather and has two little girls of his own. What, Deri wonders, is he going to do? And from worrying about Brad, Deri sees a wider question. She and Rob try to remember the latest number they've heard of how many people are working at the assembly plant. Three thousand, they think. What will all these people do?

Deri wants to watch the announcement but turns the TV off. Avery needs to be dropped off at day care. Rob needs to get to school early. By the time Deri walks into Parker, teachers are asking each other if they've heard the news. Deri makes a decision not to discuss the closing today with her social studies students. Too little is known.

But already, Deri can sense that life in Janesville is going to change. She may be an idealist, but she also is clear-eyed. And if some people in town might need to be rescued, she is going to be there for them. She just needs to watch and to figure out how.

★

Bob Borremans is cruising south toward Janesville along Interstate 39, his little runabout boat hitched to the back of his GMC Sonoma. He thought he'd be spending the afternoon on Lake Camelot, skimming across the tranquil water in the runabout, or paddling his raft to a spot where he could tie anchor and float on his back until he drifted asleep. Instead, three days into this annual respite, a call arrived from one of his staffers at the Rock County Job Center, informing him that General Motors' CEO had just announced that the company will close the Janesville Assembly Plant. As the guy in charge of the Southwest Wisconsin Workforce Development Board, based at the Job Center, Bob knows well that the greatest hovering fear has always been massive layoffs at GM. His vacation, he realizes in a heartbeat, is over. It is his obligation to forge the image and reality of responding to this long-feared calamity. This is no time to be floating on a raft on a lake named Camelot.

The Carp Swimming on
Main Street

B ob Borremans pulls into the broad parking lot of the Rock County Job Center and dashes into the warren of offices and cubicles in a former Kmart on Janesville's south side. It is here, from a small office in the center of the abandoned store, that Bob is in charge of dispensing help to the people in a six-county region who could use a job and use a hand in finding one. He runs one among hundreds of workforce development boards spread across the country, each one a conduit for a dedication by the government—engrained in federal law since the 1960s—to giving money and expertise to train Americans in need of work. The dedication includes retraining workers whose jobs go away and aren't coming back.

His role plops Bob at the epicenter of anxieties that are shooting up around town now that the head of General Motors has pronounced the worst-possible fate for the assembly plant. Bob is not a guy prone to panic. After decades of rumors and false alarms, he figures, who knows whether the closing is real? Even if it is, the GM'ers might have two more years of work—plenty of time to be ready for what happens next. No matter. Even if just as a soothing presence, he has no time to waste on getting out ahead of the situation, because, if thousands of jobs at the core of Rock County's economy are going to vanish, this will be a cataclysm dwarfing any challenge he has ever faced.

Bob has been the Job Center's director for five years. For almost a quarter century before, he was an administrator at Blackhawk Technical College, the two-year school that provides most of the job training in town. As a young man, he had been a mild, back-of-the-room kind of guy until the president of the college noticed in him a spark of creativity, promoted him to be a vice president, and helped him find his voice, which over the years grew more and more outspoken. Sometimes even now, months past sixty, his trim beard gone white, Bob thinks that people who knew him when he was young wouldn't recognize the person he has become.

Call it arrogance, call it what you want, Bob sees himself as a fix-it guy—the adult in the room, the one with a doctorate who can take on a project and do it better than anyone else. Bob is, in particular, an ace at a skill most necessary when a plant shuts down—applying for government grants.

Bob is a bureaucrat impatient with the bureaucrats in Madison and Washington who oversee the flow of job-hunting and job-training money that is the workforce agency's lifeblood. Back in his office from his cut-short vacation, Bob immediately starts to set in motion the steps the government says that people in positions such as his are to do in situations such as this. The first step is a protocol prescribed by the U.S. Department of Labor, known as Rapid Response, and Bob soon becomes a skeptic. Part One of Rapid Response calls for workforce agencies to find out in advance that a company is contemplating a big layoff and do whatever it takes to prevent contemplation from becoming eventuality. It's plain to Bob that the idea is flawed, because companies don't reveal that they are about to cut jobs before they go public with their decisions, and, in particular, the assembly plant's personnel director has zero interest in discussing with him any intervention that might keep the plant open. What Rapid Response really means, Bob can see, is Part Two—devising ways to cushion the blow. That is what he begins to do.

The personnel director is, at least, willing to share employee rosters with the Job Center. And Bob knows exactly who else he needs to enlist in this blow-cushioning effort: the president of UAW Local 95, and the state bureaucrats from whom he is hoping to borrow a few caseworkers, since this is turning out to be a most inopportune time for the Job Center recently to have lost some of its staff.

Bob anticipates that the Job Center will need to calm and inform autoworkers whose jobs have just been marked with a bull's-eye. He anticipates that he will be able to bring to town a spigot of government aid for any laid-off worker who wants to go back to school.

He does not anticipate the rains. By Wednesday, June 11, eight days after GM has unleashed the impending economic disaster, the National Weather Service predicts a natural disaster by the weekend: the worst flooding of the Rock River since the government began keeping track. Volunteers and jail inmates fill more than 260,000 sandbags. The sheriff calls in the Wisconsin National Guard.

More than seven inches fall in Wisconsin and Iowa onto land still soaked from a harsh, snowy winter. The waters spill over the downtown river wall. They inundate the entire Mole-Sadler housing development. They submerge lovely Traxler Park, and they turn farms in neighboring counties into shallow lakes. Along Main Street, whose historic brick storefronts back onto the river's banks, the waters fill shops and offices, slicking furniture with mud, soaking law firms' files, triggering mold up to the light switches.

The rains shatter records. At the measuring station closest to Janesville, the Rock River crests on a Saturday, two weeks and four days after General Motors' announcement. The river reaches 13.51 feet—4.5 feet above flood stage—smashing the old record of 13.05 feet set in 1916. It exceeds a hundred-year flood. The county estimates the damage at $42 million.

The damage, to farmland and to the sodden buildings of downtown, knocks people out of work for months. "Closed til God knows when," says a hand-lettered sign taped in the window of a Main Street barber who has been cutting hair in town since the 1950s. The sign has his home number for customers in need of a trim.

The abandoned Kmart that houses the Job Center is on high enough land to stay dry. But because the flood is stealing work, it becomes Bob's problem, too. It may be the most rain to fall on Janesville in a century, but, compared with the elusive matter of how to prevent thousands of jobs from vanishing, this is a challenge that he and his industrious city know how to tackle. Bob pivots away from the scared autoworkers to focus on nailing down an emergency grant for flood-devastated communities. The federal grant will allow the Job Center to create, in an echo of the Great Depression's Works Progress Administration, a brigade to tackle the slow, mucky work of repairs.

Yet a grant for the Job Center can't tame nature. The Rock River rushes so hard and so high that it washes fish off course. Carp are now swimming on Main Street. Near the street's northern end, in the flooded parking lot of the United Way of North Rock County, the carp find a favorite new spawning ground.

Hearing about the misdirected fish, people in town regard it as a spectacle, not a disaster. On the first dry land above the flooded street, despite the damage all around, people of Janesville—and some tourists, too—gather for days, snapping photos and laughing and cheering as the hundreds of yellow carp swim by.

Craig

General Motors did not come to Janesville by happenstance. It was brought to town one day near the end of World War I by the ingenuity of an astute manager of a local tractor manufacturer. A century later, he deserves some of the credit for Janesville's can-do spirit—for its people's optimism that they can map their own fate.

A native of western Pennsylvania, Joseph Albert Craig had moved to Milwaukee as a young man and worked as a salesman for a farm implement manufacturer until he was hired away by the Janesville Machine Company, a rival. The Janesville Machine Company was a maker of plows, cultivators, seeders, and mowers that were sold across the Midwest. In 1897, at the age of thirty, Craig became its general manager. Within a decade, the company was the largest and most prosperous among Janesville's many manufacturing enterprises, occupying a complex that stretched nearly three city blocks along South River and South Franklin Streets.

In 1909, the earliest automobile manufacturer in town began to produce Owen Thomas automobiles in old railroad shops along South Pearl Street. The next year, the Wisconsin Carriage Company formed a motor car offshoot that made the short-lived Wisco. The Monitor Auto Works arrived from Chicago and used the site of old tobacco warehouses to manufacture the city's first trucks for a few years.

Craig, however, was more interested in another recent invention—gas-powered tractors—and, under his guidance, the Janesville Machine Company branched out into making them. The firm flourished. In 1918, months before World War I was over, Craig received an invitation to Detroit from William C. Durant, General Motors' founder and president. Durant had been building GM for the past decade by cobbling together smaller automobile companies. Eager to capitalize on the growing market for mechanized farm machines—Ford Motor Co., had become the first manufacturer of mass-produced tractors the year before—Durant had purchased an ailing California firm, Samson Tractor. Durant was familiar with Craig's reputation as a savvy businessman and, that March day in Detroit, offered him a job as Samson's manager. This was when Craig executed his ingenious maneuver—and changed Janesville's fate. He refused the offer. And, before their meeting ended many hours later, he had turned the tables: Durant agreed to purchase the Janesville Machine Company, merge it with Samson, and build a new factory in Janesville to house General Motors' Samson Tractor Division. Craig would be in charge.

GM turned out its first tractors in Janesville in 1919 and, the next year, built the expansive factory on fifty-four acres the company purchased along the river's banks south of downtown. Within that first year, production swelled from ten tractors per day to 150. Craig persuaded city officials to improve streets, schools, and housing to accommodate a rapidly growing workforce. Durant himself wrote out a $100,000 check to the Janesville Improvement Association and sent it to the city's Chamber of Commerce. "In my entire experience I have never seen in a city of modest size a better spirit or a more commendable accomplishment," Durant wrote in his accompanying letter. "I predict for Janesville a splendid future."

But a farm depression and Durant's overextended finances were ruinous for GM's tractor division and, by the fall of 1921, tractor production in Janesville ceased. Then, in the first of many phoenix-like episodes over the decades, Craig persuaded the company to renovate the young factory to manufacture cars and trucks, with a Chevrolet assembly plant and a Fisher auto body division. The first Chevrolet rolled off the Janesville assembly line on February 14, 1923.

Nine years later, in the depths of the Great Depression, the plant shut down. Nevertheless, when Chicago's "Century of Progress" World's Fair opened the next spring, two hundred laid-off Janesville autoworkers had been chosen by General Motors to operate a demonstration assembly line. "Wonders of science—works of art" was the motto for the exhibit. Each day, the Janesville men were given $7 and a fresh uniform to build Chevrolet Master Eagle four-door sedans beneath a catwalk that could hold one thousand onlookers. "Of all the brilliant spectacles in the drama of modern industry," said a GM brochure for the fair, "none is so fascinating to watch as the making of a motor car."

On December 5, 1933, the Janesville plant reopened, with Wisconsin governor Albert Schmedeman on hand to buy the first truck off the resuscitated assembly line for the state.

Few events typify Janesville's calm, good-natured response to adversity as vividly as its role in one of the most important moments in U.S. labor history: the 1936–37 General Motors Sit-Down Strike. Sit-downs were a new form of strike. Instead of picketing outside factories, as the tradition had been, striking union members had discovered that they could gum up production by installing themselves inside and refusing to budge. The GM sit-down would become the most famous example of this new strike method, stopping work at seven plants in five states and, in the end, yielding a first national contract in which the United Auto Workers gained official recognition as GM workers' union representative.

In Flint, Michigan, the strike lasted forty-four days and sparked a riot one January night when company guards and police unleashed tear gas, clubs, and a few bullets on women trying to deliver dinner to the strikers, who retaliated by training fire hoses and hurling metal car hinges at the police out the plant windows.

In Janesville, by contrast, the sit-down lasted nine hours and fifteen minutes. Janesville had, by then, a city manager form of government, a

Progressive Era reform, and an adept city manager named Henry Traxler. Mere hours after the sit-down began in Janesville on that January 5, Traxler summoned the plant's union leaders to his office and made a proposal: The plant managers would promise not to manufacture any cars in Janesville until the strike was settled nationally; in exchange, workers would leave the plant. At 9 p.m. that night, escorted by the county sheriff and the city's police chief, Traxler accompanied the union leaders back into the plant to present his idea to the 2,700 striking workers, who accepted it by acclamation. At 10:15 p.m., the strikers walked out the plant's main gate and formed a "gay, noisy and cheering aggregation," as one later recalled, parading through the city's business district until almost midnight. And for the next five weeks, as Flint rioted and U.S. labor secretary Frances Perkins personally stepped in to help broker a national agreement, a little committee—the sheriff, two businessmen, and the city manager—inspected the Janesville plant in peace and presented reports to the local UAW leaders that they saw no sign of any cars being made.

The Janesville plant shut down, once again, weeks after the United States entered World War II, as the government forbade the manufacture of civilian cars and trucks. But within eight months it was back in business—this time, filled with women and older men producing artillery shells for the war effort. "Keep 'em firing" was their motto, and 16 million howitzer shells later, the War Department presented the plant with an "Army-Navy Production Award for outstanding accomplishment in the production of war materials" and a lapel pin for every man and woman at the plant to wear "as a symbol of leadership in the drive for victory." In 1945, hundreds of Janesville residents gathered to celebrate the first truck off the assembly line when peacetime production resumed.

The War Department was not alone in recognizing the quality of the work of Janesville's GM'ers over the decades. The plant and the vehicles it made won awards from J. D. Power and Associates, with plant managers sometimes ordering jackets with award sleeve patches for every employee. In 1967, General Motors bestowed on Janesville the honor of building the company's 100 millionth vehicle—a blue Chevrolet Caprice two-door hardtop, made as GM's chairman looked on. The open house that day drew thirty thousand. People ordering GM cars sometimes specified that they wanted theirs to be manufactured in Janesville.

The assembly plant went through scares. In 1986, General Motors transferred Janesville's entire pickup truck line—one of the plant's two assembly lines at the time. All at once, 1,800 jobs migrated to Fort Wayne, Indiana. Workers were told to move or, in all probability, lose their jobs. Their choice. More than 1,200 workers moved. And yet months later, General Motors announced that medium-duty trucks would soon be moving along the assembly line. Janesville was hiring again. Work was plentiful, and the pay was good, with a new union contract that created a four-day workweek with ten hours a day and the possibility of the ten hours of overtime on Fridays.

By that day in 2008 when General Motors handed the assembly plant its death sentence, the rumors that the plant would shut down had been hovering over town so long that they had become a familiar backdrop to life in Janesville—unsettling but so frequent that people stopped believing that it would happen. Just three years before, General Motors—its market share eroded, its finances in disarray—announced that it would cut costs by eliminating thirty thousand jobs. As the company's oldest operating plant, Janesville was especially vulnerable, and the months of waiting for GM to decide where the cuts would be were agonizing. But by Thanksgiving week of 2005, when Rick Wagoner—the very CEO who had now delivered the blow—finally revealed that a dozen North American facilities would be closed or decimated, Janesville was spared.

That day, the front page of the *Janesville Gazette* had a banner headline: "Whew."

A Retirement Party

Marv Wopat is a man with a lot of friends. And on the first Saturday afternoon in July, more than two hundred of them have come out to a pavilion in Schilberg Park that his family has rented to celebrate the rite of passage for which every GM'er longs. Marv has just retired.

By his final day, Marv had put in forty years and four months at the assembly plant. At sixty-one, he is a boisterous, burly man with a shock of white hair—part of an old guard that, if this closing is real, will no longer exist. He has now claimed the good pension that has been almost a General Motors birthright. But all along, he reaped the advantages of being a union man and a company man.

When he was young, through years of hard drinking that came before his sobriety, GM stood by him. It gave him the space to heal. Then it gave him the space to help heal others. For twenty-five of his forty years, until his final day, he stood at the border of the UAW and management as the plant's Employee Assistance Program representative, helping people cope with addictions and other hard-to-handle life circumstances. This made him a fixture at the plant. Plus, three months ago, he was elected to the Rock County Board of Supervisors.

Marv is a Harley rider. He is sentimental. He weeps easily. This afternoon, he is tickled that so many have come to this red-roofed pavilion in the park, an easy walk from his house in Milton, just beyond Janesville's northern edge. Yet truth be told, he is feeling wistful, conscious that he is on the safe side of a crossroads between how life in Janesville has been and something less certain.

Like many in town who are around his age, Marv had been a farm kid. He grew up on a dairy farm in Elroy, Wisconsin, and joined the navy two weeks after graduating from Royall High School, turning down college scholarships he'd been offered as a promising enough football tackle to have been chosen Most Valuable Player in the regional conference. The week between graduating and enlisting, he'd married his cheerleader girlfriend. Vietnam was raging, but he lucked out, driving fire trucks at a Texas airfield. So, when he arrived in Janesville in 1968, he was twenty-one and planning to join the city's fire department until his brother-in-law, a GM'er, urged him to put in an application. In those days, young people were coming to Janesville from the farms and small towns up north. It was where good jobs were. General Motors was eager to hire big, strong farm boys like Marv. He never worked anywhere else.

This afternoon, as his friends munch on brats and barbecue, Marv is moved to give a little speech. He has been blessed, he says, to be at the plant all those years. The best part, he says, was being able to work with people and try to help people. He does not say anything about the plant shutting down. He sidesteps this looming fact even though it is tingeing his afternoon with emotions he never imagined would show up at his retirement party. Emotions that are tipping from wistfulness into guilt. Because the reality is that, while Marv has just claimed his pension, two of his kids, right under the pavilion with him, work at the assembly plant, and they are about to lose their jobs.

*

Who could have seen this coming? Only five months ago, on a bright February morning, Marv had listened to Barack Obama, an Illinois senator with White House dreams, when he arrived at the assembly plant with a familiar message of economic hope, of Janesville's future mirroring its past.

Marv had gotten off second shift at 2:30 a.m. as usual and slept for just over four hours so that he could go back down to the plant early. As he approached the south entrance, a bomb-sniffing dog was at the doorway. Secret Service officers were waving metal-detecting wands. But the plant security guys all knew Marv and just waved him through.

Janesville is a small city, yet big enough that presidents, would-be presidents, and soon-to-be presidents have been coming through town since Abraham Lincoln stopped by during the fall of 1859. For Obama's turn, his campaign had arranged for the assembly plant to be the prop for a major economic speech. Second-shift workers who wanted to attend had been chosen, like so much else at the plant, on the basis of their seniority. Marv simply got a call from a union guy asking whether he wanted to come. He sure did. Marv is a Democrat, and he has been detecting in Obama a concern for the working class.

As Marv was waved through, the candidate already was in a first-floor conference room, huddling with GM managers and officers of UAW Local 95. By pure luck, Marv was standing alone for a moment in a hallway near the entrance when Obama came out the conference room door in a charcoal suit, crisp white shirt, and red print tie, walked right over to him, and started talking.

"How long have you been here?" the candidate asked Marv.

Marv, his wide shoulders filling out a purple UAW hoodie, told him about being about to hit forty years. When the senator asked what he did, Marv explained about being Employee Assistance rep and reached into his hoodie's front pocket for a crumpled, recent article from the *Janesville Gazette* that had featured him among fifty people in Janesville who make a difference. Obama borrowed a pen to sign the newsprint before galloping up a staircase to the second floor.

The candidate stepped over to a podium and began to speak. Wisconsin's Democratic governor, Jim Doyle, sat in the first row with Local 95 leaders and GM executives, nearly six hundred workers on folding chairs and bleachers around them. Attached to the podium was a plaque with the same Janesville Assembly Plant logo that is over the main entrance, with the words arching across the top, "People Working Together."

Work, as it happens, was the theme that Obama had come to town to talk about. The country was two months into a bad recession. Autoworkers were scared. Just the day before, General Motors had announced a $39 billion loss for 2007, the largest loss in the corporation's history, accompanied by an offer of buyouts to all 74,000 of its unionized, hourly workers. Many in the folding chairs and the bleachers were debating whether to take the offer. Marv had made his decision to retire months ago. The auto industry was shrinking, he could see; it was time for him to make room for someone younger.

Shaky though the economy and the auto industry were this morning, Obama was buoyant—fresh off primary victories in seven states and, with the Wisconsin primary next, trying to keep the momentum.

"Prosperity hasn't always come easily," he said. "But through hard times and good, great challenge and great change, the promise of Janesville has been the promise of America—that our prosperity can and must be the tide that lifts every boat; that we rise or fall as one nation; that our economy is strongest when our middle-class grows and opportunity is spread as widely as possible."

Then Obama slowed the cadence. He laid out his agenda "to claim our dream and restore our prosperity." Marv took in the candidate's words: "I believe that, if our government is there to support you and give you the assistance you need to retool and make this transition, that this plant will be here for another hundred years."

The governor and the labor leaders and the GM executives and the hundreds of workers around them were clapping, their applause swelling until it muffled the senator's hopeful words. And as they clapped, the governor and labor leaders and executives and workers, Marv among them with his four decades of plant history and retirement around the corner, were rising to their feet.

★

The morning of the closing announcement, Marv awoke to a call from a friend making sure that he'd heard. As soon as he hung up, Marv phoned his GM'er kids, his son, Matt, and his daughter, Janice, right away. He did not want them to find out from anyone else. He was the one, after all, who had taught them while they were growing up that the assembly plant was the best place for a steady job with good pay. And even though the situation was scary now, no doubt, Marv began in those very first calls to his kids to impart his conviction. Just because the company says it is closing Janesville, no reason to think that the plant won't end up getting a new product instead. Even if the plant shuts down for a while, he figured, it will reopen. It always has.

Now, under the Schilberg pavilion, Marv wants to believe that everything will work out okay. So he does not say out loud a thought burning inside him: Matt and Janice may not have the opportunity to work at the plant long enough to retire.

Change in August

At the end of his shift, Marv Wopat's son, Matt, walks alone to his locker, unlatches it, and reaches for the extra backpack that, as a careful man, a planner, he has brought for this day. It is two months and five days since the plant-closing announcement. To some, a lucky date—8/8/08. Brides and grooms around the globe are marrying so that this will be their anniversary. The Olympics are opening in Beijing. But for Matt, the date has a surreal quality that feels anything but lucky. This day is his last at the assembly plant and, when he walks out into the parking lot in a few minutes, his locker must be empty.

At thirty-seven, Matt remembers growing up with the feeling he was being raised to become an autoworker. He watched his father, Marv, go down to the plant. When Matt was little, his dad worked on the line, but he was barely a teenager when his father began his twenty-five years as Employee Assistance rep, which meant that, for most of Matt's life, his dad had been a person to whom fellow alcoholics and others with various personal troubles confided their secrets. So Matt grew up understanding GM as the best place to get good pay, good benefits, a stable work life, and—if you needed one—a sympathetic ear. As a high school junior in 1986, Matt was frustrated when the plant had a hiring spurt and he was sixteen—two years too young to be hired in. When he turned eighteen, the plant wasn't hiring. So he tried general studies at "U-Rock," a two-year arm of the University of Wisconsin in Rock County. Not finding anything he really wanted to study, he left after a year to become a manager at Fast Forward, a roller rink that his old boss from a high school job had opened in Madison. Four years later, GM still not hiring, he took a job at Lear Seating, the Janesville factory that manufactures seats for the plant.

Even when GM had openings, getting hired was a clubby thing, a matter of who you knew. Applicants needed a referral, and each GM employee was given one referral that could be bestowed upon a relative or a friend. Matt got his referral from his dad, even though his sister also wanted one, and then the plant held a hiring lottery and, on May 17, 1995, Matt finally started working where he'd felt all along that he belonged.

At six feet, Matt is just an inch shorter than his dad. Yet while Marv is broad and exuberant, Matt is slim and reserved. He is a responsible man. Once he married Darcy, four months after he became a GM'er, he adopted her little girl, Brittany. They had two more daughters, Brooke and Bria. His life felt comfortable and complete, and he liked that his General Motors wages made him a good provider.

Hiring dates have always been a big deal at the plant. Everyone carries theirs around in their head. These anniversary dates determine seniority when opportunities inside the plant come up, and they determine when a worker has put in thirty years and so is eligible to retire. This summer, they have had a crucial added significance, determining which half of the workers would lose their jobs when one shift went down, even before the whole plant is to close. Matt's anniversary date—May 17, 1995—put him just on the cusp. If he had been hired a few days earlier, his job would have been spared for now. Of course, hired a few days later, he would have been out of work already. Being on the cusp has allowed him to eke out two extra weeks at $28 an hour, and for this small fact he is grateful.

But Matt is a man of routines, and the two weeks have been topsy-turvy. He always worked second shift, but second shift has just gone away. So for these precious, on-the-cusp weeks, he has gotten up before dawn to go to a fill-in job—quality control on the torque of one hundred critical SUV components—on first shift, the only shift that remains.

Because his extra weeks have been on first shift, it is mid-afternoon when his workday ends and he unlatches his locker. He carefully places into the extra backpack the murder mysteries and old copies of *Gun Dog* magazine that he read on breaks long ago. Matt punches the time clock one last time and—after thirteen years, three months, and twenty-two days—walks the familiar path out of the plant, into the oddity at a shift's end of sunlight on a pleasant, 80-degree day.

He is now a man of routines without any guarantee of what will come next. But Matt has listened to Marv, with his forty years of plant wisdom. And even though his dad is safe, on his pension after his retirement and the shindig in the park a few weeks ago, Matt finds his words hopeful, calming. Matt is not a betting man. Still, he would bet money that it is only a matter of time before the assembly plant roars back to full strength.

★

Jerad Whiteaker's twins, Alyssa and Kayzia, have a way of feeling as if they are one person when they are trying to figure stuff out. They are fraternal twins, with Alyssa blonder and, at five-foot-five, four inches taller than Kayzia, who always thought she should have gotten a jump start by being born five minutes sooner. Though they are not identical twins, the mind meld comes naturally, and it's especially handy now because they have never faced a riddle like the one that's cropped up this summer before eighth grade: All of a sudden, even though they can sleep in a little during these lazy August days, their dad is home for breakfast.

Most of their lives and definitely the last few years, their father, Jerad, has been out of the house before they wake up. At first last month, when they found him at the round table at the end of the kitchen, the two of them discussed it and remembered that every summer the plant has its two-week shutdown. No big deal. But now that the school year is about to begin a week before Labor Day, and he's still showing up at breakfast, they sit and talk over the situation on their twin beds—Alyssa's with its wild, '70s retro green, blue, and purple bedspread, Kayzia's bedspread gray and orange with a surfboard in the middle—in the basement room that they share. They feed each other random words they have overheard their parents say when their parents think that Alyssa and Kayzia and their little brother, Noah, are not listening.

Some words—buyout, SUB pay (for the union's supplemental unemployment benefits)—make no sense. But there is one fully understandable word—*move*—that terrifies them. No way are they going to let that happen. They already had to make new friends in fourth grade, when their parents moved all five of them from Footville—a farming village just nine miles west, but far enough that they had to change schools. Switching to Janesville's schools was the whole reason for the move because they have always done well in their classes, and Footville doesn't have the AP courses that their mom, Tammy, wants them to be able to take when they get to high school. Their mom has always been doing things like that, focusing on their potential. She's been determined to prove that the doctors were wrong when the twins were born six weeks premature, and the doctors told her that her babies were so tiny that they might have trouble learning. It wasn't true, but the prediction has always given their mother extra satisfaction in their intelligence and accomplishments.

Alyssa and Kayzia conclude during their bedroom mind-meld sessions that, if they are going to ask a parent what's going on, it had better not be their dad because, whatever is happening, it must be touchy, and if he wanted them to know, he'd have told them. So they take turns asking their mom little questions. "We're trying to figure this out" is the kind of answer she gives. Not much help.

So it is from the news and from a couple of friends that they piece together that their dad must have had a bad enough anniversary date that he's part of the GM shift that's already been laid off. What they deduce is correct. He was hired on May 29, 1995, handed a referral by his father. Both their dad and mom grew up in the security of GM wages, in the same way that Alyssa and Kayzia and their brother, until this summer, have been doing.

Having solved the home-for-breakfast riddle, Alyssa and Kayzia now worry more than ever that they might be yanked somewhere else, like they were when they left Footville. Pulling on this skein of worry, they realize that Alyssa's biggest specific fear is that she might have to give up the basketball team; Kayzia fears most losing her friends.

As they work together to unravel these specific worries, the most curious thing, they notice, is their dad's mood. As long as they can remember, he has been sulky and quiet sometimes, but now he is cracking his jokes the way they love. If they watch closely, they can see that their mom is more nervous than usual—a little on edge. But their dad loves his extra sleep and, apart from a little work around the yard, is acting like the whole thing is a vacation he deserves.

★

The air is balmy, but August's mugginess lingers as Kristi Beyer arrives a few minutes before 9 a.m. at a low-slung brick building and steps inside. She wanders through a maze of intersecting hallways and finally finds room #2606. She takes a seat in a row of desks about halfway back, and looking around sees that the people are so much younger than her. She hopes she is managing to hide her jitters.

This is the first day of her first class at Blackhawk Technical College. Kristi is thirty-five, a stocky woman with sandy hair in a sensible short cut. She is on a second marriage and has a son old enough to be starting college himself if he hadn't, instead, gone straight from high school into boot camp in the Wisconsin National Guard.

By this morning in the fourth week in August, not quite two months have passed since Kristi lost her job at Lear Corp., the factory just east of the Interstate that since 1990 has been doing just-in-time production. Just-in-time has meant making car seats and delivering them to the assembly plant precisely three hours before they are bolted into GM vehicles. The same day in late June that one shift went down at General Motors, her shift went down at Lear. Now that the fall semester is starting at Blackhawk Tech, only a small trickle of the laid-off factory workers are arriving on campus. Most are Lear refugees like her. Even though they belonged to UAW Local 95, same as the GM'ers, their labor contract did not promise union SUB pay if they were ever laid off, as they have been now, so they don't have the same cushion that would have given them a while to figure out their futures.

Kristi worked on the Lear assembly line for thirteen years. If she was known for anything inside the factory, it was for designing a better version of the bib aprons they had to wear on the job. Her version had ergonomic pockets and a pull-away feature if it ever got caught in machinery. She sold her design to a local company, Lab Safety Supply, which paid her a little fee each time someone bought one of her aprons. Once Lear closed, she decided it was better to take the lump sum Lab Safety offered, because who knew if there would be workers needing aprons like hers anymore? If the apron hinted at an entrepreneurial spirit lurking inside Kristi, it never peeked out again.

Now, beyond the immediate problems that she is unemployed and her husband, Bob, will soon be losing his Lear job, too, her son going into the National Guard is raising her anxieties, because some of its companies these days go to the Middle East. She had Josh when she was sixteen. Been in a hurry your whole life, her mother likes to tease her. Kristi has always had a special bond with her mother, growing up the only girl in her extended family with two older brothers and four boy cousins. The day Kristi learned that her shift at Lear was being laid off, the first call she made was to her mother to say, "We're going down."

Being in a hurry her whole life meant that Kristi wasn't going to sit around watching TV without a job. There was government money to go back to school. Which is why she is now sitting, trying to hide her nervousness, in the first session of "The Criminal Justice System."

Sitting in a middle row near her is a woman, a little taller than her with fine brown hair and big, deep-set eyes, who is definitely not a kid. Barb Vaughn worked on the Lear assembly line, too—for fifteen years, two more than Kristi. They were on different shifts and, with eight hundred workers at the factory, their paths had not crossed.

Barb also became a mother early. A drinking, partying teenager in Whitewater, she dropped out of high school as a sophomore and was pregnant at eighteen. For a while, she was a single mom with three girls and two jobs until she got hired at Lear. With the better pay and benefits, life got easier, and she met a nice guy at the factory, Mike Vaughn, who was divorced. Yet, as life otherwise improved, being a high school dropout stayed a silent, poking shame that she carted around. She'd known Mike more than five years before she told him. Before Lear, during Lear, before telling Mike, after telling him, she kept trying to get a GED, but life always interrupted—little kids, too much work. She felt like a GED failure, too.

So, when it became clear that the closing rumors at Lear were true this time, Barb knew what she needed to do. Mike is still at Lear. He is the leader of UAW Local 95 for the factory, which means he can hang on to his job for now. But Mike hasn't been on the assembly line in years. Her body was tired of factory work. The years at Lear had torn her right rotator cuff and damaged a wrist. Two surgeries were plenty. She promised herself she was done with factory life.

As soon as she could, she signed up for a program to get Wisconsin's high school equivalency diploma. She worked harder at studying than she had at anything in her life, and took tests, and studied some more and took more tests, whipping through the whole thing with speed that shocked even her, until now, at the age of forty-seven, she is finally, *finally* a high school graduate. And with unfamiliar success-momentum pumping inside her, Blackhawk had the surprising appearance of the next logical thing to do.

This morning, Kristi and Barb do not yet know that the other is also trying to conceal her fear. As part of a first, early trickle of autoworkers at Blackhawk who have been recession-smacked out of a job, they do not know that they will need to molt, to shed old factory habits, factory ways of defining themselves, and pick up new ways.

Little in either Kristi's or Barb's pasts make them seem especially likely people among Janesville's out-of-a-job workers to be on this leading edge of personal reinvention. And yet, here they are, sitting in a middle-row desk on this first day of "The Criminal Justice System," with an instructor named Kevin Purcell explaining something called a syllabus and attendance requirements and books to buy. And it seems so alien to Kristi and to Barb, too, on this morning when neither knows yet that she is about to discover a fierce, competitive spirit inside herself and a new best friend.

To the Renaissance Center

A s the end of this recession-wrecked summer nears, Paul Ryan wishes he could be in two places at once. On the second Friday in September, a delegation from Janesville will arrive in Detroit to try to rescue the assembly plant. The same day, General Motors' chief executive will arrive on Capitol Hill to try to rescue the auto industry. Where, Paul must figure out, is it more important for him to be?

The summer, he knows, has been brutal for General Motors. Sales plunging midyear by nearly 20 percent. Stocks plunging to their lowest value in a half century. Gas prices so high that the big SUVs coming off Janesville's assembly line are especially unpopular. CEO Rick Wagoner, who gave Paul the heads-up call three months ago, has been invited to a Senate energy summit as the sole voice of U.S. automakers. Wagoner, however, has a more urgent goal in mind: In a prelude to what will become an auto industry bailout, he wants Congress to free up $25 billion in federal loans to help the industry make fuel-efficient cars. While in Washington, Wagoner has agreed to meet with members of Wisconsin's congressional delegation, who have been leaning on him to keep the assembly plant open. None is as close to Wagoner as Paul.

The timing is terrible, the confab with Wagoner in D.C. coming the day of the plant-rescue mission in Detroit. That mission will require presenting General Motors with a compelling case and great sums of money. It will also, Paul understands, require an all-hands-on-deck display of solidarity. A congressional representative should show up, and a Republican at that, and that means him.

The jobs at stake belong to his constituents, his neighbors. And like almost every family in his hometown, his has a connection to the plant. Paul is fifth-generation Janesville, part of the Ryan clan that makes up one of three sprawling families in town known collectively as the "Irish mafia" because of an outsized role in construction that made many of the Ryans wealthy. Going back to his grandfather, his branch of the family chose the law. Still, his father spent his law school summers on the GM assembly line, losing a tip of a thumb on a piece of machinery in exchange for the wages that covered his tuition and books.

On this Friday morning, Paul leaves Capitol Hill to catch a flight to Detroit.

When he lands, he meets up with Wisconsin's governor, Jim Doyle, and a small posse of civic, union, and business leaders that has come along. The posse includes the two men the governor picked over the summer to lead a GM Retention Task Force for the purpose of trying like hell to save the plant. One is a UAW leader, the other a former Democratic state senator, Tim Cullen. He and Paul have always gotten along because this is, after all, Janesville and not Congress. Moderate and unassuming, Tim had risen to become the Wisconsin Senate's majority leader, then traded politics for two decades as a Blue Cross/Blue Shield executive. He retired not long ago and won a spot on the Janesville school board. Like Paul, Tim has family roots at the assembly plant, in his case reaching back to his grandfather, who had started in the Janesville Machine Company days. His father quit high school for a job at the assembly plant and stayed the rest of his life. When Tim graduated from high school in 1962, GM was hiring workers' sons, so he paid his way through college with the wages of assembly line summers. Unlike most in town, Tim has long wondered about the plant's fate. He was on the Janesville City Council in 1971 when it commissioned a consultant to study how the city could best protect its economic future. The study's core recommendation—to diversify—came as the plant was nearing its all-time peak workforce of 7,100, and few besides Tim saw any reason to take the advice seriously. He sensed that Janesville someday would pay the cost of shortsightedness, though he had not foreseen that he would be plucked out of retirement to try to save his city from a dreadful recession.

This, then, is the plant-rescue team. Republican congressman and Democratic governor. Union leader and business owner. Federal, state, county, and local officials. A united, committed front as they approach downtown Detroit's grand cluster of curtain-wall glass towers that bears such a hopeful name: Renaissance Center.

The rescue team members ascend in a glass elevator with a commanding view of the Detroit River that glides up the side of the thirty-nine-story tower containing General Motors' corporate headquarters. At the top, they step into the marbled reception area of the executive offices and are escorted into a conference room. Troy Clarke is there to greet them. A pleasant-looking man with a trim brown mustache, Clarke joined General Motors as a co-op college student at Pontiac and has never worked anywhere else, rising over thirty-four years to become president of GM's North American operations.

In this conference room, each team member presents, in a tidy mosaic, the case they have rehearsed for why GM should continue production in Janesville. Paul knows Clarke well, speaks to him on a weekly basis. Paul's mosaic piece is a reminder to Clarke that he has fought on Capitol Hill for General Motors' concerns about its pension costs. Tim's pitch is the compelling fact that, at Janesville, the cost of producing each vehicle is lower than at a plant making the same SUVs in Arlington, Texas—a newer plant that no one is talking about closing.

Finally, the governor sums up the case: Wisconsin stands committed to preserving its relationship with General Motors. And, to fortify the seriousness of that commitment, the state and Rock County and Janesville and the local business community are honing a large package of economic incentives to induce GM to stay. General Motors is, everyone in the room knows, planning an inexpensive subcompact car model as a corporate coping mechanism in this awful recession. Wisconsin will, the governor says, make it worthwhile for the company to trust its oldest assembly plant to manufacture its newest little car.

In this room in the Renaissance Center, no one mentions the parallel rescue maneuver that General Motors' chief executive is attempting in Washington. Paul is aware that, as much as he has cultivated a relationship with Clarke, as much power as Clarke now holds over Janesville's fate, Clarke's own future—the future of the corporation in which this executive has spent his entire working life—could be on quicksand, depending on how events play out in Washington for the U.S. automakers in coming months.

At least for now, Clarke's power is intact. He listens respectfully. He says that GM will give careful consideration to Wisconsin's economic incentive package. He does not say that GM's decision to close the plant is final. For the rescue team, this passes for good news.

Tim flies back to Madison in the governor's private turboprop. Paul catches a flight to Milwaukee. As he does every Friday, he climbs into his Chevy Suburban, which he keeps parked at the airport, for the familiar seventy-mile drive home. The rescue team, he thinks, left no stone unturned. It did what it could. And yet he hasn't any idea what will happen.

Mom, What Are You Going to Do?

T he other shoe drops, sudden as the first. On the second Monday in October, an executive from Detroit is back at the assembly plant, and the GM'ers lucky enough to still have their jobs are all called to another meeting eighteen minutes after the start of first shift. The company hasn't yet figured out whether Janesville will get its new small car, but it has made another decision. General Motors is in more desperate shape than it was four months ago, when it gave the plant the 2010 death sentence. That was optimistic. Production will stop in ten weeks. Eighty-five years of turning out Chevrolets—poof! Gone. Two days before Christmas.

News like this ricochets through town, and, over at M&I Bank on Main Street, it takes no time to reach Mary Willmer. Mary is community president of M&I, Janesville's largest bank, and for weeks now she has had the unsettling sensation that, for someone in her position, the news could not be getting any worse. Four Mondays ago, she watched as Lehman Brothers, the storied investment bank, collapsed and filed the biggest bankruptcy case in U.S. history. Last Monday, the stock market crashed. By Friday, the Dow Jones Industrial Average had plunged 18 percent, its sharpest decline in a single week. On Saturday, at a meeting in

Washington a few blocks from the White House, the International Monetary Fund's managing director warned that the fragility of financial institutions of Europe and America had "pushed the global financial system to the brink of systemic meltdown."

Mary knows pretty much everyone in Janesville who matters, and she knows that, for most people in town who do not happen to be bankers, these have seemed like remote events of a distant crisis. Today, the crisis is coming home.

Mary understands the community, understands what this blow means. Closing in on fifty, she has been at M&I for nearly a quarter century, since she was hired into an entry-level position at the branch on the south side of town, right by the plant. Her customers were GM'ers or workers for suppliers. Her brother was at the plant his entire working life, a forklift driver until he was able to retire a couple of years ago. Her sister-in-law is still there.

This sped-up closing is awful, no doubt, but it's not just the GM'ers that Mary is worrying about. With Lehman Brothers and Wall Street falling apart, what about M&I's future? Her bank, headquartered in Milwaukee, is the largest in Wisconsin, not just in Janesville. She knows that M&I is well diversified, less vulnerable than some. Yet she has been thinking lately that it would be a good idea to calculate the actual risk facing the portion of M&I for which she is responsible.

With these twin pressures pounding inside her head all day—the plant, her bank—Mary is exhausted by evening when she gets home to the white Colonial she shares with her husband, an M&I mortgage manager, and their two kids who still live at home. Standing in the kitchen, she glances into the family room. Chelsea, her fifteen-year-old, is in there with some friends. Mary is used to her kids inviting their friends over to hang out in the family room with its cozy fireplace. But not like this. Ten teenagers are sitting on the floor in a big circle, no one saying a word. Some are crying. One of the criers is Chelsea.

Mary walks into the room to say "hi" and quickly picks up that these kids cannot be consoled. The best she can do, she figures, is retreat to the kitchen and get them something to eat.

The kitchen is expansive, with two pantries, hardwood floors, granite countertops, and a view of the patio and pool out back. Though Mary seldom mentions the fact in public, her life has not always been this plush. Her father was a Yugoslavian immigrant who dreamt of a Wisconsin dairy farm and reached his dream, so Mary grew up on a small farm in rural Whitewater. She was ten when her father's cancer showed up and when he died four months later. Afterward, she and her mother lived on a fragment of the farm, poor as dirt for a time. It was during that poor period that they were grocery shopping one day when her mother pulled from her wallet a kind of coupon that Mary had never seen. When she asked what the coupons were, the answer—food stamps—brought a rush of such embarrassment and fear that she has never forgotten the moment. Years later, when she scraped together money to study finance at the University of Wisconsin–Whitewater, she already had decided that becoming a banker would be a way to serve others and protect herself. Just after graduation, she lost her mother, too, to a heart attack, but went ahead with her plan to move to Janesville, where she worked for three years in a real estate office while she waited to get hired by the bank. Through her long ascent to community bank president, she has become one of Janesville's leading citizens—chairwoman of the Noon Rotary, president of the Citizens Advisory Council, chairperson of the United Way, Forward Janesville's Woman of Excellence. Still, a place inside Mary has not forgotten the darkness of fearing that she and her mother would lose what little they had.

It is that private, fearful place that Mary can still touch when Chelsea comes into the kitchen, sobbing, and tells her that half of her friends in the family room have a parent losing a job. Including the father of her best friend, Erica.

As she watches her smart, sensitive daughter in tears, Mary knows that Chelsea cannot see the scared farm girl who discovered that, without food stamps, there wouldn't be enough to eat. She knows that Chelsea is seeing the banker and leading citizen who can always be depended upon to come up with a solution for the community.

"Mom," Chelsea implores her. "What are you going to do?"

"When One Door of Happiness Closes, Another Opens"

The June floods have receded, and a National Emergency Grant is pumping federal money into temporary paychecks for mud-scraping, muck-removing, foundation-rehabilitating public works projects. So, over at the Job Center, Bob Borremans's focus is now laser-pointed where he'd expected it to be all along: on the autoworkers.

All well and good that the governor and his rescue committee are trying to salvage the General Motors plant, Bob thinks, but, even if they succeed, new products do not start rolling along retooled assembly lines overnight. In the meantime, with two days before Christmas getting closer and closer, thousands of people are facing the imminent reality of their final day of work. And with the plant's second shift gone since July, thousands of people are out of work already. Nearly a year into the recession, empty jobs are not lying around to grab. People don't know where to turn. Bob feels the weight of their anxiety, their aimlessness.

Having long prided himself on staring down problems, though, Bob is pleased with a move he already has made: creating a guide to all the resources in town that can help people who have been thrown out of work, or who will be soon. He felt a take-charge satisfaction as he and some of the Job Center's staff started contacting the leaders of organizations across Rock County to ask permission to include them in the new guide. Organizations that dispense help with job training, consumer credit, housing, health care, literacy, food, bouts of depression, bouts of addiction, bouts of domestic violence—two hundred far-flung, help-offering organizations in all.

He'd gotten this idea while attending a conference in Washington not long before, from a breakfast conversation with a woman who ran a job center like his. Her East Coast community had had massive layoffs, which prompted her to create a help guide. This was the kind of advice Bob likes—practical and levelheaded. He'd felt sorry for her community, so much less lucky than Janesville had ever been or probably ever would be. But he stored the conversation in his mind.

And now that Janesville's luck was slipping and he'd brought out the idea, it seemed useful to include in the guide, along with the listings of help-offering organizations, some tips on trying to cope emotionally with having a good job cut out from under you. So on page A8 of the guide was a box with the heading, "What to Do After a Layoff." The box had fourteen bullet points, the first of which contained a crucial antidote to lost-job paralysis. "Don't Feel Ashamed," the heading of this first bullet point said. "Being laid off is not your fault."

And scattered through the guide were words from Americans renowned for the challenges they confronted. A quote from Abraham Lincoln: "Always bear in mind that your own resolution to succeed is more important than any other one thing." And from Helen Keller: "When one door of happiness closes, another opens; but often we look so long at the closed door that we do not see the one which has been opened for us."

The help guide for laid-off workers was finished by fall. Bob was pleased. At once inspirational and handy, it was in the tradition of Janesville's good-government response to adversity—the same tradition that, seven decades before, had tamed a potentially violent sit-down strike, transforming labor strife into a nocturnal downtown parade.

As it happened, the act of checking with all these helping organizations produced an important ripple effect. The United Way of North Rock

County—whose parking lot had been the scene of spawning carp months before—and leaders of other organizations urged Bob to take a much larger step, to form a coalition to stand together in response to the mass layoffs.

An excellent idea, Bob thinks, to coordinate the help givers, to maximize their power and efficiency. Having been around town for so many years, Bob knows who he needs if this coalition is going to make a difference. He needs Sharon Kennedy, the vice president of learning at Blackhawk Tech. He needs the right people from the county's school districts and public libraries. As he is sending out his invitations to form this new coalition, Janesville's politicians in Washington and Madison hear of these plans and ask to be part of the solution—most of them Democrats, but also an aide to Republican Paul Ryan. This aide puts forth the idea of bringing in a team from the University of Michigan, which has worked as consultants to two dozen other Midwestern places knocked off their moorings by disappearing jobs.

So, late on the afternoon of December 10, Bob is at the maiden meeting of Collaborative Organizations Responding to Dislocation—CORD, as it will be known—listening to a presentation by a guy from Ann Arbor named Larry Molnar, a researcher and economy-building coach at the University of Michigan's Community Economic Adjustment Program. Molnar is talking up the advantages to Janesville of working with his program, the advantages including guidance on how to make the most of six hundred government grants that exist for the purpose of helping economically distressed communities—plus a personal introduction to people who are federal and state arbiters of which communities deserve that money.

As he listens to this presentation, Bob—a realist, a pragmatist, a sixty-year-old guy with sardonic humor—is sensing a tinge of hope. The assembly plant will close in thirteen days. Sure, General Motors will leave behind a crater. But, he thinks, the Job Center and the assistance from Ann Arbor and the banding-together help dispensers he has assembled just might be pulling ahead of the trouble.

In Bob's view, the shackle of big GM paychecks bred complacency and tethered people to the assembly line for thirty years or forty—for an entire working life, even if they hated the work. With CORD just born and so much grant money on the horizon, Bob believes, catastrophe might prove to be unbidden opportunity to help people find the work paths that would have suited them all along. Sure, people will need to retrain for this new work, but that's his specialty, and he can help them go back to school while waiting for jobs to emerge on the far side of this recession.

The Job Center together with the rest of CORD, Bob believes, can help Janesville's job-losing autoworkers discover their latent dreams.

The Parker Closet

Deri Wahlert is worrying that some of her students will have strange, sad Christmases. It is mid-December, three months since she talked her principal at Parker High into letting her start the Parker Closet. As a social studies teacher, she hadn't exactly planned on the Closet, but it had seemed more and more an inevitability ever since she had, her first year at Parker, found out the secret of why a junior named Sarah in her first-period class was late to school and losing weight. One day, Sarah confided to Deri that her mother had taken off, leaving her with her little brother in an apartment without electricity or enough to eat. Deri told Sarah's guidance counselor and a few other teachers, and they began to collect food and clothes for Sarah. And it occurred to Deri that there must be other kids who could use a helping hand.

This business of helping was vintage Deri. She had been barely a teenager when her father got the virus that left him paralyzed. He was in his forties and resented having to stop working a few years later, and her family couldn't afford it, with even his careful savings and Social Security disability checks not adding up to his lost salary. The Americans with Disabilities Act was just a year old when he got sick—new enough that wheelchair ramps were rare on sidewalks and into restaurants and offices.

Deri remembers the stares and the rumors that flew in the small town of Fort Atkinson where they lived: Did he have AIDS? No, it was just an unfortunate, ordinary virus. It taught her that even a middle-class white guy and his family could face injustice.

Early on, she began to look for people and places that could benefit from her empathy: a friend in high school who would go on to the Wheelchair Olympics, vacant lots that needed cleaning up while she was in college at the University of Wisconsin–Whitewater. A professor once told her that she belonged in the '60s with her hippie passion for righting wrongs.

When she graduated, she was committed to working toward a greener world and felt lucky to be hired by an environmental consulting firm, until the job ended after a few months. Eventually, a college friend pointed out that she was qualified for substitute teaching. She quickly sensed that she had found her calling, so she got a second degree in history and another in secondary education and landed at Parker High for her first full-time teaching job the fall of 2006, before anyone was talking about plant-closing troubles. Deri kept in her mind and spirit a favorite poem in which a wise man notices a young man standing along the shore, tossing starfish back into the sea. The shoreline is miles long, the wise man points out, and there are too many starfish to save them all. And the young man, tossing another into the ocean, past the breaking waves, replies to the wise man: "It made a difference for that one."

So Deri made a difference for Sarah and started watching closely enough to notice a few more kids coming to school hungry and tired. Lately, she was noticing kids from families that used to be middle-class until a parent lost a job. At the start of this school year, Deri's principal gave her a spare storage room two doors down the hallway from her social studies classroom, #1151. So the Parker Closet became a reality, with twelve students who ducked inside, when their friends weren't looking so that nobody else would know, to comb through donated Rubbermaid bins for toothpaste or used jeans or cans of soup.

Now, with Christmas and the plant closing soon, it has hit Deri that some of her Closet kids might not get presents at home. And as she has begun to line up special donations—the Big Give she is calling this aspect of her project—she asked a freshman named Trent what he wanted and was absolutely floored by his answer: a mattress. A mattress? "What about the one at home?" she asked, trying to keep the surprise out of her voice. That thing was older than him, Trent told her. Thin with coils poking up, and saggy. It hadn't been bad when he was smaller, but now that he was growing, he sometimes couldn't sleep at night because it hurt. And when she asked what else he might like, something that would feel like a real present, his answer was, "Can you have something for my mom, too?"

Deri's mind was still sliding around the fact of a Parker High freshman lying awake because of a shoddy bed when she bumped into Trent's twin, Mason. She told him about his brother wanting a mattress for Christmas and asked his opinion. When he said, "Definitely could use new ones," she thought, "Oh my God. How am I going to get *this*?" But Deri found a store willing to donate two mattresses, even had them delivered. Then she figured she might as well scrounge up some bedding to go along.

So, after school one afternoon, she lugs a bulky pile out of her car and up to a neat blue ranch house. Two pillows. Two navy blue comforters. Matching sheets and pillowcases. She rings the doorbell and finds herself standing in a playroom of this house where Trent and Mason live with their mother, Sherry Sheridan, who at this moment, though they've never met before, is pulling her into a very large hug. And as long as she's wrapped in a hug from this mom who seems so grateful and already has offered her something to drink as if she were a real guest and not a thirty-year-old teacher on a mission after school, Deri feels she shouldn't leave right away but should ask a little about their lives.

The pale blue house is barely a mile from the assembly plant. But it turns out that Mrs. Sheridan has never been a GM'er. She is an older mom, forty-six when the twins were born, and, since long before then, long before she kicked out the boys' father while she was pregnant, she's been running a day care. It has been a good business and has allowed her to raise her boys in comfortable circumstances. But lately the children have been leaving, one by one, and now her playroom is almost empty, because moms and dads have been hit by the recession, and it isn't just because of General Motors. One dad is a carpet layer, another a plasterer, and they can't get work, so they're home during the day and can watch their own kids. "They don't need me to baby-sit anymore," she tells Deri, and breaks into tears.

A thought leaps into Deri's head. All the plant-closing talk, she realizes, is missing something very big. It isn't going to be just the GM workers the *Gazette* keeps writing about who will be out of work. It's also going to be the people at the freight yard who won't be needed to unload parts for GM, and the little shops that won't have enough customers because people stop buying in hard times, and the construction workers who already didn't have houses to build, and the carpet layers and plasterers whose customers already couldn't afford them. All these men and women who once made up a prosperous, flourishing workforce now at home with their kids, not needing Mrs. Sheridan, this nice lady who is hugging her again and thanking her for the mattresses and navy comforters and all the rest, including the donated purse Deri has brought for her with a gift certificate inside for Eagle Inn Family Restaurant a few blocks away on Center Avenue, because even people whose day care centers are dying in this economy deserve to get out to eat, at least once in a while.

Deri wants to tell this mom what she is thinking. But she does not. Because her realization is upsetting, and even though she is a rookie at running the Closet, she already knows something important: better to let other people vent—lean on her with their anger, frustration, fear—without letting her feelings show too much. Better because, if she lets hers slip out, kids or moms like Mrs. Sheridan might feel bad that they have upset the teacher and stop confiding in her, and that would defeat the Closet's whole purpose.

So she keeps her thoughts to herself and lets Mrs. Sheridan thank her one more time. But as she gets back into her Pontiac Grand Am filled with presents, she can't stop the words running through her head: Wow, we are in for a lot of problems here. The words still whirling, she checks the list of addresses and sets out to make her next delivery.

Part Two

★ 2009 ★

Rock County 5.0

Mary Willmer has not forgotten the October night she came home to find Chelsea, her fifteen-year-old, crying in a circle with friends whose parents were losing their jobs, asking her what she intended to do about this situation. The answer begins to reveal itself in January. Just after the plant has closed, a tiny team starts to convene in secret once a week.

They often huddle in the boardroom outside Mary's office on the second floor of M&I Bank's Main Street branch. John Beckord is there as president of Forward Janesville, the city's business association, and James Otterstein as Rock County's economic development manager. Sometimes a few others. And, of course, Mary.

Their core question is as daunting as it is obvious: How to get the local economy out of its free fall? One obstacle, they quickly recognize, is that no one—not Forward Janesville; not Rock County; not the Janesville city government; not Beloit, the county's second-largest city—has any real money to devote to a muscular economic development campaign.

Amidst these weekly private discussions, John Beckord arrives at Mary's office one day for a one-on-one chat. John is a pleasant, sandy-haired man with a mustache, a seasoned economic development professional who came to Janesville from Iowa eight years ago. Forward Janesville, he tells her, really wants to move ahead with this thing. It's not just that the city's main employer has left in the middle of a recession. Janesville has become a damaged brand, known now for being down on its economic luck. Fixing the brand—raising money from the local business community, marketing, keeping companies and winning new ones—will require a strong leader. It will be a big commitment. Point-blank, he asks Mary if she will do it.

Mary has not seen his question coming and, when it comes, her doubts surface first. For all of its big talk, this little team has no concrete plan. Though she sits on Forward Janesville's board, she is not exactly an economic development whiz. It all seems too hazy.

Then, in a moment of unanticipated clarity, Mary glimpses the answer. The only way this campaign could succeed, she tells John, "is if we get our arms around this whole county. Not Janesville, not Beloit, but the whole county and really make a bold statement."

In many places, this idea would have been automatic. In Janesville, it is novel, verging on heretical. As long as anyone can remember, Janesville and Beloit have been, if not exactly enemies, then passionate rivals. Beloit is thirteen miles away, just above the Illinois line. It is a straight shot from downtown along Center Avenue, past the Job Center in the converted Kmart, and on down Route 51 until the Rock River stops meandering and the road follows the river right into Beloit. Close as they are, the two small cities have been worlds apart. The way that some towns have fevered sports rivalries, Janesville and Beloit have had everything rivalries. If you lived in one, you did not go out to eat in the other, or go shopping, or read the other's local newspaper or listen to its radio station. Janesville has almost always been an overwhelmingly white community, with real estate redlining in its past. Beloit's industry drew African Americans from the South as part of the Great Migration early in the twentieth century. But the rivalry has never been overtly about race. It has been about identity. And for the past decade, it has been about Janesville's economic superiority. The Beloit Corporation began as an iron foundry just before the Civil War and grew into the nation's largest manufacturer of paper-making machinery with 7,700 workers at its peak—more than the Janesville Assembly Plant. But it was sold and then went into bankruptcy and closed down. A fall from industrial glory to a toxic Superfund site. With all its good jobs, Janesville looked down on Beloit. But now, with GM just closed, Mary sees that Janesville and Beloit are in the same tough spot.

And so her answer to John is this: Yes, she will lead this shapeless, nameless economic development campaign—*if* someone from Beloit is her partner. They toss around various names. They agree upon who would be ideal. This is how John Beckord comes to approach Diane Hendricks, one of the wealthiest self-made women in America.

Diane was half of a Horatio Alger duo, but now she is a recent widow. One of nine daughters of parents who were dairy farmers, she was pregnant and married at seventeen, divorced at twenty-one. She was selling real estate when she met Ken Hendricks, a roofer's son and high school dropout who at twenty-one formed his own roofing company. Together, they created ABC Supply Co., Inc. in Beloit—Ken having felt shunned by the Janesville business community when he was starting out. Over the years, the Hendrickses built ABC into the nation's largest supplier of roofing and siding material. In 2006, *Inc.* magazine named Ken its Entrepreneur of the Year. They built a fortune—$3.5 billion, making him the ninety-first richest man in the United States, according to *Forbes*, by December 20, 2007—a year and three days before the assembly plant closed. That night, they returned from a business party, and, a few minutes later, Ken went to check on construction work on their garage, part of a transformation under way of their house into a ten-thousand-square-foot dream. The sixty-six-year-old roofer fell through a tarp-covered subfloor of his own garage roof. Diane found him, unconscious, on the concrete below. He died before dawn.

Since then, Diane has run the company but retreated from many of her community involvements. At sixty-one, she is lean with striking eyes and flowing brown hair. She lives on a two-hundred-acre wooded estate with a small herd of deer, overlooking the river between Janesville and Beloit, in the home she completed after her husband's death.

Mary knew Ken more than she knows Diane, and she isn't sure whether the recent widow would be up for a big, shapeless economic development campaign in the middle of a recession. But sure enough, once John Beckord asks, Diane is in.

When Mary and Diane get talking, Mary is delighted to discover how much they agree. One of their central points of agreement is that, whatever this campaign will be, local businesses need to invest in it. "We are not going to wait for the government to come in and rescue us," Diane is fond of saying. "We are not going to wait for GM to rescue us. We are on our own. Let's get this job done."

They need to move fast to explain their ideas to the county's business leaders and ask them to chip in. But first, they face a quandary: Should the initial meeting include businesses from both Janesville and Beloit, making clear from the outset this unorthodox mind-set of advancing the economic interest of all of Rock County through a single voice? Too much, too soon, Mary and Diane decide. They will start with Janesville.

The winter night they choose will be the first time that Mary has road-tested this fledgling vision for reviving Janesville's economy to find out whether the business establishment of her community will stand behind her. The evening is a fundraiser. It is a gamble. It is crucial, Mary knows, to Janesville's future. She is terrified.

Forward Janesville occasionally has gatherings at the homes of local business leaders. For this evening, the co-president of Bain's Farm and Fleet, a friend of Mary's, offers her imposing home on the river's bluff. It is an ornate home with high ceilings, a classic European feel. It is here, at tables in two rooms, that a sit-down dinner is served to more than two dozen businessmen and women. The "aircraft carriers of the community" is how John Beckord regards this gathering. As the dinner ends, he begins the evening's formal program. Then it is Mary's turn.

By the time she speaks, the barely born, public-private, Janesville-and-Beloit-together campaign that she and Diane are leading has a name: Rock County 5.0. Five key strategies. A five-year plan to heal the economy. She sketches all this out, placing more emphasis on how critical it is than on how difficult it will be. She and Diane take questions. Finally, the moment in the evening arrives at which Mary discloses the fundraising goal: $1 million. She announces that M&I Bank—her bank—is pledging $50,000. Though she eventually will contribute much more, Diane says that ABC Supply is pledging $50,000, too.

Mary waits. Will anyone else come through?

The room is silent. The entire idea, Mary fears, could die right here in this living room.

At last, one hand goes up. It belongs to the chairman of JP Cullen, the area's most successful construction firm, which has had so much work at the assembly plant over the decades, work that it will now lose. With a hand raised, others go up, one by one.

The gathering is breaking up, and Mary is thrilled and overwhelmed. She needs a minute alone. She opens the door into an elegant bathroom. She stands there, shaking, nearly sobbing with relief, on the other side of the door from the business leaders of Janesville who have just put faith and money behind this new hope—this Rock County 5.0 that is still taking form. If this evening hadn't worked out, she had no Plan B. But now, looking into the mirror, Mary tells herself, "We are off and running."

The Fourth Last Day

Machines ripped out. Assembly lines ripped out. Workers ripped out. It is April 10, Mike Vaughn's final day at Lear Corp. For almost two decades, Lear has been Janesville's largest supplier to General Motors, manufacturing the seats for every vehicle that came out of the assembly plant. Founded outside Detroit in 1917, the company eventually merged with a business formed by the inventor and business-man William Lear, who developed a car radio, the 8-track tape, and the Learjet. It has two hundred locations in three dozen countries. In Janes-ville, the assembly plant has been Lear's only client, their fortunes bound together.

Now Mike stands in the doorway, taking a long look into the shell of a factory.

Inside this space, he met his wife, Barb. With their wages combined and overtime, Lear gave them a nice, six-figure life until her job ended last summer—$22 an hour suddenly gone, though Barb welcomed a reprieve from the assembly line and sped back to school. They were managing. After today, though, they will go from one income to none.

Inside this space, too, Mike has been shop chairman for UAW Local 95, representing a workforce of eight hundred Lear union brothers and sisters. This responsibility made Mike the third generation of Vaughns to have been a leader in the UAW local. His grandfather Tom came to GM from a lead mine and worked at the assembly plant for thirty and a half years until he retired. His father, Dave, started at the assembly plant at nineteen and stayed thirty-five years until he, too, retired.

At forty-one, Mike is a plainspoken man with close-cropped dark hair and an earnest manner. He had applied to General Motors right out of high school but never got the call, so he went to U-Rock for a year. Feeling unfocused, he left for a cook's job in the Mercy Hospital kitchen. General Motors still wasn't hiring, so eventually he followed his brother, DJ, into Lear. He started on general assembly and became a relief operator, filling in on jobs throughout the factory, and then he trained other people to be relief operators. By 2000, he'd already been involved in the union for a few years when he left the assembly line, under the time-honored labor tradition of "release time," to represent 250 workers on first shift. Four years later, his fellow workers elected him chairman of the entire Lear bargaining unit. He handled grievances with management, made sure everyone knew the factory policies, represented Lear workers in the local—just as his father and grandfather had done, the union a sheltering presence.

But by this spring day, Mike has had responsibilities that his father and grandfather never imagined. He helped to prepare an application to the U.S. Labor Department to get certification for Trade Readjustment Allowances—government help for workers hurt by foreign trade—for the bargaining unit of a plant that was, in stages, going away. And as each wave of his union brothers and sisters lost their jobs, he stood alongside them. For this reason, today feels like Mike's fourth last day.

The first of those last days was fifteen months ago, when several dozen second-shift workers were laid off. It had seemed a routine enough layoff. Over at the assembly plant, production was being slowed because of the weak SUV market, so General Motors didn't need as many of Lear's seats. Mike sat with the first unlucky round of workers in human resources meetings as they were given their layoff slips. He made sure they were told everything they needed to know about unemployment benefits and

COBRA health insurance and training opportunities. He answered their questions from the union side. He was present for them on their final day.

His second last day—the same day over the summer that a shift went down at the assembly plant—stole the jobs of half of Lear's workers, ones who had been there for up to fifteen years. This time, the frightened job losers included Barb. By then, GM had said it would be shutting the assembly plant, so he knew it was only a matter of time before his own paychecks would disappear, along with hers. It was raw shock. He felt it in his gut.

The third last day was on December 23, the date the assembly plant closed. This time, the job-losing Lear workers included Mike's brother, DJ, who had long ago encouraged him to apply. As this day neared, though he hadn't done it for the two previous last days, Mike walked through the plant, meeting with small groups of his UAW brothers and sisters to say a personal goodbye. There were, at this point, 371 goodbyes to say, so he spent a few days talking to as many as he could, telling these men and women he represented that they must try to remain positive and remember that they were proud people, smart and hardworking. "You have to make the best of what comes next," Mike said over and over, "and start formulating your plan." Barb was, he knew, trying to make the best, with her high school equivalency diploma and her criminal justice studies at Blackhawk Tech. Still, as he spread his plan-formulating message around the plant floor, he sometimes cried.

As he went through all these goodbyes, Mike understood that it was not just Lear Corp., which would file for bankruptcy that summer. Not even just Lear and General Motors, which had always been resented by many workers at the suppliers in the area for having the best pay and vacation benefits, even though amalgamated UAW Local 95 included them all. General Motors was resented but acknowledged as essential, because, if not for the assembly plant, a lot of other jobs wouldn't have existed and, now that GM was closing, jobs were disappearing all around town. Two days before Christmas, the day that GM and Lear stopped production, so did the 159 employees of Logistics Services, Inc., a warehouse that sequenced parts and delivered them to the assembly plant. So did

Allied Systems Group, whose 117 workers suddenly stopped hauling GM vehicles to car dealers through the Midwest. And nearby in Brodhead, seventy workers at the Woodbridge Group stopped making the foam to be delivered to Lear, where it was stuffed into seats for GM. Woodbridge's other ninety-nine workers would be laid off when that factory, too, closed by spring. No, it wasn't only GM and Lear that, by February, pushed up Rock County's unemployment rate to 13.4 percent.

As these thousands of workers were losing their jobs, and Mike worried late at night about what would happen to them all, he carried around another piece of knowledge: When the fourth last day arrived, it would be his turn. As shop chairman, he was allowed to stay on with a small maintenance crew and a few forklift operators, just fifteen in all. Each weekday from after Christmas until two days before Easter—Good Friday—he watched as this little crew took apart the plant, piece by piece, assembly line by assembly line. A little more gone every day, until now it is empty, which is pretty much how Mike is feeling inside.

This morning, he said his goodbyes to each person in the small crew, aware that he has not been as close to them as to many who have left before. Now that it is the afternoon of his own last day, he doesn't want to get stuck in any long conversations. So he takes the one look from the doorway and, after eighteen years at Lear, is gone.

Bidding War

At 6 p.m. on June 11, Marv Wopat enters a large courtroom on the fourth floor of the Rock County Courthouse. His forty years at the assembly plant may have ended, but not his fighting spirit for the working man. Or, more precisely, for the men and women who were working until their jobs vanished and who are aching to be working again, two of his kids among them. He has been waiting for this night to make his big push.

Tonight is one of the two Thursdays each month that the county's Board of Supervisors convenes inside the courtroom. The supervisors sit toward the front of the room in two rows of seats divided by a center aisle. For the past fourteen months, Marv has squeezed his broad frame into a chair in the second row, two seats to the right of the aisle. He represents the town of Milton, just north of Janesville. For all the community work he has done—boards and commissions on top of listening to the private confidences of people with addictions screwing up their lives—this is the first time in his sixty-two years that Marv has held elective office.

It is from this cramped seat that, tonight, Marv raises his hand and is recognized by the board's leader on the courtroom's dais. In his booming voice—so loud that, whenever he picks up his microphone, the county clerk knows to keep her hand on the audio system's volume dial—Marv makes a motion to go into a closed, executive session.

This late spring evening marks a full year since the plant-closing announcement. It is weeks shy of a year since Marv's retirement. It is the first time the supervisors have met in the ten days since General Motors disclosed that Janesville is one of three U.S. assembly plants still in the running to manufacture a next-generation subcompact car, which the company is hoping will help reverse its fortunes. GM's fortunes have just crashed to a once unimaginable low. At 8 a.m. the day before it disclosed that Janesville is a finalist, and despite $19.4 billion in loans that the U.S. Treasury has ended up pumping into the company, General Motors filed for bankruptcy in a Manhattan court. As part of its restructuring, the company said it will shed fourteen more U.S. plants and 21,000 more hourly wage jobs. The government is providing another $30 million in loans. Rick Wagoner is not around to deliver the latest grim news; he was pushed out of the CEO's job in March.

Amid these ashes, Marv sees opportunity. In response to his motion, the doors are closed and the supervisors and a few managers are now the only ones in the courtroom. The agenda item is how much money the county will contribute to the final economic incentive package that Wisconsin is about to present to General Motors. Most of the supervisors believe that $5 million is plenty. The county, they say, can't afford more with its tax base hemorrhaging in this awful economy.

Marv is his blunt self. "We need to put in the best offer," he says in his booming voice. "If we don't, other places will outbid us."

Neither Marv nor anyone else fighting to reopen the assembly plant knows how much money is being offered by the two competing communities whose plants are also in the running—Spring Hill, Tennessee, and Orion Township, Michigan. Yet Marv can see that he is not the only person in Janesville who recognizes that an all-out effort is needed to prevail in a bidding war to reincarnate an auto plant with its lights out.

The city's two medical systems, Mercy and Dean, have pledged to provide discounts on workers' health insurance premiums if General Motors returns. Alliant Energy has promised to lower the assembly plant's electric bills. Some local businesses have even banded together and agreed to pay whatever it takes to buy Zachow's Tavern. To General Motors' consternation, Zachow's has been sitting for decades on a sliver of property that the tavern owned before the plant's parking lot expanded around it. If the plant reopens, the business owners are planning to convert the tavern into a day care center for the kids of working-again GM'ers.

With everyone else pitching in, Marv thunders, Rock County must not do its part on the cheap. Besides he has done a little math: Think about the payroll from one day of overtime when the plant was busy—time and a half to all the GM'ers and the Lear folks and the people who loaded and unloaded the freight trains bringing in supplies and carrying away Janesville-made vehicles. And then think about the tax revenue from all those workers' pay. It adds up to $5 million in no time at all.

This is Marv's argument. This, plus the fact that, if the plant stays closed and people stay out of work, "there isn't going to be any more money spent in Rock County." A worrisome prospect, indeed, for supervisors who have been elected by the citizens to set the county's budget.

By the time Marv finishes and the votes are tallied and someone opens the courtroom door for the public to come back in, the supervisors have agreed to offer General Motors what Marv wanted: $20 million.

This is not a fact that the public will know right away. Still, Marv is relieved. He has accomplished what he came to do tonight. He believes that $20 million—a fortune for a hurting county—will be enough to make a difference.

Sonic Speed

When U.S. automakers decide where to manufacture new products, they have come to expect that the states and communities they are considering will present enormous dowries in the form of tax breaks and other financial gifts. So, a few days after the Rock County supervisors quadrupled their offering to General Motors, Wisconsin sends off to the company its final economic incentive package to try to land the new small car for Janesville's assembly plant. The package adds up to $195 million: $115 million in state tax credits and energy-efficiency grants, the $20 million that Marv Wopat pushed through the county board, $15 million from the strapped Janesville city government, and $2 million from Beloit, plus private industry incentives, including from the businesses willing to buy out the tavern in the assembly plant's parking lot. And that isn't counting concessions worth $213 million that UAW Local 95 is willing to sacrifice in exchange for retrieving jobs.

The biggest incentive package in Wisconsin history.

The competition is still down to the three finalists—the factories in Tennessee and Michigan, along with Janesville. GM executives have said they are considering a dozen factors in evaluating which one deserves the little car and the jobs that come with it. The amount of money each finalist has proffered for the privilege is only one factor. Yet the unmistakable fact is that money counts for a company in bankruptcy court.

In the end, Janesville never had a chance.

*

At 7 a.m. on June 26, Governor Doyle receives a phone call. On the other end is Tim Lee, the vice president for manufacturing of GM North America. Seventeen months ago, the day of Obama's hope-drenched campaign speech at the assembly plant, Lee was in the front row, two seats to the right of the governor. When Obama predicted that the plant would last another hundred years, Lee stood in ovation with all the rest.

This morning, Lee's news for the governor is grim. General Motors is giving its new small car to Orion Township, Michigan.

It is crushing news for Janesville. During the Great Depression, the assembly plant had reopened after a year. During the crisis of 1986, medium-duty trucks soon replaced the pickups that vanished from the assembly line. It is hard to fathom that the plant-rescue mission hasn't rescued the plant once again.

In defeat, the governor sounds bitter. All along, Doyle says, General Motors wanted to give its new little car to the Orion plant. The company had merely used Wisconsin's offer as leverage to wring even more from Michigan, he says. "I do not believe that Michigan matched us."

Each finalist's gambit in the bidding war was a secret until now. And the governor, it turns out, is wrong. Wisconsin's offer may have been historic. But Michigan offered nearly five times as much.

Home to the U.S. auto industry and a 15 percent unemployment rate that is the nation's highest, Michigan has a governor who has been desperate to get the new car for the Orion Assembly Plant. Of more than a dozen factories that General Motors intends to close as part of its plan to climb out of bankruptcy, half are in Michigan. Orion, about forty miles north of Detroit, is one of them. Winning the bidding war would salvage 1,400 jobs for Orion and a nearby GM plant that stamps out parts from sheet metal. "We would do everything possible to get that production in Michigan,"

Governor Jennifer Granholm told GM executives right after the company declared bankruptcy.

Everything possible included setting up a war room inside the headquarters of the Michigan Economic Development Corporation in the state capital of Lansing and within a mere few weeks devising a strategy to offer General Motors the amazing sum of $779 million worth of tax breaks over the next twenty years and $135 million in job-training funds, plus water and sewer credits from Orion Township and money from a fund to help companies find good workers. In all, more than $1 billion in public money. The largest inducement Michigan had ever offered a corporation. Enough to win a small car.

Michigan's bid on behalf of Orion isn't the only stratospheric offer lately that has landed an automotive prize. When General Motors decided last year to build a Chevy compact, the Cruze, at its assembly plant in Lordstown, Ohio, that state gave GM $220 million in incentives. After the Ford Motor Company decided last year to spend $75 million to renovate a truck plant in Wayne, Michigan, in order to manufacture a compact model, the Ford Focus, the state of Michigan agreed to give Ford $387 million in tax credits and rebates. And when Volkswagen last year decided to build a plant in Chattanooga, Tennessee, to manufacture a sedan, the Passat, that company received $554 million in state and local tax breaks.

All were more than Wisconsin offered General Motors to try to get the lights back on at Janesville. Even in this high-stakes, high-priced environment, Michigan's play in the bidding war is a record-breaker.

*

In their defeat, the governor of Wisconsin and the people of Janesville were not in position to see that winning also would have had a cost. But as time went on, it turned out the price of victory went beyond Michigan's enormous public investment. The price was steep for Orion's workers, too.

GM named its new small car model the Sonic. It became the only subcompact car being made within the United State—the first subcompact, in fact, that General Motors had made domestically since the 1980s. Originally, it was to have been manufactured in China, but GM had rethought that decision as part of its strategy to reposition itself for consumers in a feeble economy. The company had decided to make the inexpensive little car in the U.S., even though many of its parts would still be made in South Korea, as GM's previous smallest car, the Aveo, had been. This decision carried with it a large question: How to make a profit while paying union wages?

General Motors had anticipated this question, and a few years earlier it persuaded the United Auto Workers to accept a big concession in a national labor contract: a two-tier wage system that allowed the company to hire new employees at about $14 an hour—half the standard $28-an-hour wage. Under the contract, as many as one fourth of GM workers across the company could be paid this lower wage.

Then, while the Orion assembly plant was shut down to be reconfigured, the UAW local there bent further than the national contract had envisioned. Worried that GM might take away the plant-preserving, job-sparing little car, the local agreed to extra wage cuts: When the plant reopened to make Sonics, two of every five workers, including some existing GM employees, would be paid half as much as men and women next to them on the assembly line. The new president by then of General Motors North America called the arrangement "very radical" and said it would "test our ability to be really competitive here." A leader of the Orion UAW local said it was "better than having the doors closed and wondering where your next paycheck is coming from."

While waiting for the plant to reopen, the company gave hundreds of Orion's laid-off workers with more recent anniversary dates a terrible choice—an option to transfer to GM's Lordstown plant, 250 miles away. If they transferred, they'd be guaranteed the regular $28 an hour. If they remained in Orion until the plant reopened for the Sonic, they'd gamble on whether their seniority would end up protecting their wages or slicing them in half.

Scores of Orion workers picketed Solidarity House, the UAW International's headquarters in Detroit. "Call a cop, I've been robbed," said the placard that one carried. Another filed a complaint with the National Labor Relations Board—not against General Motors, but against his own

UAW local for having accepted the concession without checking with its members. The NLRB dismissed the complaint.

So at 6 a.m. on August 1, 2011, when production of the Sonic began, 40 percent of the workers were paid $14 an hour. Many parts were shipped from South Korea. The engines came from Mexico. And in another innovation, some parts suppliers began working right inside the Orion plant. Their average wage: $10 an hour.

This was the price of victory.

★

The high price of victory is off in the future. On the bad-news day at the start of summer, the people of Janesville are reeling, the failed crusade to reopen the assembly plant so contrary to the community's long, proud tradition of comebacks.

Paul Ryan issues a joint statement with three Democrats in Wisconsin's congressional delegation. Among them is Senator Russ Feingold, who grew up in Janesville, too, and whose grandfather had, in 1923, bought the first Chevrolet truck that ever came off the assembly line. "It is because of the hard work, determination and coordination by all involved that the Janesville plant made it this far and was in the running until this point," Paul and the Democrats say. "We are committed to helping the working people of Rock County . . . and we will continue to work together, with the Governor and with others, to do all we can."

Their statement typifies the unified front that has lasted through the hard-fought, losing struggle. And yet, before this day ends, an ideological crevice surfaces—small at first, but over time it will deepen. The crevice goes to the core of the question that confronts Janesville now: What should happen next?

Paul believes it is pointless to wait around for General Motors to come back. It is time, he says, for Janesville to find a way to buy from General Motors the silent behemoth of a factory along the river and use it for other purposes. "We need to move on," he says.

With these words, Paul is reflecting the view of local business leaders. It is the view of Forward Janesville and Mary Willmer, who during the past few months has quietly been raising money toward the $1 million goal of Rock County 5.0—the economic development campaign, which has not yet been revealed to the community as a whole.

But to many out-of-a-job workers, this view is heresy. "Move on" sounds like an insult. They hear "move on" as a betrayal of Janesville's past and a cruel disregard for a thin silver lining on which, dispirited as they are, they are beginning to focus. The silver lining is this: When it chose Orion, General Motors could have closed Janesville's assembly plant permanently. It did not. It has left the plant in a status known as "standby"— inert but available in case GM's business recovers enough that it is needed again. In the limbo of standby, Janesville's workers find a residue of hope.

14

What Does a Union Man Do?

August 24 is coming up soon. The first day of classes. And Mike Vaughn knows he can't put it off much longer. He couldn't remember the last time he'd kept a secret from his dad, let alone a whopper like this one. But on these hot days of a Wisconsin summer, every time he imagined telling his father, he couldn't get past the disappointment that might cross his face, the very real possibility that his father, who'd always stood behind him, might not be able to stand behind him now. So Mike has waited a few more days and a few more days, until time is running out.

How do you tell your father that you're going to the other side?

The shadow of the three generations of Vaughn union history, his own included, keeps stopping him. He knows the family lore. It is his lore. It goes back to the lead mines that, in the old days, were scattered through Wisconsin's southwest corner in places with names like New Diggings and Swindler's Ridge, and the McCabe Mine in which his great-grandfather was killed. Mike's grandfather Tom tried to start a union in a mine before he came to Janesville for a GM job in the "See the USA in Your Chevrolet" 1950s, doubling his wages from $1 an hour to $2. Having wanted to be a union man all along, his grandfather talked wages and working conditions with the other UAW guys after their shifts at a gas station out on Milton Avenue. He gained their confidence to be elected a zone committeeman representing one thousand GM'ers. Years later, he helped to plan the Walter P. Reuther Memorial Hall where Local 95's offices still stand today.

Mike's father, Dave, grew up in Janesville and was still a teenager when he was hired into the assembly plant in 1967 as a spot welder. He'd been on the assembly line for just three years when a strike over raises and pensions broke out. *His* father was still at the plant, on the union bargaining committee, so that they struck General Motors together for eleven weeks. Dave became a Local 95 vice president a couple of years after Mike got hired at Lear so that they, too, overlapped in the local. Dave loves the union so much that now, with the assembly plant closed and no workers left to run the local on release time, as they always had, he and a buddy, Mike Marcks, have stepped out of retirement to reprise their old gigs as its vice president and president. This time, as volunteers.

The Vaughns are one of only two families in town who have had three generations on the Local 95 executive committee. Mike's turn lasted eleven years before it was over. He helped to resolve routine pay squabbles and larger disputes over workers' comp and the Family and Medical Leave Act. For a time, he was even on a committee for the UAW International, sizing up the merits of grievances that had arisen at other parts suppliers. Union pride runs as deep in him as in the generations before. But the truth is that his father had been retired for five years and his grandfather buried for a year by the time his wife, Barb, lost her job and his own was ending soon.

What does a union man do when there are no workers left to represent? Mike began to talk to the International about a job in Detroit. But a real offer hadn't come yet from headquarters, and the more Mike considered the possibility, the less he could imagine leaving Janesville. Why should he have to trade his roomy yard with the vegetable garden and the flowers and trees that he and Barb love to tend, with family and old friends around them—all to continue working for the union?

Still, he couldn't shrug off the allegiance. For months, he trolled unionjobs.com, scouring every listing on the site in Wisconsin, Minnesota, and Illinois. The problem was, he didn't see a single job that would let him keep doing what he loved: representing workers. The openings were all for organizers. Mike had been on two UAW organizing drives, enough to know that he wasn't cut out to knock on the doors of strangers, many of whom had been distinctly hostile once they found out why he was there, enough to have heard the stories of organizers who'd met unleashed dogs and brandished guns. And on top of the dogs and the guns, he couldn't imagine being on the road three weeks of every month. It wasn't a life for him.

This discovery he made about himself—startling to his core—came along gradually, but there it was: Deep as his UAW heritage was, there were limits to what he was willing to do to keep standing on the union side.

Nothing in his family's past had prepared him for the choices he was confronting. The reality of life was that he and Barb were both out of work, two incomes gone—poof!—and he didn't have a fix. As he struggled with what to do, he watched Barb in astonishment, her head deep into her schoolwork, turning crisis into opportunity.

The more he thought about how to handle this moment without precedent, the more an idea coalesced inside him, faint at first, then growing into a solid belief. His union experience could be a foundation. A foundation for human resources work. As it happened, Blackhawk Tech was starting an HR program, with predictions of jobs at the end. It seemed right, this chance in front of him: the federal Trade Adjustment Act tuition money he'd fought for while still at Lear, a college degree, the prospect of work he felt suited to do, the ability to stay in town. He'd be crazy not to sign up.

But the jobs weren't union jobs. He'd be management.

As he sat with this idea, he sensed himself making peace with it. On his own, he doesn't feel like a bad man. Still, what would his father think?

The moment there is no escaping comes the early August afternoon that his stepmom, Judy, invites the whole family over for his father's sixty-first birthday. As Mike knew they would, he and his dad eventually head out to the screened porch together with their smokes, his hand-rolled, his father's Marlboros. He takes a puff before he begins. Then, with the party going on without them, he turns to his father and says, "I've decided what I'm going to do."

He starts with the easy stuff. The stuff about going back to school in twenty days, and Blackhawk's new program, and the government's training money. About how, as the months have gone by, the pain of his fourth last day at Lear has grown milder, leaving inside him, even though he is nervous, a small seed of optimism about his future.

Then he launches into the part that's hard. About how he's come to see that human resources management is a way to educate workers, too. About how he figures that, if he's been doing it from the union side, how different can it be from the company side?

As he is talking, he keeps a close watch on his father's expression. Is that a flicker of sadness? Yes, it's there. But if his dad's long, grooved face betrays certain feelings, his words don't say what Mike has feared the most: that Mike was going over to the dark side. No, the old union leader tells the young union leader he is proud of him for taking this opportunity to better himself. Then his father wraps him, the last generation of the union Vaughns, in a hug.

Inside his father's hug, hearing the words encouraging him to do the very best he can, Mike knows that his guilt will fade and that, scary as college is, he must embrace what lies ahead. His passion for labor, the special place of unions in his family history—nothing can take that away.

But he must give himself the counsel that he gave to the men and women he represented on the days of walking the Lear aisles to say his goodbyes: that they must each formulate their own plan. The same advice that he remembers giving to Lear's workers years before when the plant was migrating to linear assembly, and they would no longer be building seats in modules. Look for the truth of the situation, he remembers telling his union brothers and sisters back then, and embrace it.

With his father's arms still around him, he hears his own words once again: If you don't change with the times, you'll be left behind.

15

Blackhawk

Training people out of unemployment is a big, popular idea. In fact, it may be the only economic idea on which Republicans such as Paul Ryan and Democrats such as President Obama agree, anchored, as it is, in an abiding cultural myth, going back to America's founding, of this as a land that offers its people a chance at personal reinvention.

The evidence is thin that job training in the United States is an effective way to lead laid-off workers back into solid employment. Still, there is a lack of political consensus that the government should invest in creating jobs, and there is very much a consensus that it should help displaced workers go back to school. Which is why the Rock County Job Center that Bob Borremans runs in the converted Kmart now finds itself on the receiving end of millions in federal job-training money.

This spigot of federal money is impressive for a small community, even one that has just lost thousands of jobs, and it flows together from several streams. Bob relied on his old grants-writing skill to pull in nearly $1.8 million in a National Emergency Grant for communities whacked hard by job losses. The county is also receiving almost $1.1 million from an economic stimulus law that President Obama, now ending his first summer in the White House, has pushed through Congress. Both of these streams require Bob to devote more than $4 of every $5 to job training—$2.3 million in all. In addition, Rock County is getting roughly $1 million through a fund from the U.S. Labor Department's Workforce Investment Act for training workers whose jobs are unlikely to come back. Plus, though it isn't handled by the Job Center, Trade Adjustment Act training benefits—the help for workers hurt by foreign competition that Mike Vaughn fought to get for his Lear union brothers and sisters—is providing these laid-off workers more than $900,000 this year to pay for tuition and schoolbooks and gas to commute to classes.

Counselors at the Job Center, who meet with Janesville's out-of-a-job factory workers, talk up the fact that retraining opportunities are affordable even for people whose paychecks have disappeared. This has been a mantra since the beginning, when the GM'ers and Lear employees and all the rest first showed up to register for unemployment benefits and scout out what other help might be available. But it has taken months for some—more than a year for others—for the reality to sink in that replacing one job with another is not easy around Janesville, and learning a new skill might be a good idea.

So, on the last Monday in August, the first day of the fall semester at Blackhawk Technical College, Janesville's displaced, not-finding-jobs, don't-know-where-else-to-turn factory workers descend in such numbers that they fill every space in the sprawling parking lot and leave their cars on the lawn and on the shoulders edging the cornfields along South County Road G.

A year ago, Barb Vaughn and Kristi Beyer were part of an early trickle of laid-off workers who ventured back to school. Now, when Barb's husband, Mike, arrives for his first day of classes, he is startled to find himself in a mob scene. In this mob scene, too, is Matt Wopat, the GM'er whose father, Marv, persuaded the Rock County board to quadruple its contribution to the now failed plant rescue crusade. So is Jerad Whiteaker, the GM'er who at first stumped his twin daughters by showing up at breakfast. Their trajectories at Blackhawk will diverge, but on this first day, all three are frightened and overwhelmed.

Blackhawk Tech is named for a famed Sauk Native American warrior who in the 1830s unsuccessfully fought against nearby white settlement in what came to be known as the Black Hawk War. The school that bears his name is part of a century-old network of technical colleges in Wisconsin. In 1911, they became the first system of state-supported trade schools in the United States, created to transform farm boys into labor for the early twentieth century's industrial boom. Today, these two-year schools are like community colleges, except that they focus only on instilling skills that come in handy for jobs, preparing their students to work as welders, computer specialists, medical lab technicians, or—as Barb and Kristi are studying to become—employees of the criminal justice system. Of the sixteen colleges, Blackhawk has been among the smallest. But on this first morning, August 24, the campus is being slammed with the largest surge of students in the technical college's history—a 54 percent increase.

Coping with this surge falls to Sharon Kennedy, who has the august title of vice president of learning, which means that she is Blackhawk's chief academic officer and second-in-command. Sharon is in her early sixties, with a blond bob, a wide smile, a law degree, and steely smarts. She was a seasoned college administrator when she arrived at Blackhawk shortly before anyone in town found out that General Motors was going to shut the assembly plant.

During the past few months, she has watched with amazement and alarm as the roster of new students signing up for the fall semester climbed, and climbed more. Even before the roster turns into the overflowing parking lot and the mob getting lost looking for their classrooms on this first day, Sharon anticipated that transforming factory workers into successful college students would not be easy. Unlike at some two-year colleges, where older unemployed students are treated as afterthoughts, she recognized that, for Blackhawk and for Janesville, the city's out-of-work workers were now mission number one. Since the spring, Sharon and others decided to create programs in fields that seem most likely to produce jobs sometime soon. During the weeks before this first, crowded day of fall semester, Blackhawk added an astounding eighty-eight new class sections. And in a remarkable accomplishment, Sharon was part of a team that persuaded one of Wisconsin's Democratic U.S. senators, Herb Kohl, to push for money back in Washington that he somehow managed to insert as an earmark into the federal budget: $1 million for each of two years, all for Blackhawk to lavish extra effort on trying to transform some laid-off autoworkers who aren't really ready for college into competent students and, eventually, workers of other kinds. This money won't become available until the winter, but Sharon is relieved that it is coming.

An associate's degree in human resources management, the path that Mike Vaughn is pursuing, is one of the new programs created on the premise that it will lead to jobs. Compared to most arriving students, Mike is unusual, because he is starting out with a firm direction, having gone through the reasoning that led him to decide on his own that HR would be a logical sequel to his union roots. Yet as he enters his first class this morning—psychology—Mike is worried. Does he really know how to study? Can he write a research paper? Will he be able to learn to use Word on a computer? Hovering in the background are larger questions. Now that he and Barb are both in school, will they lose their house? Will it all lead to jobs for them in the end?

Such questions are also worrying Matt Wopat. Matt is more typical of today's crush of new students, having picked something to study, not out of passion or even moderate curiosity, but because it seemed as likely a path as any back to a decent wage.

Diligent as always, Matt went to the Job Center last summer, as all GM'ers were being encouraged to do, weeks before he cleaned out his locker at the end of his final shift. He went to the Job Center even though he shared his father, Marv's, faith that the plant would come back. He went, in other words, just in case.

Matt took a test called JobFit that gauged his learning style (visual/verbal, it turned out), his numerical skill (rapid grasp of numerical information), and his sociability (comfortable working with a group or individually). Matt was then issued a "Career Compatibility Passport," which told him that he would be equally adept as a database developer, a podiatrist, or a registered nurse—his best fits out of a list of fifty occupations for which he was well suited, with horticulturist and software engineer not far behind.

Next to a box indicating that he was being recommended for a training program, a Job Center caseworker handwrote about Matt: "Currently undecided."

He truly was undecided. Matt's unemployment checks and union Supplemental Unemployment Benefits would pump out 72 percent of his GM wages for a while longer. And even when he had still been at GM, he'd had a buddy with a small roofing crew, and he would make extra money once in a while working on roofs before his shift or on a weekend. So he expected that he'd get more roofs, but neither his buddy nor a cousin with another roofing crew were getting many jobs with so few people wanting to spend money these days on their roofs. Matt was getting just a couple of roofs to work on a month.

He tried to take it easy, figuring that he might as well, before the plant opened back up. He did yardwork. And that first fall, he took drives out to some public land west of town when pheasant hunting season opened in October and deer hunting the next month. He liked being outside, walking in nature. He enjoyed teaching his chocolate Lab, Cooper, to be a hunting dog. It was peaceful. But he noticed himself worrying about what he was shelling out for gas. Could he really afford the $10 to $15 each time he went hunting?

Once hunting was over for the year, Matt began to think about whether he could convert "Currently undecided" into a decision. He wasn't focused so much on what his Career Compatibility Passport had told him. He focused on what he could study that would, in the end, pay nearly as well as GM and be certain to have a job waiting for him. The common wisdom was that good jobs would be opening up at Alliant Energy, because it had older workers getting ready to retire.

This is what led Matt to the idea that learning to climb utility poles at Blackhawk's electric power distribution program was his best bet. The prospect of working with electricity scared him. Maybe he could work for a cable company. Maybe GM would reopen and he could go back where he belonged. Worst case, it would just be a year in school for a technical diploma, not two years for a degree. It was a Plan B, after all. Just in case.

Except that Plan B wasn't so easy to set in motion. So many other out-of-a-job factory workers were hearing that good positions would open soon at Alliant that, when Matt tried to sign up at Blackhawk, the electric power distribution program was full and the waiting list long. By now, Matt was serious about his Plan B, just in case. He was noticing that, month by month, with Darcy working less than half-time, restocking Hallmark cards for just above minimum wage, and Brittany, Brooke, and Bria needing stuff, their bank account was starting to drop in a way that was not good at all. He looked into the electric power distribution program at a technical college in Milwaukee, nearly one and a half hours away. He was about to start school in Milwaukee when a spot at Blackhawk opened up.

On this first day of classes, Jerad Whiteaker is starting to learn about electric power distribution, too. He has run through the same calculations as Matt. Health benefits ending before long. The assembly plant not yet reopening. The Job Center pushing all its training money. After a while, it became clear to Jerad that sleeping in and treating his layoff as a vacation he deserved was not a realistic strategy.

Like Matt, Jerad is a year shy of his fortieth birthday, and the last time he was in school was half a lifetime ago, when he went to Blackhawk for a year right out of high school to learn to be a diesel mechanic. He finished the program, but a diesel mechanic's job never came along, and that was before Janesville was in a nasty recession with thousands tossed out of work. Fearful though he is, Jerad is also glad to have gotten off the waiting list.

Jerad and Matt are in the same program but on different class schedules. Soon, Matt settles into a routine. He brings to campus habits from his years as a GM'er, like many of the fish-out-of-water autoworkers at Blackhawk. They get to school early and shoot the breeze with the guys, as they did at their jobs. They bring to class the same work thermoses they brought to their jobs.

Jerad starts out fine, too. He enjoys going outside behind the classroom building on a nice late-summer day with the instructor, Mike Double-day, a Blackhawk graduate himself and journeyman lineman until he was hired to help with the waiting list. The instructor divides the eighteen students into groups and assigns each group to work together to create a hole twelve inches across and six feet into the ground. No problem.

On another day soon, a practice utility pole is set into the hole, and each student must take a turn climbing it. When Jerad's turn comes, he gets five feet up when a knee gives out. He slides to the ground, the rough wooden surface scraping his chest all the way down as he clings to the pole.

By the time he hits the ground, terrified, his skin raw, Jerad considers the fact that this was just a practice pole. What would have happened if he were on a real pole, thirty feet in the air, when he lost his footing and fell? How much good would he be for Tammy and the kids then? Besides, rumors are circulating that the good jobs at Alliant Energy, the jobs that are supposed to be waiting at the end of his year in school, may not be opening so fast. Instead of retiring, he is starting to hear, the older guys are hanging on to their jobs because, in this economy, their 401(k)'s are a shrunken mess. What will happen if he can't get a job at the end?

And with these fears, two weeks into this fall semester, Jerad's time at Blackhawk ends.

16

Ahead of the Class

For Kristi Beyer's thirty-seventh birthday, a month into their second year of criminal justice classes at Blackhawk Tech, Barb Vaughn gives her a present. It is a wooden plaque, with a saying painted in pale green letters on silvery raw wood: ONE ROSE CAN BE MY GARDEN . . . ONE FRIEND MY WORLD.

Barb had read the quote and hand-lettered it onto the piece of wood she found in her and Mike's garage. The saying seemed fitting, because, thirteen months after she and Kristi arrived at Blackhawk, each struggling to hide her jitters, it is clear to them both that their friendship has become indispensable. At first, they propped each other up as they morphed from factory workers to students. Now they are pushing each other forward, sometimes feeling that it is just the two of them alone, out ahead of the rest of the class.

Barb has never thought of herself as a competitive person, a striver. The one time a boss asked whether she wanted to try being a supervisor— at a factory where she worked, making golf bags, before Lear—she turned down the opportunity. But now, any grade beneath an A has become un- acceptable. She can't put her finger on where this change has come from. It is just here.

And by this birthday of Kristi's on September 22, her mother, Linda Haberman, who turned to Blackhawk herself at twenty-nine to find her way forward from a failed marriage, has never seen anyone studying so hard. Like most people in Janesville, Kristi takes the Green Bay Packers seriously. Now that football season has arrived, the living room television naturally is on for games.

Doesn't she want to put away her books, her mother asks?

"I got to study," Kristi says. "I got a test on Monday." Studying does not get timeouts. The books stay open through the Packers games.

Kristi and her husband, Bob—by now, nine months into his Lear lay-off, without a plan yet what to do about it—share their house with her mother. Seven years ago, the three of them found the yellow ranch house, blocks from Parker High School on the west side of town. Linda was already retired from her hospital secretary's job; she put her pension into the house and makes the mortgage payments. Kristi and Bob cover all the other expenses. Kristi knows her mother thinks of her as her best friend. Even so, her mother brings up now and then that maybe she should let Kristi and Bob have the place to themselves. Kristi always protests, telling her mother that she is right where she belongs. And so it was that Kristi and her mother were watching the television in the living room one night a summer ago, with Lear over just days before and Kristi uncertain which way to turn. Kristi always controlled the TV remote, so it was not surprising that a detective show was on. This night's episode happened to be about fingerprinting, and it got her mother thinking about Kristi always paying such close attention to the crime shows.

"Why don't you go into that kind of work?" Linda asked.

"Yeah, maybe I will," Kristi replied.

Kristi has always been someone who, if she was going to do something, was going to do it fast. She decided fast on Blackhawk, where she found Barb, who, it turns out, loves detective shows, too.

These days, Kristi comes home from school Mondays through Fridays, settles onto the living room couch, opens her books, and—stopping only for supper—studies until time for bed. At some point every day, even though they have been together in classes five days of the week, Barb calls

Kristi, or Kristi calls Barb. They talk over life and assignments and lessons that one or the other doesn't quite understand. Through all these conversations runs a rivalry over who has the best grades, even though the truth is that they both are getting As.

As she listens and watches, her mother has an insight about Kristi that she doesn't say aloud. Kristi needs to prove something to herself: that, at thirty-seven, she isn't too old to make a fresh start.

17

A Plan and Distress Signals

Mary Willmer and Diane Hendricks are ready to go public.

For months, the banker and the billionaire widow have been working with a tiny group of economic development promoters to flesh out their unorthodox vision of a shared destiny for Janesville and Beloit. They have invited business leaders to a few more private meetings, after the first one that left Mary shaking with relief in another woman's bathroom. Still, they have managed to keep their work hush-hush, not wanting it to leak out before the proper time.

Just before Halloween, they decide the time is right. Rock County 5.0 has not yet reached the goal of $1 million in private support. But it is $400,000 along the path. Respectable. And the project now has five well-defined, five-year strategies to buttress its 5.0 name: persuading local companies to stay and expand, attracting new businesses, offering special help to small businesses and start-ups, preparing real estate for commercial uses, and forging a workforce that employers will want to hire. This is the hopeful vision of Rock County from a business-centric point of view: moving beyond Janesville's automotive identity.

Even though the idea is to unify the entire county's fate, Mary keeps in mind, now that it is time to go public, the long, deep rivalry between the

Janesville Gazette and the *Beloit Daily News*, and the reality that almost no one living in one city reads the other's newspaper. So she and Diane invite reporters from both papers to the Beloit headquarters of ABC Supply.

The next day, on October 29, stories announcing the formation of Rock County 5.0 appear on each front page.

"It will change the culture within Rock County, long-term," Mary is quoted as saying.

"Maybe the loss of General Motors was the catalyst that's finally going to bring these communities together," Diane says. "But this is not based around the loss of GM; it's based about the needs of Rock County."

Affirmation is swift. "It's a great idea," the editorial page of the *Beloit Daily News* says the next day. Rock County 5.0 "deserves the strong support of the people, their governmental representatives and the private-sector business community. Sure, times are tough. But they won't get better without a positive attitude and a plan. There's comfort in knowing, now, we're all in this together."

This is a victory for Mary. And yet, from her perch at M&I Bank, she can't escape noticing unmistakable signals that some members of her community are having a hard time keeping their lives glued together.

These distress signals have not appeared right away. During the first six months after one shift at GM went down, wiping out jobs at Lear and the other suppliers, too, personal bankruptcies around town crept up just a little. But now, signs of people's financial collapse are piling up in the U.S. Bankruptcy Court's western district of Wisconsin. From the second half of 2007, when the recession hadn't yet settled in full force and no one knew that the assembly plant would close, to the second half of 2009, the number of people in Janesville filing for bankruptcy has nearly doubled.

Around town, "For Sale" signs are cropping up on the lawns of people who no longer can afford their homes. Of the families in which someone has lost a job, nearly one in three have missed at least one payment on their mortgage or their rent. One in six are moving in with relatives or friends to save money. Some aren't finding an escape plan soon enough; the foreclosure filings in Rock County this year—about 1,200—are running 50 percent ahead of two years ago. Nearly half of the filings will lead to an outright foreclosure. This is part of a national foreclosure crisis that has been both a cause and an effect of the recession—inflicted first by chancy subprime mortgage loans and then by shrunken home values that trap people no longer able to afford their monthly house payments on mortgages larger than their homes are now worth. At 10 a.m. every Wednesday now, in the lobby of the Rock County Courthouse, a member of the Sheriff's Department conducts a foreclosure auction of houses whose owners couldn't figure out a way to keep them.

These foreclosures, and an understanding in the pit of her stomach that people who lose their jobs in America shouldn't have to lose their homes, too, give Mary another idea. Her idea is to invite all the bank presidents and credit union leaders in the area to her office for a conversation about what they are seeing and what they might do about it. It becomes a hard conversation. By piecing together what each one is seeing, the situation looks worse than Mary and the other bankers have each noticed on their own. The conversation leads to an agreement that the banks, together with the United Way, are going to work very hard to support families, providing as much debt counseling as they can and staving off foreclosures as long as they can, giving as much as a year's grace period in hope that people can find new work that will prop up their mortgage payments once again. This is the human side of responding to the recession, Mary thinks, with the banks taking some of the hit and not loading the full burden onto their customers.

Still, the list of foreclosures in the *Gazette* keeps growing. Hard as it is for her to watch, with the girlhood memory of food stamps tucked away in a private place inside her, some people are losing their homes because their mortgages are held by national companies that aren't cutting their customers any breaks. Or because their new jobs don't come with pay that covers the mortgages they could afford in better times. Or because, with unemployment in Rock County still hovering near 12 percent by this fall, some people don't have new jobs.

The Holiday Food Drive

Even in good times, Janesville has had families that were poor, and the assembly plant was a charitable force. Around town, GM'ers were resented sometimes for their big paychecks and their fancy benefits. And yet, union and management alike, they prided themselves on a culture of giving that helped prop up the city's homegrown non-profits, filling crevices of need. Now, Christmas is approaching, almost a year since the last Tahoe came off the line. This is the season in which the GM'ers' generosity found its biggest expression, the season of General Motors' holiday food drive. This year, workers are gone. The crevices of need around town are widening. What will happen to the food drive now?

No one in town is agonizing about this question as much as Marv Wopat. For the past twenty-five years, the food drive has been Marv's baby and one of his greatest pleasures. Every December, as the UAW-GM Employee Assistance Program representative, he was in charge, together with a friend who was a plant nurse, of accumulating the donated groceries and distributing them to the families that needed them the most.

Marv hadn't started out making the food drive a big deal. It began when the nurse got a call at work late one night in the early 1980s about a family that had just been burned out of their house by a fire. It was two days before Christmas, and the family was in desperate need of help. Where better to call than the plant, with its giving culture and its lights on into the wee hours with workers making Chevy Cavaliers. Was there any way that GM could help the family for Christmas? The nurse told Marv, and they went down the assembly line that night and, by the time they got to the end, they had collected $3,000.

The second year, they helped seven families with Christmastime groceries. The next year fifteen. And on it grew, with Marv eventually getting names from the school system and the county health department, and families by now knowing that they could ask to be on the list. Over time, it became 375 families, sometimes 400.

Each year, Marv would handpick certain workers he knew were friendly and well-liked. Somebody from chassis, body shop, skilled trades—each of the departments. And the first week in December, the handpicked would walk up and down the assembly line, asking everyone to contribute. They raised $50,000, easy. The money would go into the Blackhawk Credit Union until it was time to buy the groceries. Woodman's Markets, the grocery chain that began in Janesville in 1919, the same year that General Motors began making tractors in town, could be counted on to give a nice donation. The Seneca Foods plant out near the Interstate, a factory that processes peas, corn, mixed vegetables, and potatoes, provided pallets of canned vegetables.

It wasn't just about food. Marv and some of the plant's other Harley riders would take care of getting toys, once the list of families was drawn up and sorted by the number of kids in each and their ages and whether they were boys or girls. Other GM'ers would ring bells for the Salvation Army.

The pinnacle of this generosity always came the Saturday before Christmas when hundreds of volunteers—UAW line workers and managers alike, many of them bringing their kids—would go down to the plant at 4:30 a.m. and gather in the loading dock area for the bagging operation. Pork chops were piled high in row one, chicken in row two, peanut butter in the next, and on and on. Donated Woodman's grocery bags were unfolded and given a number.

When the food was in its rows and the bags all numbered, Marv, his burly frame often in his Santa suit to delight the kids, stood in the middle and, every year, gave the speech he loved to give: "We want to thank everybody for working together—union and management—and Lord make sure everybody is safe today during the deliveries." And then, in his booming voice, he said: "Go bag!"

Within a half hour, the baggers were done, and the deliverers set out on their routes. The most beautiful assembly line you ever saw in your life, it looked to Marv.

Last year, for the food drive of 2008, the GM'ers raised enough money to provide six bags of groceries each to 350 families. Three mornings before the last Tahoe came off the assembly line, the food was piled on tables in the dock area. Some of the workers bagging food that day had been laid off the summer before and had transferred to GM plants hundreds of miles away but came nevertheless. Some of the workers had no idea whether they would be able to afford their own groceries after the plant closed.

On that food-bagging day, with the assembly plant about to shut down, Marv had an insight: The generosity that had fueled the food drive for a quarter century was about to become a lot more important. The food drive, he told a *Gazette* reporter, needed to outlive the plant. He would organize the drive in a parking lot if he had to. "You get out there and tell people you need help, and they fall out of the woodwork," he told the reporter. "It's too nice of a thing to lose in the community. We're losing enough."

Now, with another December coming and the plant silent, Marv can see the truth of his words almost a year ago. He can see the truth over at ECHO, the main food pantry in town. ECHO stands for Everyone Cooperating to Help Others. It was created in the late 1960s by a coalition of Janesville churches. Now, at its headquarters, downtown at the corner of South High and Court Streets, need is welling up even among some people who have never been poor in their lives and never imagined that they could be. This year, ECHO is giving away 1.4 million pounds of food—nearly twice as much as two years ago and six times as much as the year before that. For the first time, a few people who have been ECHO's donors are standing with shame in its early-morning line to get bread and meat and canned goods.

Marv knows that need has been showing up, too, at Community Action, Inc., part of a string of antipoverty nonprofits born in the federal War on Poverty of the mid-1960s. This need seems different than the kind that Community Action staffers have grown accustomed to seeing walk into their Milwaukee Street office over the decades. The staffers are now seeing new poor who, unlike the old poor, don't want to hear about Food-Share, as food stamps are called in Wisconsin, or BadgerCare, as Medicaid is called, or any other kind of government help for people low on money. These new poor are stressed to the max, having topped out their credit cards and raided their 401(k)'s and sometimes moved out of where they were living and moved in with relatives. In their stress, there is one very specific kind of help that these new poor want, and that is leading them to swallow their pride and call Community Action. Almost all of them want advice on how to find a J-O-B. Not as easy to find as the phone number for FoodShare.

Marv has been in Janesville as long as ECHO has been in town and almost as long as Community Action. Now, with another Christmas coming, and the need rising and rising, he has looked at the question of how to keep the food drive going from every angle he can think of. And the unexpected truth it comes down to is this: How can the drive go on without the workers to chip in when the handpicked walk the assembly line, or to arrive at 4:30 a.m. for the stacking and the bagging and the delivering? How can it go on with some people in town bitter now about GM leaving, and some people having no money to donate for other people's food?

He hates to admit it. It can't be done.

So when Marv is quoted again in the *Gazette*, he says that the end of the drive will leave a big hole—in the community and in his heart.

Part Three

⋆ 2010 ⋆

Last Days of Parker Pen

Eight days into 2010, the last vestige of Parker Pen in town begins to pack up and move to Mexico.

The following Friday is Linda Korban's final day of work. Her final day arrives three months after she has reached a personal goal. In the fall, after the retirement of a co-worker, Linda became #1 in seniority among the 153 who still have jobs. To reach #1 has taken her forty-four years.

Her relationship with Parker began in 1966. That spring, as in every spring in those days, members of the Parker Pen personnel department chose graduating seniors to hire by coming right into Janesville's only high school at the time. The Parker personnel people brought along a test of dexterity and speed that it offered to any senior who wanted to try it. Most of the students who took the test were girls, because the understanding in town back then was that young men lucky enough to be offered a General Motors job would go to the assembly plant. And young women lucky enough to be chosen by Parker Pen would go to work at Arrow Park, a clean, friendly factory in which the making and assembling of pen parts required fine motor skills. Good work for women's hands.

Linda took the test. It required her to insert pegs into a board. She was one of only about twenty in her six-hundred-member graduating class whose hands were nimble enough to get her hired. She started on August 1, and, even these forty-four years later, she can still remember being eighteen, slim with her dirty-blond hair cut short, and the pride she felt when people around town asked what she was doing, and she could tell them that she was working at Parker Pen. Being able to say that was an honor. It was a time when a prestigious Parker fountain pen or even a nice ballpoint was an especially meaningful gift around Janesville, because the giver perhaps had made it or worked with someone who had made it or, at the least, knew someone working at Parker Pen.

Now that her final day, January 15, is arriving, it is hard for Linda—indeed, for many in town—to fathom that the name Parker Pen will soon remain only as a fragment of Janesville's history.

★

The Parker Pen Company was founded by a man whose life trajectory traced a perfect arc of the American Dream. George Safford Parker was born during the Civil War in rural Shullsburg, Wisconsin, sixty-eight miles west of Janesville. His family went back on his father's side to a couple who had arrived in Connecticut from Dover, England, in 1632. Parker grew up on an Iowa farm, yearning to see the world. At the time he was coming of age, it was popular for young men with ambition and wanderlust to seek jobs as telegraph operators on railroads. He was a lanky nineteen-year-old when he arrived in Janesville with $55 for the tuition at the Valentine School of Telegraphy. Run by two brothers of that name, Valentine was the only telegraphy school in the nation that held contracts with railroad companies. Parker was an able student. When he graduated, he was pleased to be hired by the Chicago, Milwaukee and St. Paul Railroad, until he learned that his job would not be riding the rails that traversed the American West, but holed up in a station in a backwater of South Dakota. So when Richard Valentine asked Parker months later to return to the school as an instructor, he jumped at the chance. Back in Janesville, he taught young men just a few years younger than himself and, on the side, was an agent for an Ohio pen company, selling fountain pens that his students needed in their studies to transcribe telegraph code. The John Holland Co. pens tended to leak, and Parker developed a specialty in pen repair and alteration. "It will always be possible to make a better pen," Parker said in 1888, the year he formed the Parker Pen Company. He was twenty-five. The following year, he secured his first pen patent and, five years after that, another patent for the writing instrument that would catapult Parker into a company with an international reputation—the Lucky Curve.

By 1900, his business had large contracts to sell pens to the federal government and a Main Street address for its four-story factory and sales office, before it eventually moved into a handsome, steel-frame factory along Court Street. As his business grew, so did a paternalistic generosity that Parker showered on his workers, typical of the welfare capitalism of the day intended to foster loyalty and ward off unrest. A clubhouse for employee parties. Camp Cheerio on the grounds of his summer house on the river's bluff. A housing development, Parkwood, for company executives. By the 1920s, he was patron of the Parker Pen Concert Band, purchasing instruments for musicians if they needed help and furnishing company vehicles to convey players to concerts. He instructed the personnel in charge of hiring Parker Pen's factory and office workers to check with the band's director about the kinds of musicians he could use; applicants who could fill a vacancy in the band were to be given hiring preference.

Parker satisfied his childhood yen to roam, traveling the globe to open export markets—the first in the Netherlands in 1903. When, after his death, the Arrow Park factory opened in 1953 on Parker Drive, it had flags outside from each of the eighty-eight nations in which the company was, at the time, selling pens. Parker wrote books about his travels, on the South Seas and China's Yangtze River, and brought home an enormous ivory collection that he was fond of showing to friends, including the architect Frank Lloyd Wright.

Parker pens showed up at defining moments of the twentieth century. During World War I, the U.S. War Department awarded Parker a contract for a "Trench Pen," with dry pellets that turned into liquid ink when soldiers in the field added water. In May of 1945, the treaty of German surrender that ended World War II in Europe was signed with a pair of Parker 51 fountain pens belonging to General Dwight D. Eisenhower, the Supreme Commander of the Allied Forces, who held up the two pens for the cameras in a V for victory. At the 1964 World's Fair in New York, a Parker pavilion sponsored the biggest international letter-writing program that had ever been undertaken. It featured an early "electric computer," which could, within seconds, match a fairgoer with a pen pal of similar age and interests overseas. Uniformed women known as Pennettes, from Janesville and around the globe, handed out pens, postcards, and stationery.

Two years later, the year that Linda was hired, George S. Parker II, a grandson of its founder, became the company's president and CEO. He was the last Parker to run Parker Pen, and he presided over a long, slow decline as the market for high-end pens waned. In 1986, he sold the company to a group of British investors affiliated with a British firm based in a town along the English Channel, Newhaven, where Parker pens had been manufactured since shortly after World War II. Pen making continued in Janesville under the name Parker Pen Holdings Ltd. Then, in 1993, the Gillette Company bought out Parker Pen Holdings Ltd. Six years later, the pen business was bought out again, by Newell Rubbermaid—specifically, by an offshoot of its office supplies division known as Sanford Business-to-Business, which customizes pens for promotional purposes. So the final 153 workers, Linda among them, have been working for a company called Sanford, not Parker. They have no longer been making pens. They have been printing the logos of pharmaceutical companies and other businesses onto the sides of pens that were made overseas.

*

With the British Parker Pen and then Gillette and finally Newell Rubbermaid's Sanford B2B, more than a name was surrendered. Gone, too, was the relationship that workers had with a local, family-run business and that the family that owned the business had with the community in which its workers lived.

Inside Arrow Park when Linda was hired, there was no mistaking the factory's family feel. Girls followed their mothers into Parker Pen the way that boys followed their fathers into the GM assembly plant. The work had seasonal ups and down, with pens in high demand for gifts as graduation season and Christmas neared—and sometimes temporary layoffs in between. Parker sent women home, too, when they were pregnant and hired them back once their babies were a year old. Linda, married at twenty and divorced five years later, did not have children, so her seniority was uninterrupted.

Late every Friday afternoon, just before Linda and everyone else went home for the weekend, a song came over the loudspeaker:

> *May the good Lord bless and keep you*
> *Whether near or far away . . .*

Listening to the song, Linda felt every Friday that the Parkers cared about her. Even before the song, Fridays were special, because that was the day that workers dressed up a little more and that some departments had their check pools, with everyone kicking in a dollar and betting on the last digits on their paychecks.

And there was never an employee birthday without a cake or a Christmas season without a smorgasbord. The Parker Pen employees created two cookbooks of their favorite recipes. Every day, break time began with the arrival of a woman who wheeled a coffee cart through the factory, with fresh hard rolls and squares of cheese, and sometimes even baked apples and donuts, depending on the season. To encourage exercise, the company gave a walking award, and employees strolled the grounds at lunchtime until their miles earned them a charm shaped like two tiny feet. Managers understood if a worker had to stay home with a sick child. And once a year was Family Day, when husbands and children toured the plant and everyone could take home a pen—a Jotter ballpoint or, once it was invented in 1982, a Vector rollerball. In the summer, Parker Pen sponsored its company picnic at different parks around the county, including sometimes at Thresherman's Park, with free rides on a model steam engine train and fresh sweet corn from a nearby farm set into a cattle trough and cooked in the engine's steam. And there were elaborate Parker Pen floats for Janesville's Labor Fest parade, with the float in 1994 constructed right at Arrow Park, where workers tucked blue crepe paper into a long cylindrical frame of chicken wire to look like a giant Jotter, commemorating the fortieth anniversary of one of Parker's most successful writing instruments.

For years, Linda bowled in one of the Parker Pen leagues. In the summer, she played on the Parker Pen golf league. Working at Parker was about philanthropy, too, with a Charitable Giving Committee of workers who, each year, were selected to decide which of the many social service organizations in town deserved $5,000—sometimes $10,000—that the company's annual budget allocated for good works. Managers encouraged workers to do their part. Linda raised money for the Humane Society.

She had been hired into the department that made the fountain pen's nibs—solid gold for their durability and smooth writing feel. Over the years, she moved to the department that inspected for quality control and then to the stock department, which, once she got there, she felt was her calling because it drew on her orderliness and allowed her the freedom to move throughout the factory. As long as Parker Pen was still in the Parker family, almost no one quit for a different job.

It did not occur to Linda to leave even when Gillette took over and the blessing song stopped coming over the loudspeaker on Friday afternoons. When the song stopped, she felt like just a factory worker, one of 650 at Arrow Park by then, none of them special anymore. She was still doing her stock work on January 19, 1999, the day that a corporate man from Gillette arrived and announced that the company was closing Arrow Park and told everyone to take the rest of the day off and come back the next morning for a few more months, until their jobs would end.

The last day of making pens was the Friday before Memorial Day that year. Before then, some of Linda's co-workers had to take all the little pen pieces and glue them to wooden boards in the correct sequence, to be shipped to Newhaven in Britain so that workers near the English Channel would know how to assemble properly the pen models that no longer would be made in Janesville. Before Arrow Park closed, Linda and others in the stock department had to crate up and send free shipments of surplus pens. They were mailed off to a pen factory in California, a loyal department store in New York, and other distant destinations, until a little delegation of stock department workers asked their bosses whether some of these pens could stay in town, going to the food pantry, ECHO, and the Salvation Army and even Janesville schoolkids, because who wouldn't want a nice Parker Pen? Finally, it was down to a few beautiful ballpoints, in sterling silver, which were going to be shipped away, too, until one of Linda's co-workers marched into a supervisor's office and said, given that the stock room women were among the last still working at Arrow Park, shipping pens after production had stopped, didn't they deserve a silver pen? On their last day, Linda and the others each got one.

By now, Linda was fifty-one and single and needed a job. She had never thought of working anywhere else. So, when the new owners, the Sanford B2B division of Newell Rubbermaid, said that they needed sixty-five people for the logo-imprinting on pens made elsewhere—working in a manufacturing space, much smaller than Arrow Park, on the north side of town—she applied. The sixty-five workers were handpicked and, as she had when she graduated from high school, Linda felt honored to be chosen.

For eleven years, as the sixty-five workers grew to 153, Linda continued to do stock work, becoming a stock lead, which meant that she supervised and stocked, too. A muted camaraderie returned among the workers who remembered the Parker days. Her pay, right around $18 an hour, was among the highest. So it was fine, until last August 19, when, without warning, the top Sanford guy in Janesville came out onto the plant floor. He set a wooden crate upside down for him to stand high enough that everyone could see him. He announced that the corporation had decided to close the plant. Just as Gillette had done eleven years before, he told everyone to take the rest of the day off.

At Newell Rubbermaid's corporate headquarters in Illinois, a decision had been made a month before to close the Newhaven pen-making factory in England. Then, on this August day, a corporate public relations manager issued a press release. The Janesville plant, it said, was a casualty of excess capacity. A factory in Mexico, doing the same kind of logo imprinting, could take on all the work. "This decision is a response to structural issues accelerated by market trends," the press release said, "and is in no way a reflection on the highly valued work performed by our Janesville employees over the years."

To Linda, it isn't structural. It is personal. Close to a half century of her life. She is about to turn sixty-two, old enough to collect Social Security after the severance pay she would get if she left now. So, although she could stay while this manufacturing space is taken apart, as Arrow Park was taken apart years before, she decides to move aside. Let someone younger than her eke out a few more months.

Her departure, just as this year is beginning, counts as a layoff, not a retirement. And so, for her forty-four years, she does not get even a retirement cake.

It hurts at first, after all the birthday cakes and the Christmas smorgasbords of what used to be such a friendly, family-feeling factory back in the Parker Pen days. But now she is at peace with this uncelebrated leaving.

She is ready to leave, because she does not want to do what some of her co-workers will do during the next few months. Like them, she has been offered an opportunity to be paid longer if she were willing to fly to Mexico and train workers there. Linda has given training over the years, and she knows that she has a knack for it. If she were being asked to train someone in Janesville, she would, naturally, say yes. But to train someone in Mexico—*Mexico!*—to take over her job? After her forty-four years, she doesn't have the heart for that.

Becoming a Gypsy

Just get going, Matt Wopat whispers to himself. *Go.* He is in his Sierra pickup, in his garage, merely a few feet from the open doorway to the laundry room where Darcy and the girls are crowded together. He watches them as if in a picture frame. They're crying. They're blowing kisses his way.

He sees his daughters turn away from the doorway. He sees Darcy, as if she can't take it anymore, wave a last goodbye and shut the door. He is alone, fighting tears himself. He's tried hard to sound reassuring, to convince them that everything will be fine. Now he wonders how persuasive he's been, because, frankly, he isn't sure he believes it himself.

A twist of the key in the ignition, and Matt feels the aging truck's familiar idle. His hand drifts to the gear shift, but he can't make himself shift into reverse. And he knows why.

A weight is pressing on him, the kind of weight that presses hard on a man who is on the cusp of his fifth decade when he discovers that doing everything right is not enough. Not enough to live by Plan A, as his father has done, and his father-in-law and his uncle, and the thousands of men a couple of generations back who counted their days and months on the assembly line until the years added up to thirty, and they could retire. He came up with a Plan B, learning to climb utility poles, just in case the assembly plant fails to reopen, even though his dad, Marv, still insists that it will. Plan B isn't looking good, either.

By this Sunday afternoon, March 7, seven months have gone by since Matt began to study electric power distribution—finding himself in the throng of out-of-a-job factory workers who pivoted to Blackhawk Tech. Peculiar and embarrassing as it had seemed at first, he made peace with the nightly ritual of spreading his schoolbooks on the kitchen table after dinner, along with Brittany in twelfth grade, Brooke in ninth, and Bria in seventh, all four of them doing their homework and him sometimes even asking Brittany for help with his math. A good example, he felt he was setting for his daughters—an example of working hard and making the best of a bad situation.

His main instructor, Mike Doubleday, had grown up on a farm that grew corn and soybeans in Clinton, a small town fifteen miles southeast of Janesville, and, after high school, he had taken over the farming because his father had gotten hurt. His farming days, though, didn't last long. He went to Blackhawk as a student in the same program in which he is teaching now, then found a job building and repairing power lines for the town of Evansville, twenty miles to the northwest. For fifteen years, he was an apprentice and then a journeyman lineman until he heard that the college needed an instructor to help with the backlog of people wanting to become linemen like him. The change appealed to him. Mike had been teaching for only a year by the time Matt arrived, but he already had an instinct for predicting, a few weeks into a semester, which of his students were going to succeed, which would drop out, and which were the middling ones who could go either way. In Mike's view, Matt had what it took to succeed. Like most of the guys, Matt had trouble with the algebra formulas for electrical theory. But he hung out with five other GM'ers in class, including one especially good with the math, until they each worked out the solutions. Matt impressed Mike as honest and straightforward, a hard worker who wasn't outgoing but wasn't afraid to ask questions when he didn't understand and was eager to help other guys if he grasped a concept first. Plus, his roofing experience gave Matt some background that would come in handy. He was going to make a good lineman somewhere, Mike felt pretty sure.

What Mike Doubleday could not see in Matt was that, as he was puzzling out electrical theory with some of the guys in class, he also was worrying. Matt is a deliberate man, and deliberate men do not let their mortgage payments slip behind, but there it was. He and Darcy had lived near the edge of what General Motors' $28 an hour could buy, as so many GM'ers did, paying $270 a month on their camper, trading in cars for newer models, even dipping into their 401(k) once in a while to take the girls on trips. So even though, as a GM'er, Matt was lucky to get his union SUB pay on top of his unemployment checks, and the federal government was covering his tuition and textbooks and gas mileage to campus and even the right clothes for climbing utility poles, it didn't add up to anywhere near $28 an hour. The reality was that he and Darcy didn't have much cushion, and his SUB pay was about to be cut in half, and his GM health benefits were going to run out.

He just needed, Matt told himself, to hang on until May. When he got his technical diploma, he could grab on to the kind of job that Mike had given up to become an instructor. But that's where the rumors came in—the rumors getting louder that the linemen at the local utility company, Alliant Energy, whose average age was about fifty-five, might not be retiring, after all, so that jobs might not be opening up. And that is why, when another GM'er learning to climb utility poles mentioned to Matt that he'd heard that GM jobs were coming open in Indiana, Matt felt he needed to pay attention.

By this winter, hundreds of Janesville GM'ers have morphed into GM'ers working far from Janesville. Their UAW contract gave them these transfer rights. Nearly two hundred are working at a General Motors plant in Kansas City—so many that people in town now joke that Kansas City has become Janesville West. Almost 140 are at a plant in Arlington, Texas—Janesville South—which is still turning out the Tahoe SUVs that Janesville had made. So far, fifty-five have transferred to Janesville

East—Fort Wayne, Indiana—to assemble Chevy Silverado trucks, which are so popular that the plant is adding a third shift and is sending job offers to sixty-seven more Janesville GM'ers, including Matt.

GM gypsies, these out-of-town Janesville GM'ers are called, because even the ones in Arlington, nearly one thousand miles away, have, for the most part, left their families behind and are commuting home as best they can. Matt has been firm that he was not going to become any gypsy. No way.

But he and Darcy don't want to move, either. They have had long, soulful, repeated conversations on this subject. They were in agreement. Close as they are to both their families, how could they leave? Darcy going over to her father's house, ever since her mother died, to pay his bills out of his GM pension and balance his checkbook. The girls on their sports teams in school. That was the whole reason Matt began doing homework at the kitchen table—to retool so that he can get a different job so that they can all stay together in town.

But that was before the mortgage payments started slipping behind, and his benefits were going to get cut, and the GM jobs opening up were in Fort Wayne, which, while four and a half hours away, is closer than Kansas City or Arlington. That is why, one day, Matt and a bunch of the GM'ers learning to climb utility poles with him decide that it is time to stay after class and ask their instructor, Mike, a tough, pointed question: If they stay in school to graduate, will linemen's jobs be waiting for them or not?

Mike starts by laying out the benefits of electric power distribution. But the more he talks, the more he feels he needs to be a straight shooter with these guys who already have lost so much. The truth is, he has to admit, not many of his Blackhawk graduates got jobs last year. The outlook still isn't great. Jobs exist in the utility field but not many of them in southern Wisconsin. He tells them they might end up in the Dakotas or Texas or somewhere in the Southwest.

Listening to this straight shooting, one thing the instructor says, in particular, burns into Matt's mind: "If I were you guys and had an opportunity to get GM wages, I would run and not look back."

That is when Matt understands that the option he'd rejected is the only choice he has left. He couldn't even call it a choice, because he feels that it has all come down to either Fort Wayne or maybe even bankruptcy sometime soon, and responsible men don't file for bankruptcy.

As his mind churns on this jam he is in, the strangest thing is that he can find absolutely no one to blame. Not the instructor who, poor guy, was just leveling with him. Or the government, dutifully paying for classes for a job he might never get. Not GM, shelling out for his benefits even as the company had gone bankrupt itself. Certainly not Darcy, trying her damnedest to find a job better than restocking her Hallmark displays a couple of days a week. Not even himself, because every time he has rethought the exceedingly hard question of whether he missed a clue, whether he overlooked some narrow passageway that would have led him out of the maze, he came to the conclusion that he had not.

Nine weeks of classes to go before he is to get his diploma, Matt leaves school.

So now, in less than twenty-four hours, he will be working at a GM plant he's never seen in a city he's never visited. He couldn't think of anything he wanted to do less, or anything he needed to do more.

He and Darcy and the girls have just finished Sunday lunch, and he's stood in their warm, bright kitchen, insisting that it won't be so bad. It will be just five days, Mondays cruising toward Fridays, he said as he hugged them all, and he'll be back every weekend. And who knows, maybe, sometime soon, something decent in Janesville, something close to $28 an hour, will finally come along.

Now, sitting in the Sierra with his hand on the gear shift, it is time to pull out of the garage and head south to the Wisconsin border and on into Illinois, past the Belvidere Chrysler plant—not hiring, of course—and then east into Indiana all the way to Fort Wayne, where he will crash on the couch of another Janesville GM'er—another guy who quit learning to climb utility poles a couple of weeks ago—because Matt doesn't have a clue where he's going to live.

It is time. But he sits there five minutes. Ten. Just brooding, staring at nothing, the only sound the idle of the pickup in his garage. Matt still remembers a long-ago moment when he was younger than even Bria is now. Money was short because his father was drinking in those days before he became Employee Assistance rep, and he was riding around town in his dad's rusted-out boat of a Cadillac, feeling as if he was in the only wreck in a new-car-proud town. A friend of his was on the sidewalk, and he'd been so embarrassed about the Caddy that, pretending to tie a shoelace, he'd ducked down.

It is so plain: He can't let his kids feel that kind of money shame. Plan A, Plan B, or whatever plan it takes, he will at least be the man he's always understood himself to be. Who would rather put himself out than his family. Who always keeps his word when he says he'll do a job. Who understands that, in order to protect his family, he has to leave them.

He grips the steering wheel, shifts into reverse, and backs out of the garage and down the driveway.

Family Is More Important than GM

S pring has just returned to southern Wisconsin when Jerad Whiteaker grabs a buyout from General Motors like a brass ring. It isn't
much—about $4,000 and six more months of health insurance. At
least it's something.

As he signs the paperwork that seals the deal, Jerad trades away the
possibility of another job within General Motors, somewhere, sometime,
for the certainty of this small severance package right now. He is transforming himself from a GM'er who happens to be on an indefinite layoff
into an ex-GM'er. Not much difference, it might seem. Except that, for
Jerad, whose father and father-in-law put in their thirty years at the assembly plant and now live on their comfy pensions, he is signing away the
future he has expected for himself.

The decision was not easy at first. He and Tammy talked over their
choices, at moments when they hoped that the twins and Noah wouldn't
hear. None of the choices were any good. Of their need for the cash and
the insurance there was no doubt. The early days of layoff life, when Jerad
treated the curious absence of a job as a deserved vacation, seemed far in
the past. Of all their bad choices, this one, at least, had the virtue of being

in line with the basic understanding of his life that Jerad carries around: Family is more important than General Motors.

Family being more important than General Motors is the kind of mantra—terse yet sturdy—typical of Jerad, whose feelings for the people he loves are often cloaked in a taciturn nature. And so, when he says, "To me, family is everything," the twins, Alyssa and Kayzia, understand what their dad is saying, even if he doesn't come out and say it. They understand that their father has never quite gotten over the night of December 22, 1986, when he was sixteen, growing up in Footville and just a year older than they are now. His parents were finishing Christmas shopping, so he was the only one home to open the door to a police officer who was standing on the front steps. Jerad's brother, Michael, had just been killed in a car crash. The car brakes, it would turn out, probably had failed as he was driving in a rural part of Janesville's west side, so that he plowed through a stop sign and into another car. His girlfriend was with him; she was killed, too. Michael was twenty—Jerad's big brother. His death left their parents with only one living child—and left Jerad with a gloom that arrives before every Christmas.

With his family-is-everything attitude, Jerad disliked his second year at the assembly plant. After having been hired into the paint shop, he was bumped to second shift, which started at 4:30 p.m. and ended at 2:30 a.m. He disliked not eating supper or spending evenings with Tammy and the twins, in the days before Noah was born, leaving him time with them mainly on weekends. He so hated being away from them that, after a year, he managed to switch to the plant's medium-duty truck line, even though the work was harder on his body, because medium-duty had only one shift in those days and it was first shift, which meant that he could punch out at 3:48 p.m. and go home. A few years later, once the medium-duty assembly moved from Janesville to Flint, Michigan, Jerad had enough seniority that he could stay on first shift when he slid over to Tahoes.

These days, Jerad cannot imagine living the way his best friend, Kevin, now lives. Kevin took a transfer to GM's Fairfax Assembly Plant in Kansas City, five hundred miles away. He has a family that he loves, too, and he drove the seven and a half hours each way, back and forth, every weekend until Fairfax started giving overtime, so that now he drives back and forth one weekend a month. No way to live, Jerad thinks.

When Jerad got his chance to transfer, like his friend Kevin and like Matt Wopat and hundreds of others, the idea didn't seem worth thinking about. Tammy and the kids didn't want to move. He wasn't going anywhere without them. Besides, his own mother, Lucille, already felt too far from her only son and her only grandkids. Jerad's father, Randy, had retired from the assembly plant on the day before his fiftieth birthday; after a while, they'd moved three hundred miles up north to a small town, Spooner, in an area speckled with pretty lakes. Even if Tammy and the kids wanted to go, which they didn't, Jerad couldn't pull his family further from his parents, his girls further from the grandmother they adore. Family is everything.

So late last summer, just around the time he slid down the wooden practice utility pole in his electric power distribution class, when Jerad got a job offer, he took it. It was his first offer since he'd begun looking, an offer when jobs weren't coming along in Janesville. "The heck with school," Jerad thought after the pole-sliding, chest-scraping, nerve-jangling incident. "I'm going to work."

He was aware that this wouldn't be a perfect solution. The job is at a local company called GOEX, which makes plastic sheeting and plastic rolls. The fact that his new job is in a factory making plastic, not automobiles, is not a problem. The problem is that the work comes in twelve-hour shifts, 6 a.m. to 6 p.m., on a rotation that requires him to work every other weekend. While he is still living with his family in Janesville—and not in some apartment near a GM plant hundreds of miles from home—he can't go to his kids' events after school or, half the time, on a Saturday or a Sunday. For this family-disrupting work, Jerad is paid $12.48 an hour—less than half his old $28 GM wages.

With this skimpy new pay, trying to scratch together enough money to live on has become a family project. While raising three kids, Tammy has been working part-time from home, typing in data on a laptop for a company called Home Entry Services. The rules of her job say she can work up to six hours a day. It often turns out to be less. The work is piecework.

She averages $10 an hour, but the amount of work is unpredictable week to week. And after volunteering and making a point of getting to know the principal, she finally got hired as a part-time teacher's aide at the kids' former elementary school.

Alyssa and Kayzia have begun to chip in, too, now that they are fifteen and go to Parker High. Wisconsin allows teenagers as young as fourteen to work three hours on school days and eight hours on weekends. Alyssa goes first, managing to get hired as a hostess at Texas Roadhouse on the north side of town for $2.33 an hour, plus her tip share. Kayzia starts as a cashier at minimum wage at Culver's, home of the ButterBurger and frozen custard, and soon Alyssa switches to Culver's, figuring that it's easier for them to work at the same place, plus Culver's is close enough to home that they can walk. They are saving for cell phones and used cars; no way their parents can help pay for these basic props of Janesville teen-age life. But they listen carefully to the conversations their parents hope they can't hear. Soon, without their parents asking, they begin to offer some of their small paychecks from serving up ButterBurgers and frozen custard to help cover their family's bills, even if the phones will have to wait a little longer.

Because the truth is that a low-pay plastics job and piecework home data-entry plus part-time as a teacher's aide are not enough for a family of five to live the normal, middle-class way that the Whiteakers have lived. When Jerad was laid off from GM, he and Tammy had about $5,000 in savings. After more than one and a half years of pulling out a bit at a time to keep up with the mortgage and the utility bills, the savings are gone.

They have cut back as much as they can. The $200 a week that Tammy used to spend on groceries is down to $200 a month, with more pasta and less meat. No more going out to eat. No more of their favorite weekend afternoons, with all of them piling into the car for a drive into the country-side, nowhere in particular. Wasting gas money on a country drive is now out of the question. No high school dances for Alyssa and Kayzia, unless they pay their own way.

Tammy and Jerad can see that their family is not the only one cut-ting back. Around town, "For Sale" signs have been cropping up on boats and campers and other grown-up toys that were trophies of middle-class lives. And as more houses have gone up for sale, Tammy and Jerad talk over whether to try to sell their raised ranch with its backyard pool and find something smaller to rent. They bought their house for $140,000 in 2004. Then, back in the days of Jerad's GM wages and ten overtime hours most weeks at time-and-a-half, they took out a second loan to fix up the basement for the twins and Noah to have their bedrooms downstairs. They owe $160,000 on the house, which was fine when it was appraised at $161,000 in May 2008, a month before GM announced that the plant would become a goner. But it is no longer fine at all. Last they knew, the house was worth just $137,000—and that's if anyone were buying houses in Janesville these days. Every time Tammy and Jerad talk about it, they end up in the same place: Trying to sell a house with a mortgage underwater in a crummy real estate market doesn't make sense.

If they cannot sell their house, they can at least join the rush of people around town selling off belongings. Jerad and Tammy already have sold their snowmobile and two four-wheelers. Now Tammy gets rid of her Harley in a garage sale. But much as they need the cash, she draws a line: She will not sell the oak, glass-shelved curio cabinet that sits in the far corner of the living room, the curio that she always wanted as a girl and that Jerad bought for her when they were first married—he twenty-two, she all of eighteen.

Curio or no curio, something has to give. The buyout begins to seem like a good deal. It is a good deal for General Motors, too, because, for the past five years, one tool the company has been using to try to straighten out its finances is to coax workers to leave—saving GM the expense of their benefits and pensions. In March 2006, a few months after the major cutbacks that unnerved yet spared Janesville, GM offered buyouts to 113,000 hourly workers. Nearly 35,000 took the offer, including about 900 from Janesville. In February 2008, the day before Obama arrived in town for his campaign speech at the plant, GM offered a "special attrition program" to all 74,000 of its remaining hourly workers. Nearly 19,000 took that buyout. If Jerad had taken the buyout then, he would have lost his benefits right away but received $140,000 in cash—$136,000 more than he is getting through the buyout he signs for now. If only he'd jumped sooner, but who knew the plant was going to close?

The buyout cash now won't put him ahead. The few thousand dollars is about the same amount of money as the SUB pay that the UAW contract would have provided him anyway until later in the year. And the buyout means that he'll never be eligible for a General Motors pension. Retirement benefits, though, would have been years away, and the clincher for taking the buyout is now. The clincher is the health insurance; for six more months, Jerad and Tammy will not need to buy health insurance through GOEX. Of all their bad options, the buyout seems best.

As it turns out, when Jerad signs the paperwork converting him into an ex-GM'er, he happens to be doing himself and his family a favor. General Motors may have been given nearly $50 billion in government loans for the bailout and the bankruptcy, yet it still is trying to shrink its workforce. In May, the company will give its remaining out-of-a-job Janesville GM'ers one more opportunity to transfer to a plant out of town—to Lordstown, Ohio, eight hours away. This transfer opportunity will be different from the one that Matt Wopat took when he began driving to Fort Wayne on Mondays and back home on Friday nights, or the ones that led hundreds of others to Arlington, Texas, or Kansas City, where Jerad's best friend is working. This will be a forced transfer, allowed under the contract when laid-off workers have already turned down three transfer offers. Janesville's remaining GM'ers will need to report to Lordstown. Otherwise, they will be severed from General Motors with nothing except a slim chance they might be rehired if the Janesville plant ever reopens.

So the cash isn't much, and the insurance won't last long. But by the time the Lordstown transfer comes along, Jerad is feeling clever to have grasped for the last brass ring when he could.

★ 22 ★

Honor Cords

The Dream Center is the Beloit auditorium in which Blackhawk Tech holds its graduations, and Barb Vaughn feels as if she's pinch-me dreaming, seated in a black cap and gown amid rows of caps and gowns. Draped around her neck are a golden Phi Theta Kappa sash and honor cords, royal blue and gold, their tasseled ends dangling past her waist. Wisdom, aspiration, purity. The honor society at two-year colleges such as Blackhawk takes its name from the initial letters of the Greek words for these virtues. Barb is having trouble absorbing that the shame she lugged around since she was a sixteen-year-old dropout is gone, her ferocious studying and string of As having earned her a place in this virtue-named honor society and, within a few moments, an associate's degree.

Barb is not seated next to her friend Kristi. The 268 students, to be handed their diplomas in gold-trimmed black cases on this day, May 15, are organized by program. Within each one, they are seated alphabetically. So Kristi, wearing her own sash and honor cords, is near the front of the criminal justice degree earners and Barb is toward the rear. When the time arrives that Blackhawk's president calls out, "Criminal Justice," they rise in unison and move toward the steps that lead onto the right side of the curved stage. They share the same outsized pride, even though, in the end, Kristi edged out Barb, who hasn't forgiven herself for the lone A-minus—in their juvenile law course—that sullies an otherwise perfect record.

In their pride and their graduation regalia as they approach the stage, just under two years since they left the Lear Corp. factory floor, Barb and Kristi are part of what is notable about the Blackhawk graduating class of 2010. This year's graduates include the first Great Recession refugees who turned to Blackhawk. Even before the throngs of laid-off autoworkers and laid-off other workers—including Barb's husband, Mike—descended on the campus a year later, this first wave began to reshape the school. By the spring of Barb's and Kristi's first year, the little campus surrounded by cornfields had 850 more students than a year before—a 20 percent increase—most of them fresh out of factory jobs.

So it is fitting that this morning's commencement address is delivered by an American Dream story herself—a woman named Tiffaney Beverly-Malott, who lifted herself from the overnight shift in a jelly-making factory to the boardroom of a network-marketing firm. In the process, she became a millionaire selling cosmetics. She gives a lot of motivational speeches. When she takes center stage at the Dream Center, in an elegant cream-colored suit with ruffled lapels, she aims her words straight at this morning's unlikeliest graduates, including Barb and Kristi, who had never expected that a recession would steal their factory jobs. "There were many reactions, I'm sure, to the dire circumstances facing the economy of this community," she tells the graduates. "Many people complained, many people cried, many people gave up. Some waited for things to go back to the way they were. . . . But there were a vital few that decided to create a new future for themselves and this area. They decided to use the economic obstacles as an economic opportunity. Those people were all of you."

Blunt though she is, there is a piece of the story that the American-Dream-in-a-suit commencement speaker leaves unspoken. Many of the former factory workers who turned to Blackhawk veered off course before today. Of the laid-off workers who arrived at the college in the fall of 2008 with Barb and Kristi, nearly half left without finishing what they'd begun. Of the three hundred or so who, like Barb and Kristi, aimed for an associate's degree—the highest degree that Blackhawk offers—just over one third will stick around to finish within a few years. And of the thirty-one laid-off workers who began to study criminal justice with Barb and Kristi? Just half are collecting diplomas today or will graduate next year.

Such bumpy outcomes are not unusual at two-year colleges in general. In fact, at Blackhawk, more of this first wave of laid-off workers finished their studies than did their classmates who hadn't lost a job. Still, the point unspoken in the Dream Center today is that, even when people desperate for a job try to retrain, as the Job Center has been encouraging, they don't always succeed.

Paul Ryan, now chairman of the House Budget Committee, and President Obama remain unlikely allies in cheerleading for out-of-work Americans to retrain for new jobs. Still, the people at Blackhawk know a grittier, ground-level truth: Retraining laid-off factory workers is not easy. Even at a little college like Blackhawk, which has been trying like hell.

Sharon Kennedy, Blackhawk's vice president of learning who arrived in town months before anyone knew that the assembly plant would close, believes in job retraining. She also believes in candor. In her scant spare time, she has begun to research a book on Midwestern assembly line workers who go back to school. Not long ago, she drove up to Madison to the Wisconsin state capitol, where she told lawmakers eager to build Wisconsin's workforce the story of her baptism by fire and the frenzy of her staff as they raced to figure out how to help dazed, confused, out-of-a-job factory workers trying to transform themselves into students. Even that first year, the year that Barb and Kristi arrived, before the bigger crush, Sharon testified, they arrived in numbers "too overwhelming to do business as usual."

That is why Blackhawk added the eighty-eight extra class sessions; hired extra instructors such as Mike Doubleday; borrowed financial aid officers from other schools; and—when it ran out of classrooms—added courses at night and on Saturdays, along with a "Nighttime Is the Right Time" marketing campaign to attract students to these unpopular hours for sitting in class. It hired a mental health counselor for students and created stress-reduction sessions for instructors and administrators. And it wasn't enough. Just before the fall semester of 2008, Sharon and the staff tried hard to foster a welcoming feel for laid-off workers who hadn't been in school for a long time. Blackhawk had a community picnic for families, with games for kids and a chance for about-to-be students to talk with deans and instructors over hamburgers and hot dogs. At the picnic, staff members brought computers for anyone who wanted to register for classes on the spot. Sharon was startled at how few registered. "This," she later told the legislators, "should have been our first clue as to a looming problem."

Because to Sharon and Blackhawk's instructors, the most surprising fact about these arriving factory workers was how many of them didn't know how to use a computer—didn't even know how to turn one on. "We were caught totally off guard by the minimal skills most have, and they were caught off guard by the need to have these skills in order to be a student in today's world," Sharon testified. Blackhawk's staff was nimble. They hustled to create a computer boot camp, and on short notice they created a Student Success course on how to study. Even so, some students dropped out as soon as they found out that their instructors would not accept course papers written out longhand.

So, when Jerad Whiteaker left school after two weeks, his decision wasn't unusual. By the time Matt Wopat left Blackhawk, nine weeks before this graduation day, to reclaim General Motors wages, he already had stayed in school longer than many who had started classes with him.

For the men and women in caps and gowns on this cool, clear late morning, even the ones who aren't wearing Phi Theta Kappa sashes and honor cords, the fact that they are walking across the Dream Center stage makes them standouts.

By the time Barb and Kristi remove their regalia and head off together, with their husbands and Barb's in-laws and Kristi's mom, to celebrate graduation with a late lunch at Olive Garden, they are double standouts. They have just graduated with top grades. They are about to start good jobs.

Back in December, as they were finishing their third semester, both added their names to a list of applicants for four openings at the Rock County Sheriff's Department. Given all the people in town who still need a job, the list was long—about one thousand names. The Sheriff's Department invited four hundred of them to take an application test. Barb and Kristi were among them.

The jobs are entry-level—correctional officers at the County Jail—but they pay $16.47 an hour. Nearly $6 an hour less than at Lear, it is better than most places in town offer these days. Plus, correctional officers are state employees, with solid health insurance and vacation time. And these jobs are in the criminal justice system—exactly where Barb and Kristi have been aiming in school. When their instructor, Kevin Purcell, got a call for background checks, he said he was impressed, not just by their grades, but also by how well they had done in their internships. Kristi's internship was at the Beloit probation and parole office, Barb's at a halfway house that worked mainly with sex offenders just out of federal prison.

"You are nuts if you don't hire them," Kevin told the Sheriff's Department.

So Kristi will be starting her job at the jail in six days. Most of all, her mother, Linda, is thrilled that someone in their shared household will be getting a paycheck again. "Oh wow," had been her mother's first reaction when Kristi told her the job offer had arrived. "We will keep the house."

With her badge and her Sheriff's Department khakis, Kristi will become an instant role model, an inspiration for Janesville's out-of-work workers who can't figure out how, in a still bad economy, they will get a new job. "Kristi Beyer Turns Hardship into Victories" is the front-page headline of the June 1 issue of the newsletter produced by CORD, the group formed by Bob Borremans at the Job Center to help prop up Janesville's unemployed. In the article, Kevin, the criminal justice instructor, says that she was the best student he has taught in his ten years at Blackhawk. Kristi has "an incredible drive to succeed and true desire to learn. She has been an inspiration not only to her fellow students but to me as an instructor. She re-set the bar!"

Less than two months from now, Barb's job offer at the jail will come through, too. And Kristi will be profiled again, in the *Janesville Gazette* this time, by a reporter who meets up with her coming off a Sunday shift at the jail. "Every day that I put on this uniform, I'm more and more proud of it," Kristi tells the reporter. "I'm doing what I set out to do. I'm helping keep the community safe."

For the staff of the Job Center in the abandoned Kmart, hungry for good-news stories to lighten the caseload still struggling to find work, these two best friends will be proof that the American faith in reinvention is still alive in Janesville. And Barb and Kristi will be filled with pride over their success, never imagining that their paths from here will not lead where they expect.

The Day the White House Comes to Town

Over at the Rock County Job Center, Bob Borremans has scored a coup. Just before 9:30 a.m. on Friday, June 11, he is waiting in the Job Center's broad lobby for a man named Edward B. Montgomery to arrive. Montgomery is an economist and, more particularly, he is executive director of the White House Council on Auto Communities and Workers.

Bob has been maneuvering toward this visit for more than a year. It has not been easy.

The eight hundred miles from Janesville to Washington often seems a long distance to Bob. Steering people toward jobs in a wrecked economy is not a simple matter, and he wishes he were more than a speck in a labyrinthine government apparatus that has too many rules about how to spend the federal money that flows into the Job Center. Bob is dogged, though, and he watches carefully for every new opportunity for help that pops up in the nation's capital. So it did not escape his notice when President Obama, barely two months after he was sworn into office, gave a big speech about fighting for the 400,000 Americans who had lost jobs in the past year in the hemorrhaging auto industry.

A lot of the speech was a justification for sending more money to General Motors, along with Chrysler, both of which had already started to collect their billions in emergency federal loans. The auto industry, he said, was "an emblem of the American spirit" and a "pillar of our economy that has held up the dreams of millions of our people," so these companies deserved another shot of federal aid and a brief chance to restructure. As a sign of the changes at GM, the president announced, Rick Wagoner was stepping down as CEO right away. (The White House had pushed him out, though he was leaving with an estimated $23 million in pension and benefits.)

For Bob, the attention-grabber—more than the extra billions for the companies or the push-out of the CEO—was Obama's promise, late in the speech, aimed straight at "all those men and women who work in the auto industry or live in countless communities that depend on it." The president pledged to give communities struck by "the storm that has hit our auto towns" as much caring attention as the government devotes to places wiped out by tornadoes or hurricanes. The specific form of this caring attention would be the new White House Council on Auto Communities and Workers and a new Labor Department office helping those places and people recover. To guide them both, the president said, Ed Montgomery was the man for the job. Montgomery had a successful career that toggled between government and academia, rising to become Labor's deputy secretary during the Clinton administration and now a University of Maryland dean. In both worlds, his sensibility had been shaped by a Pittsburgh childhood as the steel mills were about to go to rust.

Bob was not clear on what exactly Ed Montgomery was supposed to do inside the White House; rebuilding communities struck by the auto storm seemed more complicated than sending billions of dollars to the companies that had ended their jobs. His role seemed to involve new initiatives and busting through bureaucratic barriers among federal agencies. And Montgomery was planning "listening sessions" around the country.

Right away, Bob knew that he must find a way to bring Montgomery to Rock County. Bureaucracy busting was a favorite theme of Bob's. He couldn't wait to get this new man in the White House focused on the specific fact that Janesville's economy had sunk through the floor and was having trouble getting up.

Bob presented the idea to CORD, the coalition he had built in Janesville's classic good-government style to coordinate help for displaced workers. CORD's members could see that this was, indeed, an urgent mission. Bob sent off letters to Janesville's congressional delegation, including Paul Ryan's staff, asking for help in arranging a visit. Preferably an all-day visit, because there was a lot to discuss with the White House's auto communities man. And preferably by summer's end, because, if the government could send relief to the hurting auto community that was Janesville, there was no time to waste.

*

By the time that the executive director of the White House council gets to Janesville, he has toured twenty-six other auto communities in the past year. The all-day visit Bob envisioned has been trimmed to three and a half hours.

Still, it is a thrill when Montgomery walks through the Job Center's double glass doors, wearing pinstripes and accompanied by thirteen officials from eight federal agencies. Bob thanks him profusely for coming to Rock County and whisks him and the entourage on a tour of the warren of cubicles in the former Kmart. The staff is working, just as on any normal day on which the White House's top Auto Communities man isn't peering around, because what Bob wants Montgomery to see is how busy this Job Center is, with fifteen thousand visits a month, on average, because of all the services it provides and all the people who still need its help.

After the tour and a quick press conference in the lobby, Bob escorts Montgomery and everyone else to a forum at the UAW Local 95 hall, a couple of blocks away. More than one hundred people are waiting there—Rock County's leaders from every imaginable vantage point, including Mary Willmer, representing the Rock County 5.0 economic development campaign. Bob has invited the area's congressional delegation to be present on this day, but the only member here in person, rather than having dispatched an aide, is a liberal Democrat from Madison. After working on the failed plant-rescue mission and voting for the auto bailout, Paul Ryan's attention has been drifting away from his hometown's needs. He has been amplifying his role as a voice of the right on federal fiscal policy, bashing government spending, bashing the national debt. This morning he is in Washington, a guest on a conservative talk radio show aired nationwide, hosted by a guy who dubs himself the "Voice of Tea Party Patriots."

Montgomery is seated at a small skirted table, along with Wisconsin's labor secretary and the Democrat from Madison. On the wall behind them is a large black-and-white photo—a nighttime scene from the great 1936–37 sit-down strike. The picture was taken moments after Janesville GM'ers agreed to the clever plan that averted violence, and it shows men cheering as they poured out of the assembly plant.

This is a listening tour, so Montgomery listens to laid-off workers who can't for the life of them find a job. He listens to state legislators and union officers and economic development specialists who explain about the county's soaring foreclosures and bankruptcy filings and public assistance cases, and its plummeting building permits because almost nobody is building a new home, and the crisis at the United Way of North Rock County, where General Motors used to account for almost 40 percent of the annual giving but isn't giving anymore. Montgomery listens to a choreographed presentation of eleven creative, economy-enhancing ideas—flashes of the old can-do—that the Job Center and Blackhawk Tech and the local school systems and various community organizations would like to set in motion, if only the federal government could give enough money and freedom for spending it. These grant ideas add up to nearly $40 million for three years, on top of the job-training money and unemployment benefits the government already funnels into town. The most ambitious idea is called Workers4U. It is a $12 million plan, reprising an early federal manpower development strategy of the 1960s, to create five hundred jobs for Janesville's laid-off workers by subsidizing their pay at first at companies willing to hire and train them. Some employers in town are still laying people off, but Bob thinks that others might be poised to grow—ones in innovative manufacturing techniques, health care, or food processing, for instance. A version of this very idea will, in fact, be part of the American Jobs Act that President Obama proposes sixteen months from now. But as of this day when the White House's auto man is in town, neither federal job-training programs nor unemployment benefits allow money to be spent for this kind of on-the-job training.

During his wrap-up, Bob begins in Janesville's old-time, can-do way, telling Montgomery: "At no time do I feel that anyone in this room has felt defeated or unwilling to step forward to try and make a difference." Then Bob's words turn darker, more pointed. "At times," he admits, "we have felt overwhelmed by the challenges. We have felt isolated and overlooked. We have been frustrated by government regulations and bogged down by the rules and red tape.

"The one thing we are asking for most," he tells Montgomery, "is recognition that best solutions to local problems come from the creativity and ingenuity of communities."

It is now early afternoon and, in a few minutes, Montgomery and the entourage are heading east to Kenosha, because Kenosha is becoming a hurting auto community, too, with a Chrysler engine plant due to close in the fall. Before he leaves, Montgomery does not promise money but he promises prompt help in reviewing Janesville's ideas, in nudging them forward. He uses the word "partnership" a lot. His is a message of hope and pragmatism, a message he has been bestowing on every hurting auto community to which he has listened. Communities can rebuild, he says, but that rebuilding will happen one brick at a time.

The brick-by-brick metaphor is one that Montgomery has used often in this job. But as it happens, he will not stand with Janesville to help piece together the bricks. On the day before he is in town, Georgetown University, two miles west of the White House, has announced that Montgomery will become the university's next public policy dean. Janesville and Kenosha, it turns out, are his last listening sessions before he leaves the Obama administration in a couple of weeks.

★

Three days after Montgomery's visit, President Obama says that his administration will "move quickly to find a replacement." Another year will go by before the job is filled. By the time it is given to the mayor of Youngstown, Ohio, the White House will have disbanded the council that Montgomery led, with its leverage to coordinate among federal agencies, to bust through their bureaucracy. The new guy in charge of helping auto communities and workers will not report to the president. He will be inside the Labor Department.

During the year that the job lies vacant, the federal Government Accountability Office will issue a harsh critique of the White House's Auto Communities council and the Labor Department's recovery office. The report will conclude that they were useful as listening posts—but that no one kept track of whether any hurting auto communities got extra federal assistance as a result.

And Bob? After working so hard to arrange the visit, he soon feels exasperated. Montgomery had a goal of ensuring that each stop on his listening tour got some help from the government. For Janesville, though, it turns out that the supposed red tape cutters have no scissors. As Montgomery is leaving the government, a young man who works in the Labor Department is instructed to add Rock County to the communities for which he is to serve as a liaison. Bob presents this young man with the eleven grant ideas to which Montgomery listened at the UAW union hall. Bob asks for advice on which federal agency would be the best place to pursue each idea, expecting that the liaison can be an advocate and a conduit, shepherding these ideas to the right places to help open fresh spigots of federal money. Except no advice arrives. No money flows.

After a year or so, Bob and the liaison stop chatting altogether.

Labor Fest 2010

On the first Sunday of September, a clear day in the mid-70s for the middle of Labor Day weekend, Main Street is holiday-quiet. Tomorrow, crowds will fill the sidewalks, as they always do, for the 1 p.m. parade. But today, the action is on the south side of town, at the Walter P. Reuther Memorial Hall, the headquarters of UAW Local 95. This is the union hall that Mike Vaughn's grandfather helped to plan, that the White House's Auto Communities man visited three months ago. It has been on this spot since 1971 and is named for one of America's most influential labor leaders—the autoworkers' president for nearly twenty-five years in the mid-twentieth century. It is a low-slung structure of sand-colored brick, surrounded by broad, grassy grounds that, on this weekend, are studded with tents and stages and a beer garden for Labor Fest.

Janesville always has made a big thing of Labor Day, magnifying it into a three-day celebration of the well-performed work and well-mannered labor relations in which the community has long taken pride. Labor Fest is sponsored by several unions in town, not just the UAW, and some business, too. But the UAW grounds are always the site of the festivities: live music, mud volleyball for teens, clowns, a rock-climbing wall, a puppet show, and, of course, in a town that produced cars for eight and a half decades, an auto show.

This year, there is something extra. It comes late in the afternoon, during the spot in the festival's schedule between a break-dancing troupe and a Madison show band called Little Vito and the Torpedoes. Surrounding the main Labor Fest stage, hundreds of men and women are holding up orange signs that match the slogan they are chanting. JOBS NOW!

Jobs are becoming political. Unemployment, hovering in Janesville around 11 percent over the summer, is stoking anger. The chanters are workers and out of work. In the middle of the crowd is Marv Wopat. It has been two years since Marv retired and began to draw his GM pension. Still, he has come out as an act of solidarity and to hear the speeches.

This "Jobs Now!" rally is a regional warm-up for a One Nation Working Together rally in Washington next month that will spill down the steps of the Lincoln Memorial and onto the National Mall. The Midwest Territory of the Machinists Union came up with the idea of this warm-up and, together with the Wisconsin AFL-CIO and the Rock County Labor Council, organized this show of labor's force—its vestigial force, really, in a state in which only one of seven workers still belongs to a union, in a nation in which only one in eight workers still belongs. The machinists could have picked anywhere in the Midwest for "Jobs Now!" They picked Janesville because it has become a poster child for the need for more jobs.

Marv listens as most of the Democratic candidates in the area take turns on the Labor Fest stage, along with a slew of union officials. When it is his turn, Milwaukee's mayor, Tom Barrett, has pulled a black T-shirt with the machinists' logo over his checkered, button-down shirt. Barrett is running for governor, because Wisconsin's present governor, Jim Doyle, who tried to bring the assembly plant back to life, is not seeking a third term. The days are gone, Barrett says from the stage, when all it took to make a decent living were "a good back and a good alarm clock." Fighting for good jobs, he pledges, will be his top priority in Madison.

The next afternoon, a Monday of brilliant September sunshine, unions and jobs are on President Obama's mind, too. Since his campaign speech inside the assembly plant, he hasn't returned to town. But he is back in

Wisconsin, speaking at another Labor Fest, seventy-five miles northeast of Janesville, on Milwaukee's lakefront. The president's shirtsleeves are rolled up by the time he walks out onto the Henry Maier Festival Park stage and unfurls a $50 billion job-creating plan to refurbish the nation's roads, rails, and runways. He wraps the plan in a hymn to the labor movement, his voice on a crescendo as he recites, one by one, the improvements in working conditions that unions fought for and won across the span of the twentieth century. He is nearly shouting, his arms pumping, and the sunshine-bathed crowd clapping as he arrives where this recitation has been leading. "The cornerstones of middle-class security," he shouts, "all bear the union label." From here, Obama presses into his political point: In tough times, his administration has stood by America's workers. And the workers he invokes as evidence of his administration's solidarity are the nation's autoworkers.

"Today that industry is on the way back," the president says. "We said yes to the American worker. They're coming back!"

As the president is speaking, the Labor Fest parade is coming along Milwaukee Street and turning right onto Main Street in Janesville, where no auto jobs have come back at all. Since this is an election year, political candidates are out marching in full force. In his trademark Kelly green polo shirt, with his wife and blond kids in tow, Paul Ryan is a familiar figure, running for a seventh term as his hometown's congressman.

Less familiar is another dark-haired Republican, his navy blue polo matching the campaign signs that a retinue of supporters is carrying behind him. This is Scott Walker, who is trying to win the primary, eight days from today, to become the GOP candidate for governor. If Paul's conservatism, his distaste for Obama's ideas, is cloaked back home in Janesville in a genial demeanor, Scott Walker is emerging as a firebrand. His campaign issues a statement today that derides, with stinging rhetoric, what the president is saying in Milwaukee: "Obama's spend-o-rama stimulus-fueled $810 million boondoggle train . . . It seems like every time the president opens his mouth, he spends another $50 billion of our money to 'create jobs' but instead we continue to see spiraling unemployment."

Walker is the Milwaukee county executive, but he grew up in Delavan, a small town just east of Janesville. He tells a *Gazette* reporter today that, when he was a teenager, he and his friends liked to hang out at the Janesville Mall and eat at the Shakey's Pizza that stood just off Milton Avenue for three and a half decades. The Shakey's closed in February 2008, three days before Obama's campaign speech at the assembly plant.

Walker has not yet won the primary. Yet already he tells the *Gazette* that he has a plan to deal with Wisconsin's budget deficit: eliminate state jobs that are now vacant, and require public employees to pay in toward their future pensions, as private sector workers lucky enough to have pensions often do.

In this gathering political storm, on this sunniest of days along Main Street, another figure marches in the parade, too. He is wearing a white polo shirt and khakis, a baseball cap over his gray hair. And he is being trailed by two guys holding up each side of a large campaign sign whose slogan is devoid of pizzazz: "Tim Cullen. Effective for Us."

Tim is trying to recapture the State Senate seat that he first won three dozen years ago and that he relinquished twenty-four years ago. The crusade he led to rescue the assembly plant, though unable to outmaneuver the big money of Michigan, has renewed his faith in something else. In the possibility of coalitions. Political right and left, public sector and private, all striving toward a common goal. If he returns to the State Senate, Tim has been saying lately, his seasoned, moderate voice can help forge the kind of bipartisan trust that helps to bring jobs. On this Labor Day, Tim is hopeful again.

Project 16:49

In the shadows of town, hundreds of teenagers are becoming victims of a domino effect. These are kids whose parents used to scrape by on jobs at Burger King or Target or the Gas Mart. Now their parents are competing with the unemployed autoworkers who used to look down on these jobs but now are grasping at any job they can find. So, as middle-class families have been tumbling downhill, working-class families have been tumbling into poverty. And as this down-into-poverty domino effect happens, some parents are turning to drinking or drugs. Some are leaving their kids behind while they go looking for work out of town. Some are just unable to keep up the rent. So with a parent or on their own, a growing crop of teenagers is surfing the couches at friends' and relatives' places—or spending nights in out-of-the-way spots in cars or on the street.

The idea of homeless kids in Janesville is disquieting. It is so out of kilter with the community's self-image that most people prefer to pretend that the problem of hard-luck teenagers does not exist. But this being Janesville, with its tradition of constructive civic response to adversity, some well-meaning people in town and in Beloit formed a Homeless Education Action Team. And the team thought up Project 16:49.

The name comes from Beloit, where 16:49 is the number of hours and minutes between the end of one school day and the start of the next. The point is that these hours and minutes can feel like an eternity to kids without a safe, steady place to do homework, eat supper, or go to sleep. *Sixteen Forty-Nine* is also the name of a documentary that has just been finished by an aspiring local filmmaker. It is a work of art and advocacy. Its purpose is to smash through the community's denial about the homeless kids in their midst. And on a Thursday evening in mid-September, the documentary is having its premiere.

An hour before showtime, a tall blond woman, one of the main people behind Project 16:49, is standing in the empty U-Rock lecture hall, where the premiere is being held. She is a social worker named Ann Forbeck, and, as the Janesville school system's homeless student liaison, her mission is to help these kids try to keep their lives hinged together enough, at least, that they do not become dropouts as well as homeless.

Ann is good at dealing with the unexpected, at staying cool, at juggling—necessary skills in her job and her life. At home, she has eight-year-old quadruplets, plus a son in middle school. Still, she works day and night, helping her brood of homeless teenagers with small crises, such as losing bus tokens to get to school, and larger crises, such as having been kicked out by a relative who was letting them stay for a while. Ann can work these crazy hours because her husband creates novels and videogames, so he is a work-at-home dad, making it possible for her to spring into action on behalf of kids who aren't lucky enough to have a social worker and a writer as parents to provide them a stable, loving home.

Though she feels as if she is always in motion, helping as many kids as she can, as much as she can, Ann can see that the problem is getting worse. The school system has more than four hundred homeless kids this year, many more than before GM closed. The hardest cases are the "unaccompanied youth," the government's polite term for homeless kids trying to fend somehow for themselves. Ann feels awful every time she gets a call from a panicky teacher, asking whether she knows of a place where one of these solo teens can stay for a while. The truth is that Ann never does, because the adult shelters in Janesville are pretty full and, even if they weren't, they do not accept teenagers on their own. And no foster care in Rock County will accept a kid older than fifteen. That is why the Homeless Education Action Team has created a goal of opening two emergency shelters for teenagers. A shelter for girls and one for boys. Safe havens.

The team's goal is to open these shelters a year from now, which means that Project 16:49 is a Herculean test of Janesville's spirit. Ann, together with another social worker for homeless kids in Beloit's schools, have scoured for grants for homeless shelters for kids and reached the conclusion that government grants for this purpose do not exist. So they need to raise $700,000 to create the shelters and $210,000 a year to keep them running.

They are social workers, not fundraisers, but they really want this, so they are hoping that the new, denial-busting documentary will be so upsetting to people in town—especially to people who have not lost jobs themselves and are doing okay—that they will be motivated to commit acts of generosity. Which is why, an hour from the premiere of *Sixteen Forty-Nine*, Ann is feeling nothing like her normal calm under pressure. She is a nervous wreck. She is uncertain how many people will come, or how the people who come will react.

When the time comes to turn off the lights, Ann is amazed. Every one of the one hundred seats is filled. People are sitting in the aisles. They are squeezed, standing, along the back wall. There must be two hundred people crammed into this lecture hall.

In the front row, three people are younger than the rest. Kayla Brown, Cory Winters, and Brandon Lucian are Rock County teenagers who are homeless and the documentary's stars.

Once the room is dark and the film is rolling in public for the first time, there is Kayla on-screen, standing against a school hallway's cinder block wall, telling about being kicked out by her mother on her eighteenth birthday. And Cory, who has been couch surfing for most of his teenaged years, looking into the camera and saying, "You feel like you are by yourself, that you are a weirdo, not human." And Brandon explaining that since his out-of-work father committed an act of violence against his stepmom, who was supporting them, he's been on his own, just trying to get by.

Ann appears on screen, too, explaining about the teachers' calls and having to tell them each time that she doesn't have anywhere to put kids in an emergency. Ann is talking about trying to create temporary "safe homes." And then the Beloit social worker, Robin Stuht, is on-screen, too, saying that, without emergency shelter for these kids, "I'm constantly in fear of losing them."

The film is nearly over, when Brandon appears on-screen one last time, saying that he has talked recently to his mother, who has told him that she is happy that he will be done with high school soon, but, no, she isn't coming to see him graduate.

After thirty-four minutes and thirty-nine seconds, *Sixteen Forty-Nine* has ended, and everyone in the audience is on their feet, clapping hard. As the lights come up, Ann can see that many of these people on their feet have tears on their cheeks, and some are crying still. Finally, one woman in the audience says she'd like to ask a question. As she starts to ask, her sobs come back, so her question is down to a single word: "Why?"

26

Figuring It Out

T he year's shortest days are nearing when Barb Vaughn, honors graduate of Blackhawk Tech, correctional officer at the Rock County Jail, begins to have trouble dragging herself out of bed. Morning after morning, she feels a weird dread. She dreads brushing her teeth, dreads eating breakfast, dreads putting on her khaki uniform, dreads driving down Milton Avenue and making the right onto Route 14 that leads to the jail.

This dread is unfamiliar and perplexing. Barb knows she has handled plenty of tough stuff in her life better than she is handling this. Being a single mom to three girls. Working two jobs. Getting laid off from Lear.

Deep inside, Barb understands what is going on. But the solid lineup of A grades that she earned at Blackhawk never came with a lesson in this. What are you supposed to do when the job for which you've invested two years of your life studying, the job for which you beat out four hundred people as desperate as you were for $16.47 an hour and state benefits— what are you supposed to do when that job is pressing you down into a depression?

When she started at the jail in late July, two months after her friend Kristi, Barb was so relieved. With Mike just halfway through his

Blackhawk courses in human resources management, at least one paycheck was coming in again. His stepmother, Judy, had been bringing over
meals to save them money on food. Last year, Judy announced that no one
really needed to be buying anyone Christmas presents. Now, maybe life
would slide toward normal.

Barb could handle her rotating schedule at the jail, shifts starting at
different times of day or night. In the fall, she made it through six weeks at
the criminal justice academy, with its pepper spray and restraining holds
and the time she had to crawl forward on the floor while a role-playing
"prisoner" clutched at her leg. Some days during those six weeks, Barb
had to tamp down a question in her mind: "Is this really what I want to
do?" Still, rough as some of it was, the academy was school. The academy
classes were even held at Blackhawk. And Barb knows by now how to be
in school. She came out the far side of the criminal justice academy with a
state certificate that made her a full-fledged correctional officer.

The dread began once she was out of the academy and back at the
jail. At Blackhawk, her instructors had drilled into her that fighting with
a prisoner was a last resort. She doesn't know how to cope with some officers who seem to have a different style. But that isn't the worst of it. The
worst is feeling as if *she* is in jail.

Kristi knows that Barb sometimes goes home and cries. She wonders
whether Barb has enough toughness for the jail—enough toughness for
the inmates' taunts and the name-calling. Barb wants to believe Kristi telling her that, sure, it is a different world. That she just needs to give it a
little more time. But the voice inside her—the "is this what I want to do?"
voice—is getting louder. The morning dread is getting worse.

Busy as he is studying for his own As at Blackhawk, Mike notices.
He keeps telling Barb that he hates to see her depressed. And then one
day, Mike says to her something so startling that she never would have
dreamed he would think of it, let alone say it out loud.

"Just quit."

If they lose their ranch house and their garden, Mike tells her, they
can move somewhere cheaper. Being depressed is no way to live. "We'll
figure it out," he says.

Barb is seven years older than Mike. She is now scared as well as depressed. How can she give up $16.47 an hour, knowing that the odds of finding pay like this again are slim?

All this time, since graduation in May and the jail job coming through in July, the studying fiend she'd discovered inside herself has not been quiet. It has been telling her to push forward, to keep studying until she has a bachelor's degree. Of course, the degree that Barb has been planning to start working toward, at Upper Iowa University with a branch right at Blackhawk, is in criminal justice. But now Barb is learning something important about herself. From day after day at the jail, she realizes, she would rather help people who need help before they get into trouble, rather than guarding people once they've gone wrong. Social work is the bachelor's degree that she wants.

A dream, though, is no substitute for a paycheck. Miserable as she is, she cannot believe that Mike is right. Then one day, with Christmas coming soon, she suddenly sees her life in a new way. She sees that she spent fifteen years at Lear playing the game, staying somewhere she wasn't happy, just because the money was too good to leave. Maybe she is too intelligent, too educated now, to play the same game again. Maybe toughness is recognizing what isn't working in your life and fixing it.

Scared though she is, Barb does something she has never done at any job since her very first job as a teenager. Without any work in sight or a clue what will happen next, she decides to leave. Barb turns in her Sheriff's Department badge.

27

Bags of Hope

Early on Saturday morning, a week before Christmas, Tammy Whiteaker hears a knock on the front door of the raised ranch that she and Jerad have decided is not worth trying to sell. Tammy answers and, to her surprise, finds on the steps a couple she has never seen before.

"We have groceries for you," the man tells her.

Tammy's surprise swells into something more, because the next thing that happens is that this husband and wife walk back over to their dark SUV—General Motors, of course—that they have pulled right into the Whiteakers' driveway. They begin to pull out paper bags of groceries, ask Tammy where they should go, and bring them through the garage and into the entryway. It takes a few trips because the bags are full, and there are lots of them. Twelve in all.

Tammy is in such shock that, after a small thank-you, she just closes the entryway door. By now, Alyssa and Kayzia have come upstairs to check on what is going on. And, if their mother has no clue as to the origins of this bounty that will fill their cupboards and refrigerator, the twins have an idea. Parker High and other schools, they have heard, now have something called Bags of Hope.

Bags of Hope is a stand-in, of sorts, for the holiday food drive that Marv Wopat led for a quarter century until last year, when he had no choice but to face the fact that, with the assembly plant closed, the drive couldn't go on. Janesville's school system has decided to try to fill the void. The new version is carried out at a distribution center on the east side of town, instead of on the assembly plant's loading dock. Bagging begins at 6 a.m., instead of at 4:30. But the basic idea—to provide struggling families enough to eat around Christmastime—is intact. Plus, schools around town now hold Bags of Hope fundraisers. One at Parker before Thanksgiving raises $269 by selling lengths of silver duct tape to students and teachers for the privilege of tying the principal to a brick column in the school commons.

The volunteers include Mary Willmer, taking a break from the work of Rock County 5.0. On this Saturday morning, she is delivering bags of groceries with her fifteen-year-old son, Connor. At the last house on their route, the man who answers has several children who line up in a bag-carrying brigade. He keeps thanking and thanking Mary and Connor.

"You don't have to thank us," Mary tells him. "Being able to do this means more to us than you can know." Yet the man tells Mary that he does need to thank her because he never imagined that he would be on the receiving end and is so grateful. As they are talking, Mary glances over at one of the man's sons, and notices tears rolling down his cheeks. And she looks over at Connor in time to notice his eyes welling up, too. In a flash, Mary is back to her own childhood, to the months when her father was sick with cancer and after he died. She is reminded that you never know when one unexpected event will transform you into "the person on the other side."

*

For Tammy, it is one thing to know that Jerad isn't making enough money anymore. But it is another to think of herself as part of a struggling family, a person on the other side. Opening her front door to find herself on the receiving end of an act of charity is, in fact, quite a role reversal. Tammy is a Christian. She is a regular at Central Christian Church and a doer of

Christian deeds. She has gone on trips with church groups to Haiti for mission work. Charity is something that Tammy does for others. It has never before arrived at her front door in the form of an unfamiliar couple with a giving spirit and enough groceries to last until New Year's. Charity has not been about receiving, even though the federal government is, by now, paying for Alyssa and Kayzia and Noah to get free lunches at school. Even though Tammy has become skillful at calling the kids' teachers to ward off field trip fees that she cannot afford to pay. Even though her mother-in-law, on the periodic visits that Jerad's parents make to their only living son and their only grandkids, now goes shopping every time and buys as many groceries as can be crammed into the kitchen. But strangers bearing a dozen bags, filled with bread and milk, chicken and Saltines, canned corn and applesauce, and that's just the beginning of what is inside these bags—this is charity of a more explicit kind.

And yet Tammy decides that, given their situation, she will be happy about these groceries and not embarrassed by them. Last summer, Jerad quit the bad-pay, bad-hours job he'd started a few months before at GOEX. He'd found another job—a bad-pay job that he likes better in the warehouse of Patch Products, a toy and puzzle maker in Beloit. Patch pays him $12 an hour—48 cents less than GOEX. But he likes the work, the people, and the hours. If money were everything, he tells himself, he would have stayed at General Motors and taken a transfer. Patch is a company he could imagine staying at, except that his job has a big flaw: no health insurance. Which has been fine during the extra six months of GM insurance that he claimed by signing the buyout papers but will, starting New Year's Day, not be fine at all.

Tammy doesn't know who put her family's name on the school system's food drive list. But on this December morning, gazing upon her twelve Bags of Hope, she decides that any day when groceries show up at their house is a good day.

Part Four

★ 2011 ★

The Ambassador of Optimism

O n the first Tuesday of the year, Mary Willmer is in a cheerful mood. This morning, the *Gazette* has published a guest column she has written in hope of setting the proper tone in Janesville for 2011. The column is featured in the upper right corner of the newspaper's Opinion page. It reminds people of the efforts Rock County 5.0 has been making to lift the local economy, but the message is less about strategy than about state of mind. "We need to be proud of our community," Mary has written, "and we need to all be 'Ambassadors of Optimism.' "

This mantra about being an ambassador of optimism is an idea that Mary came up with during the early weeks of Rock County 5.0's existence. She was concerned that, in a manner contrary to Janesville's can-do spirit, she was hearing around town a lot of we're-falling-apart negativity. She first talked about being ambassadors of optimism to the 5.0 leadership team, telling them that they needed to embrace the credo that Rock County is a wonderful place with an improving economy. And then, she told them, they had to move the optimism outward. No one has tried to move it outward more than Mary herself. She has mortified her daughter, Chelsea, now a Craig High School senior, and son, Connor, a sophomore, when they go out to eat and she walks up to complete strangers in restaurants and starts her pitch about what a great place Janesville is to live and work. Mary believes that it is her mission to live this faith and that, if she does, her faith will become infectious and others will become optimists, too. She even walks into the hotels just off the Interstate and asks front-desk clerks to talk up the good things about Janesville to guests checking in. So it seemed only natural to Mary to write her guest column, spreading the ambassadors of optimism gospel to the *Gazette*'s readers.

Seeing her words in print is not the only reason that Mary is pleased. She got home late last night from downtown Madison, where she was because Diane Hendricks snagged her a ticket to the inaugural ball of a governor who is, Mary can see, as determined to set a new tone for Wisconsin as she is for Janesville. Diane, the Beloit billionaire who is the co-chair of Rock County 5.0, is a major contributor to Republican causes and candidates, so it was no surprise that she had tickets. The ball was at Monona Terrace, Madison's "dream civic center," as its architect, Frank Lloyd Wright, envisioned the dramatic, curved expanse jutting over the lake. Mary had fun watching the state's new first couple show off the results of their recent dance lessons, starting off the dancing with a song that Frank Sinatra used to croon: "The Best Is Yet to Come."

Mary watched the dancing just hours after Scott Kevin Walker had taken the oath of office that made him Wisconsin's forty-fifth governor. It was a splendid ceremony, the north gallery of the State Capitol's ornate rotunda bunting-draped for the occasion. Four previous governors were in attendance, plus the outgoing Democratic governor, Jim Doyle, shaking his successor's hand. A Boy Scout troop from Walker's hometown of Delavan leading the Pledge of Allegiance. A brass band playing the fight song, "On Wisconsin." And, in a curious touch for the inauguration of one of the nation's most incendiary social and economic conservatives, the Notre Dame Academy swing choir from Green Bay preceding the oath taking with a medley from *Hair*, the tribal-love rock opera of the 1960s counterculture that premiered on Broadway when Walker was four months old.

When the time came for the gubernatorial inaugural address, Walker's main campaign promise—to create 250,000 private sector jobs—was front and center. "My priorities are simple: jobs, jobs and more jobs," the brand-new governor said. Directly behind him, seated in a chair next to a glass case containing an 1848 copy of the Wisconsin constitution, Janesville's congressman, Paul Ryan, applauded with all the rest.

Walker is a firebrand. He railed in his campaign against state taxes, spending, and regulation. But in his inaugural address hours before the ball, he said that he is not the governor of one political party, that he is the governor for all the people of the great state of Wisconsin. By nightfall, however, it already was plain that not all the people of Wisconsin are for the governor. As Mary and Diane watched Walker in his tuxedo gliding across the Monona Terrace floor with his wife, Tonette, in her glittering taupe gown, about 350 progressives were a few blocks away at the historic Majestic Theatre, listening to live bands at an alternative party they were calling Rock the Pantry. The progressives—of which Madison has many— chose their party's name as a dig at the governor. The name was meant to draw attention to the fact that profits from the $50 inaugural ball tickets were going to help defray Walker's campaign expenses and to support the state Republican Party—unlike Doyle, who had used the profits from his two inaugural balls for charity, the Boys and Girls Clubs of Wisconsin. To show up Walker replenishing the GOP coffers, the Rock the Pantry organizers are giving their own ticket revenue to the Second Harvest food pantry and the Wisconsin chapter of Feeding America.

This dig at the governor on his inauguration night was the start of a year of anger. The anger builds soon in Madison, but not only there. It builds in Janesville, tearing at the town's trademark civility. As the year goes on, Deri Wahlert is singed by part of the anger—a part that the governor stokes against public employees, including schoolteachers. Paul Ryan is singed by a different part of the anger—a coalescing movement called Occupy that lashes out at economic inequality, at politicians aligned with business interests. This morning after the inaugural ball, when her column appears, Mary does not realize that she is about to be singed, too.

The anger that rises against Mary is local. It rises because she has neglected to notice a basic fact: talking up a town to people who can still afford to go out to eat, to travelers checking into the Hampton Inn or the Holiday Inn Express, is not quite the same as telling everyone who reads the *Gazette* that the only thing they need to do for the economy to recover is to become an optimist. And telling them this near the start of a month during which Rock County's unemployment rate, even two years after the assembly plant shut down, stands at 11.2 percent. Not the same at all.

Mary is slow to sense the anger rising against her. She ignores readers' online comments in the *Gazette*. But Chelsea and Connor do not ignore them. And they report to her things like: "Mom, eight people just totally blasted you."

Once they clue her in, Mary feels stung. This bitterness feels personal, her hard work for the community's improvement and her good intentions getting shot down by people she doesn't even know. This is tough on Mary. Painful. But soon she notices that, the greater the volume of angry comments, the stronger her resolve. All this cynicism about optimism is stiffening her resolve because, she realizes, she is a role model. Her kids are watching her, and her team at the bank is watching her. This is, she decides, a real opportunity to show them what leadership looks like.

Coward's corner. That is how she begins to describe the cynicism about optimism by people who do not attach their names to the *Gazette*'s online comments or its call-in phone line.

"I am an ambassador of optimism," Mary tells herself. "I am not going to let them get to me."

*

Two weeks and a day after Walker is sworn in, Mary stands with Diane just inside in the entrance of ABC Supply, Diane's company, awaiting the new governor. He is setting off this morning on a tour of the state's borders, the purpose of which is to affix new rectangular plaques to the bottom of wooden "Welcome to Wisconsin" road signs and to snap the governor's photo next to each one. The plaques say OPEN FOR BUSINESS, a slogan signaling Walker's intention to lower taxes, lessen regulations, and otherwise create a hospitable climate for what he and some other Republicans have started calling "job creators."

The first photo-op of the governor standing next to a freshly nailed OPEN FOR BUSINESS sign will be right in Rock County, at the rest stop along Interstate 90 in Beloit, ten miles south of Janesville. Before that, his day's schedule begins with a visit to meet with Mary and Diane and other leaders of Rock County 5.0. When he strides through ABC's sliding glass doors, Diane's arms are outstretched. Walker leans in for an embrace, then steps back to shake Mary's hand. Before they take the elevator upstairs, Diane asks, could they talk for two seconds about some concerns that are best not to raise in front of the group?

"Okay, sure," the governor says.

Diane stands close and looks him straight in the eye. "Any chance we'll ever get to be a completely red state and work on these unions and become a right-to-work? What can we do to help you?"

"Oh yeah," Walker replies. "Well, we're going to start in a couple weeks with our budget adjustment bill. The first step is, we're going to deal with collective bargaining for all public employee unions, because you use divide and conquer."

"You're right on target," Diane says, as Mary looks on.

By the time they get up to the boardroom, there is no more union talk. The leaders of Rock County 5.0 have decided that widening the Interstate, from the Illinois line to Madison, would be one of the best boosts for the local economy, and they are thrilled when Walker tells them that he supports this idea, hard as it will be to find the money for it in his lean, lean budget.

Invoking his father, a Baptist minister, Walker says that he and Rock County 5.0 are preaching to the choir, because his tax-lowering, regulation-lessening goals are the same strategies that Diane and Mary and the rest of the 5.0 leadership team believe will bring jobs to replace ones that General Motors took away.

"You've made our job a whole lot easier," Mary tells the governor.

From Beloit, Walker goes on today to have his photo taken next to OPEN FOR BUSINESS plaques in Dickeyville and Hudson and Superior, the first of twenty-three towns along Wisconsin's borders at which such plaques will be nailed onto welcome signs.

Mary types on her BlackBerry a message that she posts on her Facebook page: "Great morning with Gov. Walker. We are so lucky to have him."

The Opposite of a Jailer

Later the same week that Mary Willmer drives to Madison for the glitz of the governor's inaugural ball, Barb Vaughn drives over to Blackhawk Tech. Barb is out of work and jittery about what will happen, now that she has quit her job at the County Jail. She has not been on Blackhawk's campus since the endurance test that was the criminal justice academy last fall. Today, she walks into an unfamiliar office along a corridor off the college's main atrium.

This office belongs to Upper Iowa University, a school based nearly two hundred miles west of here in Fayetteville, Iowa, that specializes in long-distance learning. It is through Upper Iowa that Barb, jittery though she is, is determined to go forth and keep studying until she becomes a person who has a bachelor's degree. Her friend Kristi has been saying, since their Blackhawk graduation with their honor cords last spring, that she wants to go on for a bachelor's, too. Something about the way Kristi says it has made Barb begin to think that it might be just talk. Barb can see how much Kristi likes the jail paychecks. Always buying clothes and planning house renovations. So, odd as it seems to think about college without Kristi alongside, Barb figures that she is on her own. The courses leading to a social work degree, she knows, will be tough—partly online and speeded up into eight-week terms, with no breaks in between. But by now, she trusts herself with studying. She is weeks from her fiftieth birthday. Having made a mistake once by choosing criminal justice, she is determined not to aim wrong again.

But she has thrown $16.47 an hour out the window, with Mike still studying human resources at Blackhawk until the spring. And now she's just taken student loans. Barb has been trying to find something—anything—to tide her over while she is back in school. She has spent hour after hour on the computer, scouring the slim job listings. This week, she notices a new posting by something called Creative Community Living Services, which turns out to be a Wisconsin company that provides intensive help for people with developmental disabilities. "Residential coordinator/community protection" is the name of the job that is advertised. Barb applies.

To her surprise, she gets the job. It means that she works one-on-one with a client with a history of difficult behaviors. Her criminal justice background will come in handy, after all. The client has been institutionalized until now. Her first mission is to go into the institution where her client has been living and help move him into a group home, his first home in years. From there, she learns to prod and teach and motivate and soothe as she tries to help him become as independent as he can be. She is someone for her client to lean on, to trust. The opposite of being a jailer, it seems to her. It does not take long before her fragile, stubborn client and his struggles for self-sufficiency start to pull on her heartstrings.

None of this is easy. The job is full-time. She is taking her sped-up, eight-week, no-break courses at night. That's okay. Barb knew she would be working hard. Still she had expected that, once she had her associate's degree, she'd go back to keeping everything neat at home—the ranch house filled with houseplants and decorated with the Americana that she and Mike have collected. She's looked forward to dusting and vacuuming as she used to. Well, that idea turns out to be premature.

There is one other catch. Being a residential coordinator/community protection pays $10.30 an hour. Nearly 40 percent less than she was making at the Sheriff's Department. Less than half her wages at Lear.

This Is What Democracy
Looks Like

J anesville's teachers have a day off on Friday, February 25, and Deri
  Wahlert is excited as she drives up to Madison with her partner,
  Rob Eastman, a Parker science teacher, and Avery, their three-
year-old son. They grab an early lunch at Quaker Steak, a favorite spot. It
is midday as they approach Capitol Square, the highest point of the land
between two lakes on which downtown Madison is built. Avery is riding
atop Rob's shoulders, his small, blond head high enough that it will be
caught by an MSNBC news camera, so that Deri will later glimpse her
own son on television once they get back home.

It is Day No. 11 of protests against the new governor, Scott Walker. The
next day, a Saturday, will bring out up to 100,000 protesters in a snowstorm,
the biggest demonstration in Wisconsin history. But even today, thousands
have descended on the square from throughout the state and beyond. As
Deri approaches with Rob and Avery, the crowd is thick and the din loud.
She thrills to the sights and sounds. One chant, to the staccato beat of a
drum, delights her in particular: "This is what democracy looks like!"

Until these protests broke out, Deri had wondered, ever since she
was a girl learning about the civil rights movement and the Vietnam War

demonstrations, whether anyone in America still had the heart and soul to come together and fight for what they believe. This is the first time in her thirty-two years, Deri is thinking, that she has witnessed people coming together to put their First Amendment rights to use. As she watches, bagpipers and snare drummers lead a solemn brigade of firefighters, who carry aloft red and white signs, "Firefighters for Labor." Off-duty police officers toting "Cops for Labor" signs are out in big numbers, too. Construction workers and nurses, teachers and college kids, manual laborers and PhDs, they stand in the thin February midday sun and lift their voices, thousands-strong. In solidarity. In chant. "Kill the Bill! Kill the Bill!"

*

The bill in question is the first big-deal legislation that Walker put forth during his maiden month as governor. He is calling it a Budget Repair Bill. In the past, that has meant a slight fiscal tinkering. Not this time. The governor wants to carve and reshape the state government, saying that his bill is necessary to pull Wisconsin out of its recession-driven deficit. He also, it turns out, wants to shred most collective bargaining rights of most Wisconsin public sector unions. This was the plan about which he hinted to Diane and Mary the morning he met with Rock County 5.0. He had never mentioned it during his campaign.

The bill would unwind Wisconsin's own history. At the turn of the twentieth century, the state had become a hub of the Progressive movement, with the election in 1900 of Robert M. La Follette as governor. La Follette was known as "Fighting Bob" for his pursuit of reforms to help citizens in a society that was increasingly urban, industrial, and prone to capture by special interests. As part of this Progressive tradition, Wisconsin became a leader in workers' rights. In 1911, a dozen years before the Janesville Assembly Plant began turning out Chevrolets, the state created the nation's first workman's compensation law for employees injured on the job. In 1932, the year the plant closed during the Great Depression, Wisconsin was the first state to establish a system of unemployment benefits, three years before Congress adopted the federal Social Security Act that spread a similar system nationwide. It was in Madison in 1932, too, that a group of state employees formed a union that would, within a few years, grow into the country's main labor organization of state and municipal workers. And in 1959, Wisconsin became the first state to pass a law guaranteeing collective bargaining for public employees.

The surprise, labor-weakening aspect of Walker's Budget Repair Bill is the reason that a considerable, sustained expression of fury has amassed at Capitol Square.

*

Deri teaches U.S. history to teenagers and grew up in Wisconsin and certainly knows about its labor traditions. She considers herself a middle-of-the-road person—someone who tends to see both sides of a situation. In this case, her self-interest was in line with the protesters and not with the new governor's plan. The Budget Repair Bill would take away from unions that represent state and municipal workers and public school teachers the right to bargain over working conditions, and it would cap wage increases. She and Rob would lose money if they had to start pitching in toward their retirement pensions and paying more for their health insurance, as the governor wants. Losing money this way, she understands, would mean that the odds that they could afford to have another kid, as she has been thinking about lately, would go downhill.

Still, she has not come to Madison today to protest. She has come as the history teacher she is. The protests are big national news—destined, she can tell, to become an important moment in her state's history, in U.S. labor history. How could she miss seeing this dramatic chunk of history with her own eyes? With this history-in-the-making wonder, and because her little boy has never before seen the State Capitol, Deri and Rob and Avery, still on his dad's shoulders, work their way through the crowd and up to the granite-domed building. They open the capitol's heavy doors and step inside.

*

From TV news, Deri learned that the interior, its rotunda and halls normally tomb-quiet even when the legislature is in session, as it is now, had become a well-organized, if slightly stinky, twenty-four-hour encampment. But being inside in person is something else. A union of graduate students from the University of Wisconsin campus a mile away are in charge, more or less, of organizing the space. The grad students have designated the rotunda and each of the four wings for purposes vital to around-the-clock occupation: sleeping areas filled with air mattresses and sleeping bags, segregated for families with kids and for smooching college couples; a children's play area; a first-aid station; a cell phone charging station; a training area for lessons in nonviolent civil disobedience; and, because this was Madison, an area for yoga.

There is a hub, too, for food, which is plentiful and has, for days, included free deliveries of Ian's Pizza, which is just a block up State Street from the capitol. Ian's has been deluged with phone calls and online orders from protest sympathizers from all fifty states and two dozen nations, who, in acts of long-distance solidarity, are paying for the pizzas to be delivered to the capitol so that the demonstrators do not go hungry.

The backs of empty pizza boxes have been converted to protest signs, mimicking the larger signs that are lining the capitol's limestone walls. Despite the designated sleeping areas, the protesters that Deri notices seem pretty sleep-deprived, because of drum circles and strobe-lit dance parties and renditions of "Solidarity Forever" and other old-time labor songs that have gone on into the wee hours of the morning and are going on still as Deri and Rob and Avery make their way through the crowd. No matter what side of the fence you are on, Deri is thinking, it is neat to see so many people fighting for a cause.

★

Deri and Rob and Avery happen to have arrived on a pivotal day in the protests. While she delights in the spectacle inside the capitol, the mood among the pizza-fueled protesters has become grim. At 1 a.m., the Republicans in the Wisconsin Assembly, the legislature's lower chamber, abruptly ended sixty nonstop hours of debate on Walker's budget bill. Without a motion to end the debate, and with fifteen filibustering Democrats in line to speak, the Assembly's Republican leaders began the vote on the governor's plan. The vote lasted ten seconds. Before most of the Democrats even realized what was going on, the bill passed. The groggy GOP legislators then filed out of the chamber, separated by capitol police from the Democrats, who wore orange T-shirts, with "fighting for WORKING FAMILIES!" scrawled across the front and who hurled sentiments seldom heard in civilized times among state legislators: "Shame!" "Coward!"

By the afternoon, the Assembly's passage of the governor's bill is not the only reason that the protesters are in a sour mood. The capitol police are now saying that the encampment inside the capitol must move out by 4 p.m. on Sunday, two days away. The protesters want to stay. The sneaky vote by the Assembly Republicans shifted the drama to the legislature's other chamber, the State Senate, whose Democrats have already executed a sneaky move of their own. Wisconsin's Democratic state senators have fled the state.

★

Early on February 17, two days after the protests at Capitol Square began, Tim Cullen received a sad, but not unexpected, phone call at home. An old friend and mentor, a former state senator and State Supreme Court judge, had died the night before. Aware that his friend was terminally ill with cancer, Tim had promised that, whenever his death occurred, he would serve as the family's spokesman. Now he needed to run up to Madison to hand out obituaries and talk with the press.

It has been three months since Tim, who poured his heart into the losing quest to reopen the assembly plant, won election to his old seat in the State Senate. He is sixty-six and had not been a legislator for twenty-four years. Now, at 8:30 a.m., he was about to leave for Madison when he got another call, this one from Mark Miller, the State Senate's minority leader. Miller was calling to tell Tim of a decision that the Senate's Democratic caucus made moments before at a meeting that Tim missed.

With the vote on the governor's budget repair bill expected that day, the Senate Democrats had decided to flee to Illinois. This disappearing act—dramatic, bizarre, without precedent—was prompted by a small parliamentary fact: In Wisconsin, votes on legislation with fiscal implications

require a quorum of twenty senators. The nineteen Republicans held the
majority of the Senate's seats, but they were one short of the quorum, unless at least one Democrat was in the chamber. If all fourteen Democratic
senators were out of state, there could be no vote on the governor's bill.

The timing, Tim told Miller, couldn't be worse. He had to keep his
promise to his friend's family. So he raced to the capitol, thronged with
protesters, to handle the obituary, managing to slip out just before the
Senate convened for a voting session. As Tim dashed home to pack, Miller
called again to warn him not to take Interstate 90 to Illinois. The governor
may have stationed state police at the border to prevent Tim from leaving
Wisconsin.

Using back roads, Tim met up with his Democratic colleagues at a
Rockford, Illinois, hotel. He had made it out of the state, but he had a
dilemma. Tim is a friend of labor. He also is a believer in political compromise. Fleeing across state lines to avoid a vote was distinctly not an act
of compromise. And he quickly saw another problem, when he asked his
colleagues about the morning's caucus meeting he had missed. "Did you
talk about a strategy to get us back to Wisconsin?" The subject, it turns
out, had not come up.

So began three weeks during which Tim moves with his fellow
Democrats from hotel to hotel across northern Illinois. True to his nature, he tries during this time to negotiate a compromise to end the political crisis—a compromise that, in the end, neither side wants. They are
staying at a La Quinta Inn in Gurnee, Illinois, when Tim and a fellow
Democrat slip back into the state. Having received assurances that state
troopers would not pick them up and cart them back to the capitol, they
drive to a McDonald's outside Kenosha, a half hour away, for a negotiating
session with the Senate's GOP majority leader. No progress. On the next
Sunday, Day No. 13 of the protests and two days after Deri and Rob and
Avery are in Madison, he and two Democrats return to the McDonald's
at 9 p.m.—this time to meet with the governor's chief of staff. Tim senses
that some compromise might be possible. On March 6, Day No. 20, after
the Senate Republicans held the Democrats in contempt and authorized

the sergeant-at-arms to use police force, if necessary, to drag them back, the governor's chief of staff dips just below the Wisconsin line to meet with Tim and a fellow Democrat in South Beloit, Illinois. This negotiating session ends with a tentative list—not a deal, but a few ideas for softening the bill's effects on unions. Tim thinks the list does not go far enough but might give the Democrats a graceful way to return to Madison. The rest of the caucus isn't interested.

Walker and his staff are growing impatient. No more talk of compromise. On Day No. 23, the Senate Republicans employ a parliamentary trick, stripping out the fiscal parts of the bill so that a quorum no longer requires twenty senators—just seventeen. Early in the evening, without a single Democratic senator in the state, the Senate passes the sections of the bill that cripple public employee unions. The Assembly approves this version the next day. And, on Day No. 25 of what is, by now, the longest protest in Wisconsin history, as well as the largest, Governor Walker is jubilant as he signs the bill into law.

★

Many people in Janesville have always regarded Madison as a place of nutty activism. The protesters' yoga and drum circles were no surprise. In other circumstances, the white-hot political events there might not have threatened Janesville's proud tradition of good-natured calm in the face of adversity. Yet as winter yielded to spring, the boiling acrimony spilled down the Interstate, melting some of Janesville's trademark civility.

The night of the State Senate vote, the union to which Deri belongs, the Janesville Education Association, told its members to wear black the following day. Soon, the teachers' union became one of the organizations around the state agitating for a special election—a recall election to try to pry the new governor from office.

As for Tim, true to type, he tried to make peace. With the protests over and the Democrats back from Illinois in defeat, he proposed amending the state constitution to make it illegal for senators to repeat such state-fleeing tactics ever again. Still, in mid-March, Tim attended a rally in the Rock County Courthouse parking lot at which union members and their supporters denounced the governor. Tim spoke out against Republicans' moneyed interests.

And where was Paul Ryan all this time? The day that the Democratic senators left for Illinois, Paul gave an interview to MSNBC in Washington, where he was working on his ideas for reining in federal spending. These budget-cutting ideas meant that he and the governor were ideological allies. With the marble pillars of the U.S. Capitol towering behind him, Paul told the MSNBC interviewer that he and Walker were good friends and had even traded emails since the protests broke out. Paul's disdain for the protesters was palpable, his sympathy for public union members absent. Public workers, he said, already get such generous benefits that, even with the cuts the governor had in mind, they would still be better off than most Wisconsin workers.

"And he's getting, you know, riots," Paul said of the governor. "It's like Cairo has moved to Madison these days." It was a reference to the mass protests in Egypt—part of a broad movement known as the Arab Spring—that days before had toppled Egypt's president of thirty years.

The argument that Paul set forth, that public employees were getting more than their fair share, was at the core of Walker's political calculation in going after organized labor his first winter as governor. Among certain people in Janesville, this argument, that government employees were overpaid and overindulged at taxpayer expense, held appeal. In a community in which so many had lost so much, some people were starting to regard public workers, including the city's teachers, as fat cats in comparison.

Janesville may be an old union town. But with the shuttered assembly plant and the supplier companies having destroyed so many UAW jobs, the ground was shifting. Twice as many people in Rock County were former union members as current union members. And opinion was split in the county on the question of whether unions help the U.S. economy or hurt it.

The timing of this swelling resentment against public workers was curious, coming just as state budget cuts and an overall drop in local tax revenue forced the Janesville school system to announce the first major layoff of teachers in its history. And yet the anti-teacher hostility kept coming. While so many in town had crummy jobs or no jobs, most teachers, after all, still had their jobs and their summers off and their pensions, even if Deri and Rob and all the rest would soon have to pay more for them.

The hostility has welled up in the most ordinary places. One morning this summer, the teacher who is president of the Janesville Education Association, Dave Parr, is confronted in the twenty-four-hour Walmart at 4 a.m., with his family waiting in the car. They are getting an early start on the three-hour drive for a weekend at his father's in La Crosse, and he has stopped to pick up earbuds for one of his kids. And because it is before dawn, just one cashier's line is open, so Dave cannot escape the guy in front of him, who apparently recognizes Dave, who has appeared now and then in the *Gazette*. "I told you, you were gonna get yours," the guy yells at Dave. "I knew you were gonna get yours." The guy does not stop, even when the cashier suggests that maybe he should calm down. The night manager comes over and eases him out of the store.

A Parker High colleague of Deri's, Julie Bouton, who has taught business classes for thirty-one years—and sponsors a business co-op program that is helping students whose families need an extra paycheck—didn't go up to the protests. Still, people she has known for years are coming up to her in Woodman's grocery and complaining about "that teacher thing" in Madison. She is tired of hearing that teachers have it better than everyone else—hearing it from people including some GM retirees with pensions of their own. Julie hates this bad-mouthing. She has begun to wait sometimes to go to Woodman's at night, when the grocery aisles are emptier.

And one night, Deri gets a call from her mother, who sounds upset. Her mother, Judy, lives a half hour away in Fort Atkinson, where Deri grew up, but her doctor is in Janesville. And during an appointment that day, the doctor made small talk by asking how Deri and her younger sister, Devin, were doing. Her mother reminded him that Deri was teaching. He rolled his eyes. Her mother asked him why. And the doctor told her that he didn't have anything nice to say so probably shouldn't say it. He finished examining her quickly, and she was out the door. But the sting lasted. The doctor barely knows Deri, her mother is now telling her on the phone. Who is he to criticize her choice of profession?

Deri is sad that her mother has been seared by this quiet hostility.

31

On Janesville Time

At the end of every shift, just before he rushes out of the Fort Wayne Assembly Plant into the Indiana night air, Matt Wopat stops for a heartbeat at one of the time clocks, mounted on poles in the terra-cotta-tiled lobby. He slides his ID badge through the card reader, so that General Motors will know when his eight hours have ended. Each night, unless he's had a lucky, extra-long shift with overtime, the clock punches Matt out moments after 10:45 p.m.

Now that eastern Indiana's winter is melting into spring, Matt has been punching out in the Fort Wayne lobby for a year. Long enough that he has gotten mortgage payments straightened out and otherwise propped his family back up into the middle class by working almost three hundred miles from Darcy and the girls. Long enough that he no longer is aware of the oddity that, when he hustles through the vast parking lot, hops into the fourteen-year-old car he keeps down here, and starts the engine, the digital clock glowing red on the dashboard says just after 9:45 p.m.—the Janesville time.

Keeping his clocks and his watch on Central Time—Janesville time—springs from the same impulse inside Matt that leads him, each night when he turns left out of the plant parking lot, to be careful to tell himself that he is going back to the apartment and not to tell himself that he is going home. He is conscious of thinking "the apartment," because, in Matt's mind, even though he is in Fort Wayne five days a week and four nights, he has only one home, and it certainly is not the rented unit in the Willows of Coventry that he shares with a guy named Kip, another GM gypsy who wishes that he were still working in Janesville.

It is almost a taunt every time Matt drives into the apartment complex, with its entrance sign that says: "Willows of Coventry. Welcome Home." Still, he and Kip have a nice apartment with two bedrooms, two baths, and a fireplace that they have used only once—at Christmastime, when Matt came up with the idea that maybe they could cheer themselves up during the first Christmas season away from their families by decorating an old fake tree that Kip had been planning to throw out and, while they were at it, putting on some music and lighting a fire. Making the best of a bad situation. For the most part, though, the apartment is a shrine to Wisconsin.

When Matt unlocks the door and steps inside, his first sight, high on the wall directly across, is a stuffed buck's head with an impressive rack of antlers. He shot the buck on a hunting trip near his grandfather's farm in Hillsboro, up north. Mounting it in the apartment works out well because Darcy does not want the large head hanging in their house, and also because it gives Matt a quick jolt of home feeling whenever he opens the door. In Matt's bathroom are neatly folded Green Bay Packers towels—in the same dark green as the Packers blanket that, on the other side of the apartment, is smoothed across Kip's bed. In Matt's room are a single day-bed and a dresser whose surface is covered with photos of everyone in the family.

For this apartment that Matt wishes he didn't need, he and Kip split the $704-a-month rent. Matt thinks it is unfortunate that, even though Fort Wayne has gotten him back to $28 an hour, plus a $30,000 transfer bonus if he stays for at least three years, money is tighter than if he were still living at home full-time. Without the rent. Without needing a car here, even though the black 1997 Saturn was about as cheap as he could find. Without the gas money to get home to Janesville after the Friday night shift and back to Fort Wayne before Monday's shift, even though he carpools with other Janesville guys to save on the gas, chipping in $20 each way. He and Darcy seem to be arguing more about money than when he was living at home.

Matt knows that he and Kip probably could have found a lower-rent place, but he figures it's already hard enough, sleeping away from Darcy and their bed more nights than not. So sleeping in some dump would only have made things worse. Besides, the Willows of Coventry has a number of units occupied by GM gypsies, including others from Janesville, and he likes the familiar faces.

Matt is part of what turns out to be a large tribe of GM gypsies who have converged on Fort Wayne. Since it opened in 1986, when it inherited the assembly of pickups that had been made in Janesville, Fort Wayne has been a truck plant. And after the General Motors bankruptcy nearly two years ago now, the company decided to move to Fort Wayne, too, the heavy-duty pickups from a plant in Pontiac, Michigan, which closed as part of GM's restructuring. So, Fort Wayne added a third shift last year and, to keep trucks moving along the assembly line around the clock, imported nine hundred workers who had been laid off, just like Matt and the other Janesville GM'ers. The imported workers came from twenty-five GM facilities in eleven states and, while some arrived with their families, many are gypsies, like Matt. In fact, the plant manager goes home on weekends to Dayton, two hours away. The personnel director goes home on weekends to Chicago, a three-hour drive. Gypsy or not, many of the imported workers arrived with their all-important anniversary dates earlier than those of some workers who already were in Fort Wayne, which meant that their greater seniority let them claim better shifts and better jobs in the plant. Matt is a second-shift team leader on the trim line, coordinating a small group of workers just after the truck bodies have emerged from the paint shop. On this part of the assembly line, they install the weatherstrip, the insulating mat that goes under the carpet, the seatbelt bracket, the sunroof. Second shift is what Matt thought was best, because it means that his workweek doesn't start until Monday afternoon, so he can sleep at home Sunday nights.

The gypsies from all these plants and states work side by side, yet their loyalties stand apart. Until he came here, Matt never really thought about the fact that some autoworkers might be Republicans. And sports allegiances are serious and in plain view on the factory floor, with baseball caps and T-shirts making clear who roots for the Indianapolis Colts or the Chicago Bears or the New York Jets or, of course, the Packers. Matt likes wearing his Packers cap, but in general he is not one of the gypsies who are having a good time while away from home. His roommate, Kip, plays cards at a guy's house on Tuesday nights and sometimes goes to Wednesday game nights at the local UAW hall. Matt isn't in Fort Wayne to have fun. He lives as cheaply as he can. Lives pretty much on cereal, Campbell's soup, and ramen.

And lives with guilt, because Darcy is dealing alone with the house and three kids, and he can't cook for them, or load the dishwasher or help the girls with their homework, or take them to their doctor's appointments. He feels useless. Yet he has to kill his nonworking hours somehow, so, when the weather is decent, he and a couple of other gypsies go midmornings over to the Donald Ross Golf Club, since the golfing comes free with his rent at the Willows of Coventry. And when the weather is hot, he sometimes sits at the Willows of Coventry's pool before it's time to get ready for his shift. And that is when the guilt is strongest, sitting by the pool, a few hundred miles from the chores he wishes he were doing at home.

He knows that Darcy understands this helplessness that he feels and doesn't resent his time by the pool, since his afternoons and nights at the Fort Wayne Assembly Plant are keeping them all afloat. But the guilt lingers, along with the loneliness for his family. He and Darcy have come up with ways to help feel close, as best they can. On Monday mornings, just before the drive back here, he sometimes leaves "miss you" greeting cards under her pillow, but not so often that she'll come to expect them, and the surprise will be ruined. And through the week, they play games together on their smartphones. Darcy beats him almost every time at word games. It's okay with Matt, because the point isn't winning. It's the connection, so the best part is getting text messages from Darcy at unexpected moments during the day. The text, "YOUR TURN," has become curiously heart-warming.

And every night, as Matt is taking the left turn out of the plant parking lot and heading north along the highway for the short drive to the apartment, he calls home. Except that, even though it is just before 10 p.m. on his car clock and in Janesville, an hour earlier than it is around him in Fort Wayne, the time is late enough even in Janesville that, if he talks with his girls for more than a few minutes, he will make them late for bed.

32

Pride and Fear

The backpack slung over his shoulder is light as Mike Vaughn walks out of Blackhawk's classroom building and crosses the asphalt expanse toward his Chevy pickup. It is mid-May, and Mike isn't toting any books tonight. Just an attendance slip he needs to turn in to the Workforce Development agency that has paid for all his classes, and a few sheets of notes he'd brought along in case he wanted to study just before his final exam. Mike has always gotten to his classes and his exams a half hour early, as he did for shifts in his factory days. Now, as he walks toward his white truck, it is near 9 p.m., and the exam for his business law course, his last final exam, is over.

By this night, twenty-six months have gone by since Mike took the brief, nostalgic glance back at the empty Lear factory floor. In that time, he has stayed in touch less and less with the hundreds of union brothers and sisters he represented at Lear, easing each round through their layoffs as best he could. Just a few friends and people he runs into now and then around town. It's not that Mike doesn't think about the times and the people of his past. But those times are gone, and no point dwelling on them.

His father, Dave, the middle generation of the union Vaughns, is still active in the union. Nearly a decade after he retired from General Motors, he is still volunteering as vice president of UAW Local 95, as he was when Mike broke the news that he was going into HR. The local's membership has shriveled, the number of units whose workers it represents dwindled from sixteen companies to five, given the suppliers that closed along with GM. And the workers who remain cannot claim paid "release time" from their jobs to help run the union—as Mike did at Lear and Dave before him at General Motors—which is why the local's officers these days are retirees like Dave.

While his father is helping to lead what remains of the union, Mike has found that it's best to stay focused on what lies ahead. On this Wednesday night, what is immediately ahead is his graduation on Saturday at the Dream Center, just like Barb's a year ago. So, with graduation three days away, Mike is walking to his truck with pride and fear.

The pride is easy to understand. Mike is excited that he did it—twenty-three courses in all, pulling twenty-one As, an A-minus, and one B. Like Barb before him, he will be wearing with his cap and gown a golden sash and honor cord. He will tell a *Gazette* reporter: "I got decked out. At 43, I'm proud of my accomplishments."

The fear that runs alongside is because Mike cannot avoid the sense that a moment of truth has arrived. When he handed in his exam a few minutes ago, he completed a gamble, to which he has devoted two years of his life, that the Job Center's retraining gospel was worth believing. Certainly, the gospel has been spread wide. Last year, when he started at Blackhawk, 543 other out-of-a-job factory workers in Rock County—and about 100,000 nationwide at a cost to U.S. taxpayers of $575 million—got the kind of Trade Adjustment training subsidies that Mike helped to negotiate for Lear's workers as it was shutting down. Nationally, nearly half the trainees who got this help last year, and about one third this year in which he is graduating, will not quickly find a job.

Two months ago, Mike began to apply for jobs. Dozens of jobs. He figured that his résumé might get noticed, with his near-perfect grades and his decade on the union side of human resources work, including five years as the shop chairman of an eight-hundred-person factory. He would get noticed, he figured, because of the contracts that he negotiated, the grievances he handled, the employee contract language he interpreted, the Kronos workforce management system that he already knows how to use. Union side or management side, he figured, the work is similar, and companies would surely notice that he had been doing it for years.

Mike is surprised that all he has gotten are rejection letters, when he has heard anything at all. Company after company telling him that they are looking for someone with a bachelor's degree and three to five years' experience in human resources management. He understands that companies can afford to be choosy when so many people want these scarce human resources jobs, want *any* job. Yet Mike can't help but be nervous that, three days before graduation, he hasn't gotten a single callback.

Proud as he is of his accomplishments, his mind-set is not helped by the fact that, in March, for reasons unfathomable to him, his unemployment checks stopped arriving. His unemployment benefits were supposed to keep flowing as long as he was in school. He knows other out-of-a-job workers who were laid off earlier than him and are going to be in school longer than he will and are still collecting their unemployment. But try though he has, he cannot persuade anyone in the Wisconsin agency that handles unemployment insurance that the status someone assigned to him—"exhausted time period for benefits"—must be a mistake. He and Barb have been dipping lately into their small savings, because trying to live on her $10.30 an hour, from her new job helping a developmentally disabled client, isn't the same as living on her $10.30 an hour plus his unemployment checks.

So finding a job as soon as he graduates is a matter of urgency to Mike—such urgency that he has even started to apply for laborer's jobs, just in case the human resources management plan in which he has invested these two years of his life does not pan out. He has started to stare hard at the question of how far he is willing to commute each day if a job were to come along. Is Madison too far? Rockford, Illinois? Further away? As Mike walks toward his truck, his last exam just behind him, his graduation just ahead, a large question jostles in his mind: "What's next?"

This pride-fear combination will linger inside Mike for precisely two more weeks. Two Wednesdays from now, he will go for an interview at

Seneca Foods Corporation, a vegetable processing plant in Janesville that happens to have an entry-level position in its human resources department. That Friday, he will get a call to come in on Monday for a pre-employment physical. On Tuesday, he will be told that he can start work the next day. And so, on June 1, Mike will not be thinking much about the fact that he has to work the overnight shift, or that he will be dealing with workers and interpreting labor contract language from the corporate side and not the union side, or that he and Barb will, between them, be earning just over half the money they had made at Lear.

Mike will be thanking his lucky stars that, after twenty-eight months without a job, he is starting a new career.

★

This summer will mark three years since the assembly plant and its supplier companies, such as Lear, began to shut down—long enough that most people who wanted to retrain have gone back to school. By this summer, the laid-off workers who went to Blackhawk will be faring less well than their laid-off neighbors who did not.

Counterintuitive as it may seem, the out-of-a-job workers who went to Blackhawk are working less than the others. Nearly two thousand laid-off people in and around Janesville have studied at Blackhawk. Only about one in three has a steady job—getting at least some pay every season of the year—compared with about half the laid-off people who did not go back to school.

Besides, the people who went to Blackhawk are not earning as much money. Before the recession, their wages had been about the same as for other local workers. By this summer, the people who have found a new job without retraining are being paid, on average, about 8 percent less than they were paid before. But those who went to Blackhawk are being paid, on average, one third less than before.

Most startling, the group whose pay has fallen the most are people like Mike, who stuck it out at Blackhawk until they graduated. These successful students tended to have had higher wages before the recession.

For that reason, the decrease in their pay is especially steep, dropping by nearly half.

At the Job Center, through which so much federal money has flowed in support of the job-training gospel, Bob Borremans has been noticing that not everyone who went to Blackhawk has emerged with a job with good pay. Or with a job. This is not what he expected. He has a mystery on his hands.

Did some out-of-a-job workers snap up the few jobs that came along while some of their out-of-a-job neighbors were back in school? Is part of the problem that people like Mike, who had eighteen years at Lear, are now starting out at the bottom rung of a new field? If so, will their pay go up if they move up the ladder over time?

Whatever the reasons, Bob is becoming aware that the retraining gospel that the federal government and the Job Center's own caseworkers have been spreading is based on a rock-bottom premise that hasn't turned out to be true—at least, not yet. The premise is that this recession would be like past recessions and that jobs would come back at the pace that they have before. It is not happening. So Bob is aware that the Job Center, with good intentions but wrong expectations, has sent people into what he is starting to regard as a double whammy. They lost their jobs. They went to school to equip themselves with new skills, and they still can't find jobs.

*

At Blackhawk, Sharon Kennedy, the vice president of learning, has been trying hard to ward off the kind of double whammy that Bob is recognizing in the Job Center. Sharon has urged Blackhawk's staff to confer with executives and personnel directors of the companies still in town about where jobs are likely to appear. The college's tiny, overloaded crew of counselors has tried to navigate dislocated workers into studies to prepare for those fields.

Blackhawk's most remarkable effort, though, has been through the little program Sharon and the staff built with the $2 million gift that one of Wisconsin's Democratic U.S. senators, Herb Kohl, managed to wangle from Congress for the college. With this money, Blackhawk created

CATE—Career and Technical Education—for the specific purpose of heaping extra help onto a small batch of out-of-a-job workers. CATE started the winter of 2010 with just 125 students. At the start, they took tests, which found that some were ready for college, but others could read, write, or do math at only a middle school level. Each of the two groups was allowed to pick programs in just a few fields that Sharon, Bob, and their staffs all agreed were the most promising fields for finding a job. The out-of-a-job workers who were ready for college could train for computer work or clinical lab technology. The unready students could train for work as nursing assistants or welders or certain kinds of business jobs. They got a lot of handholding, with tutors and twenty hours on campus each week.

CATE was expensive—$8,000 to $10,000 per student. Yet, despite the care devoted to deciding what these students should study, despite the intense coaching lavished on this small batch of laid-off factory workers, the results were modest. And the grim reality was that, even in those fields selected as most promising by Sharon and everyone else who built CATE, the out-of-a-job Blackhawk students who studied for these fields haven't had any more luck in finding a job than the others. By this summer after Mike graduates, about half will be working—about the same as everyone else.

★

On occasion these days, Mike runs into people from Lear who went to Blackhawk. Some of them are still looking for work, and some are doing work nowhere close to what they planned. A guy who studied computer IT is bagging groceries. That kind of thing. So, by the afternoon of June 1, as he gets ready to go to Seneca Foods for his first overnight shift, the pride-fear jostling inside him has turned into pure pride—a feeling that his life has become a best-case scenario.

Yes, he will be making less money than before. But that is part, he believes, of accepting that the old times are gone. Part of not dwelling on what you can't change. Part of being grateful for what you have. In these new times, what Mike sees when he looks over the sweep of his life is, not the loss of his union office, but a gamble on human resources management that has paid off. He has a job. It is in his field. It is in Janesville.

Labor Fest 2011

The Labor Fest parade begins marching at 1 p.m., as it does each year, along Milwaukee Street and bends south onto Main. This afternoon, September 5, has postcard skies, but the mood isn't right. As the stuntmen of the New Glarus Fire Department scale their ladders in the street, as the classic Chevys roll by, a palpable anger marches alongside the parade. The anger has descended in a straight line from last winter's protests against Scott Walker's anti-union, budget-cutting first weeks as Wisconsin's governor. The anger flouts Janesville's long, proud tradition of civility, its good-natured responses to adversity.

In his sixty-seven years, Tim Cullen has never seen anything like it. Since the State Senate Democrats hiding out in Illinois returned to Madison in defeat, Tim has been trying to smooth partisan relations. He thought he was making a peace gesture with his proposal to outlaw legislators fleeing the state from now on. Instead, Republicans mocked his idea, and his fellow Democrats derided him as a patsy. The *Wisconsin State Journal* in Madison and the *Gazette* have chronicled Tim's olive-branch efforts with two Republican state senators willing to try to heal working relationships by visiting each other's districts. "It is all part of a plan to prove to someone, somewhere, that bipartisanship is not dead in

Wisconsin," the *State Journal* wrote in July. Tim often feels alone in his faith in the virtue of rekindling a tolerant, bipartisan spirit in Madison. He often feels out of step. And now, on this cool, breezy afternoon, he is walking along Milwaukee Street in his hometown parade. He looks to the crowded sidewalk on one side of the street, and about twenty people are cheering him as he walks by. He looks toward the crowd on the other side. A guy is giving him the finger.

The finger? In the midst of the Labor Fest parade? Right on Milwaukee Street in nice, can-do Janesville?

Tim can't believe it. He doesn't know whether the guy resents him for hiding out in Illinois or resents him for being too moderate. Either way, he thinks, these few seconds sum up everything that is wrong in Wisconsin politics today. Everything that is tearing down Janesville's trademark civility.

Tim is not even getting the brunt of the worst of the anger that is marching alongside the parade. The worst is marching alongside Paul Ryan. It is standing with Paul before he and his family begin to march. The anger arrives in the form of a young man with tousled brown curls and a blue zippered sweatshirt. The young man, Todd Stoner, is a twenty-five-year-old labor organizer and a member of the nascent Occupy Wall Street movement, which is denouncing the richest one percent of the world's population and the sorry state in which the concentration of wealth is leaving everyone else.

Stoner begins politely enough, extending his hand as he approaches. "Congressman Ryan," he says.

Paul shakes Stoner's hand before putting his own hand back on the handle of a double stroller, holding it steady for small, blond Sam, at six the youngest of the congressman's three kids, to scramble into one of the stroller's twin seats. "I'm sorry," says Paul, who is looking every inch the Wisconsinite in a striped Green Bay Packers polo shirt and khakis. His cell phone is clipped to his belt, just as it was on the night, more than three years ago now, that he got the heads-up, plant-closing phone call. "Nice to see you. I apologize. We are just getting started here."

Next to Paul, his wife, Janna, her blond hair pulled into a ponytail, is standing with their two other kids, Liza and Charlie. Around them are supporters in Kelly green T-shirts with "Ryan" in small white letters on the front and larger white letters on the back.

Stoner is not deterred. "I just really need to ask you a question."

"Not right now," Paul repeats, " 'cause we are just getting started." He hands Stoner a cream-colored business card, as young Sam waves a small American flag from his stroller seat. "Do me a favor. Go to my website," Paul says, but the young man, becoming less patient by the second, cuts him off.

"I have. I've read it."

"Well, then you know what I think we need to do," Paul says.

Stoner says he is not happy with what he has read.

"We are just going to disagree on that, okay?" Paul says. "Take care. I hope you do better. I want to get jobs. We just have a different opinion about how to get 'em, okay?"

Stoner's voice rises, his tone more strident. "What should I have to work for to get a job? Should I have to work the same wages as in China? Should I have to work for $1 an hour?"

Janna's hand is resting on the stroller, too, a smile pasted on her face. Charlie, who is eight, is watching. Finally, Janna turns to the young man and wishes him a nice day. Paul wishes him a nice day, too.

"Would you like some candy?" the congressman asks. His kids have hard candies they are going to toss to the parade-goers if they ever can start walking.

"No," Stoner says, sounding incredulous that this is what he is being offered.

"Would you like a Packer-Badger schedule?"

"No."

As Stoner veers into a monologue on the dangers of deregulation, Paul is now facing away from him, his lips pulled tight. Janna is still wearing her smile. A man in a Kelly green Ryan T-shirt chimes in. "C'mon," he tells the heckling young man, "we are all here to have a good time."

Stoner does not mention that unemployment in Rock County last month was still above 9 percent, with six thousand fewer people working than before GM and all the rest shut down. But he might as well have said it, because he says: "How can we be at Labor Day when there is so much unemployment? This is a *sad* Labor Day!"

Finally, Paul and his family and his Kelly green entourage start down the parade route. By the time he passes the Main Street reviewing stand, near the end of the mile-long route, his Labor Day hasn't gotten any better. Paul is still shouting out, "Everyone, happy Labor Day," and waving as he walks. On the sidewalk, behind the parade-goers in their lawn chairs, Stoner's curly-headed figure is visible. He is with friends. Several of them are from a group called Wisconsin Jobs Now!, which formed last spring, after the protests against the governor. This is the group for which Stoner is an organizer. The group's activism is being paid for by a large labor organization for which he also has worked, the Service Employees International Union. In fact, Wisconsin Jobs Now! has a float in the parade. The float is a flatbed, being towed behind a station wagon with "Unemployed Workers United for Good Jobs" written along the side. Sitting on the flatbed are a few out-of-a-job and low-wage workers from Paul's congressional district.

"Paul Ryan. He's the worst. He puts corporate interests first," Stoner and his friends are chanting, as the object of their anger nears the end of the parade route.

"Stop the attacks on the middle class!" Stoner yells, as he holds up one edge of a white sheet, hand-lettered with the words: "Ryan ignores WORKING people."

"Where are the jobs? Where are the jobs?" the protesters are yelling, as Paul opens the driver's door of his blue Suburban—a Chevy, of course, in his hometown that no longer makes them. Janna finishes hugging people in the Kelly green T-shirts, and she and the kids pile inside. As Paul drives off, a few blue and white signs are still visible in the mid-afternoon sun: "Save the American Dream."

★

Days later, Janesville's fortunes get a fresh dent. Yet again, it comes from Detroit. That Friday night, General Motors and the United Auto Workers reach a tentative agreement on a new four-year labor contract. These labor negotiations have been GM's first since Presidents George W. Bush and Obama agreed to the federal auto loans, since the GM bankruptcy and the restructuring that was its recovery strategy. During these negotiations, a minor issue has been the future of the company's only two assembly plants that are on standby—Janesville and the one in Spring Hill, Tennessee, a bit south of Nashville, a newer plant that opened to make Chevy Saturns in 1989 and was making SUVs until production stopped two years ago.

To the people of Janesville, the issue is not minor. At the Job Center, Bob Borremans still sees the longing in clients for the assembly plant to reopen, with the ripple effect it would bring along of so many other jobs. Realist that he is, Bob likes to believe that most people are no longer really banking on this phoenix. Still, some do—people such as Marv Wopat, retired for three years by now after his quarter century as the plant's employee assistance representative. Marv still holds a passionate belief that the plant's reopening, which would end his son Matt's workweeks in Indiana, is just a matter of time.

On the Friday night, word begins to slip out that the tentative contract would reopen Spring Hill. Janesville would stay closed.

As vice president of UAW Local 95, Dave Vaughn rushes to Detroit with Mike Marcks, his friend and fellow retiree who is the local's president. Throughout the negotiations, the local has been urging the union international's leaders to get the assembly plant reopened or—failing that—at least to keep it designated on standby, because standby is better than closed. Now they listen to the UAW's president lay out the tentative terms. By the end of the month, the union's members ratify the contract. General Motors announces that the new contract will create 6,400 jobs in the United States over the next four years. It will add just one percent to the corporation's costs and give bonuses and larger profit-sharing to its workers. General Motors' chief executive, Daniel Akerson, calls the contract "a win-win for both membership and the company." It is, he says, "further evidence that this is really a new GM."

And in Janesville? Disappointment, sure. Yet the old optimism, the old can-do flickers. Dave Vaughn and the other local officers are relieved that the UAW shielded the plant from a permanent death sentence. The same flicker of hope appears in the *Gazette*. If Spring Hill is going to re-open, a newspaper article reasons, doesn't that mean that Janesville, General Motors' only plant left on standby, is next in line?

Discovering the Closet

AP Psychology is Kayzia Whiteaker's seventh-period class, her last of the day. At 3:20 p.m., which is when seventh period ends, Kayzia is about to reach down for her pink mesh backpack so that she can put her book and notebook and folder inside. But as she starts to reach down, she feels, of all awful things, tears sliding down her face.

Kayzia is mortified. She and Alyssa, her twin, are by now juniors at Parker High. Kayzia is a disciplined member of the debate team and, last year as a sophomore, was already a varsity debater who helped Parker get to the state tournament. She is a believer in neatness and self-control. Not a person to cry in public. And at this moment, as she is realizing that she is not making any crying noises—thank goodness!—she knows that she must get these tears to stop.

She gives her tears a talking-to. "This is not the time or the place," she tells them in her mind. "You just can't cry in the middle of class."

The tears keep falling.

She keeps her head down, hoping that the other kids will be too busy with their own backpacks and whatever is on their minds to notice her wet, streaky face, which she knows isn't really being hidden by her curtain of straight brown hair. No one in her class seems to be paying attention.

But her desk is near the front of the room, against the wall and facing the middle. It is, in other words, near Mrs. Venuti's desk.

Amy Venuti has been teaching social studies at Parker for four years, and she works closely with Deri Wahlert, whose classroom is on the same hall as hers. Amy has just finished today's lesson on psychological disorders, and she happens to glance over at Kayzia and sees what is going on. She asks Kayzia if she has a minute to stay after class.

She is careful to wait until the other kids have left before she sits down in the desk next to Kayzia's and, in a quiet, motherly tone, asks what is happening and whether there is any way that she can help.

Kayzia doesn't have a clue what to say. In the past three years, she and Alyssa have become experts at hiding what is going on at home. They have become skillful at poking through the clothes at Goodwill to find designer jeans that look as if they got them new. At going along when their friends want to go shopping without drawing attention to the fact that they aren't buying anything. What's going on at home is not something to discuss with their friends.

Well, Alyssa's boyfriend, Justin, knows. He knows that Alyssa appreciates hanging out at his house, because there is less talk about money, and she can ride with him on a four-wheeler and just feel like a teenager for a change. And last year, Kayzia had to tell Ryan, a senior who was her debate partner, when they qualified for state. She had to tell him that she couldn't go. The team needed two hotel rooms near Ripon College, one for the three girls and one for the two boys, and she had to tell Ryan because she couldn't afford her share. So he told the coach, and somehow—she still isn't sure how—it was worked out that Kayzia could pay just a little and still go. And she made sure to be extra helpful, trying to make it up to whoever was paying so she could be there, even though the tournament was in the midst of a blizzard and the drive, which took longer than the two hours that it should have taken, frightened her.

So they had barely told friends, and, if they didn't feel it was proper to talk to their friends, how could Kayzia possibly tell a teacher?

How could she tell Mrs. Venuti that her dad, Jerad, was now on his third job since GM, after having been out of work for over a year after he was laid off from the plant? Or that she had started to worry that he might lose this one? This third job had seemed lucky at first. He was a guard at the County Jail, where Barb Vaughn used to work and Kristi Beyer still does. It had taken almost a year after he applied for the job to come through, and it probably hadn't hurt that the dad in a family they are close to, with Kayzia and Alyssa baby-sitting their kids since they were infants, is a Sheriff's Department sergeant. Jerad works mostly the second shift, before Kristi comes on duty for overnight, and he does not know her. Jerad is grateful for the pay—almost $17 an hour, which isn't GM pay but is better than $12 at the Patch Products warehouse, where he would have loved to stay if it had come with health insurance the way the jail job does.

Soon, though, Jerad has a problem with his jail job. Kayzia has been noticing that her dad seems different lately. Nervous. He seems almost scared to go to work. And the problem was getting worse over the summer, when he was putting in as much overtime as he could get, filling in when other correction officers were on vacation, to bring home the extra money. And even though almost $17 an hour is better than at Patch, Kayzia and Alyssa still hear their parents talking a lot about money, at the moments when they think that the girls and Noah can't hear, with Noah getting more into sports and uniforms costing so much, plus the high deductibles on the jail's health insurance which means that they have to shell out a lot for Kayzia's doctors' appointments to try to figure out why she is having so much pain in her abdomen. And Kayzia knows it's hard on her parents to have gone from middle-class and figuring that GM would last forever, the way it had for her grandfathers, to lower-middle-class and maybe lower than that. She feels that she should be helping them more, but she isn't sure what to do.

At school, Kayzia tries to keep her mind on her classes and not on what is happening at home. But in this unit on psychological disorders, the way Mrs. Venuti was talking today about depression and anxiety made Kayzia think of the changes in her dad. And putting two and two together in a way that she never had before, she felt during the last part of class as if a lump was stuck in her throat until she realized that the tears were coming out. In public.

Mrs. Venuti is being so nice in asking, and Kayzia doesn't want to be rude, but she doesn't think it is right to drag her personal life into class. So she waits a minute, trying to figure out what to say. She doesn't want to say any of it; she knows she has to say something.

"My family situation's not the greatest right now" is what she comes up with. And right then, she totally loses it, her silent tears becoming large, gulping sobs.

"We can help," Mrs. Venuti is saying.

"Well, I never received help before. We don't qualify for that," Kayzia is telling her. While she is saying that, she is remembering her mom's eyes looking red after trying and trying to get help from ECHO, the food pantry, where the staff kept telling her mom that her family's income each month was just a few dollars above the cut-off line.

Mrs. Venuti is telling her that you don't have to qualify for this kind of help.

She tells Kayzia to take her stuff, so Kayzia picks up her hot pink backpack, while Mrs. Venuti grabs her key chain from the top of her file cabinet. They walk out of the classroom to a closed door, across the hall and two doors down, which Kayzia has never really noticed before. When Mrs. Venuti unlocks the door, Kayzia can't believe what she sees: shelves filled with jeans and shoes and school supplies, and open cabinets stocked with food and body washes and toothpastes. The Parker Closet.

What amazes Kayzia is not just that this room exists. What amazes her most is the avalanche of a realization she is having that, if this room exists behind the door that Mrs. Venuti has unlocked for her, that must mean that other kids at Parker are from families whose situations are not the greatest either.

Hard as it is to imagine, in Janesville where thousands of people have lost jobs and some are still out of work and some, like her dad, are job hopping and not earning enough money, it has never occurred to Kayzia before that what is going on in her family is going on all over town. That is what happens when she and Alyssa have decided that this is not a subject to discuss with friends, and other kids, who used to be middle-class, too, have decided the same thing. So, now, Kayzia is overwhelmed by this thought that is hitting her, all of a sudden. "There's more kids like me!"

Amy Venuti has seen this "it's not just me" astonishment before. Since she started at Parker, she has been helping Deri with the Closet as it has grown from its dozen students the first year to nearly two hundred. Even if she doesn't do as much as Deri, she has, lately, been introducing a couple of dozen kids to the closet each year. From the kids before Kayzia, she has learned that she is not just offering used jeans and toothpaste. With this offer, she knows, she is wrenching their understanding of their lives into a new and different meaning: as needy. One girl got angry and started to cry, insisting that her family didn't need help. A boy whose parents were divorcing refused, too, until Amy came up with the idea of telling him that he now had to be the man of the house, and he couldn't be working because his full-time job was to be in school and to play his sports, so he needed to take some stuff home as a small way that he could take care of his family.

She has to find ways to make it palatable, Amy has learned.

While Amy is seeing Kayzia's shock as normal, Kayzia is on to her next thought, which is that someone is going to a lot of trouble to provide kids with this help that she never knew existed. People are taking time out of their day to be kind and to help, not just her, but her whole family, and not just her now, but her chances of reaching her goals of becoming a general practitioner and someday being in a position in which she will be able to help someone else.

It seems to Kayzia too emotional to be thinking all of this, so she doesn't say it all out loud. She just asks Mrs. Venuti, "Well, where do you get this stuff?"

Donations, her teacher tells her. People in the community who chip in.

Mrs. Venuti is asking what she needs, but Kayzia is still focused on the amazing fact of this secret place in school that no one knows about unless they get into a situation where they need to know. And when she focuses on "needs," she gets stuck on the fact that she and Alyssa and Noah have been taught at home to be giving people. Giving and independent people. She doesn't want to take too much.

She picks out Suave shampoo and conditioner. She has learned that it's cheaper to go without conditioner, but it will be nice to have some. And because it's good to be a giving person, she takes an Old Spice deodorant for Noah.

When Mrs. Venuti asks whether she needs anything else, Kayzia tells her that this is enough. Before Mrs. Venuti locks the door again, a well-dressed boy Kayzia has never seen before, from a younger grade, ducks in for a minute and gets a few items, too.

She walks alone the few blocks between Parker and home, thinking about this discovery and about Mrs. Venuti telling her not to be afraid to ask if she needs anything else. When she gets home, Alyssa is at work, so Kayzia leaves the shampoo and conditioner and deodorant on the kitchen counter, between the table and the stove. She walks over for her 5 p.m. to 9 p.m. shift, serving up ButterBurgers and frozen custard in a blue Culver's apron and cap.

When she gets home from work, Alyssa asks, as Kayzia knew she would, where the stuff has come from. Kayzia knows that her sister won't like the answer. If they need something, they have been taught, they work harder for it. Or they do without.

Kayzia explains about Mrs. Venuti taking her to a room, about their school having something called the Parker Closet. As she is explaining, she knows that, even if they need it, Alyssa will not be easy right away with the idea of accepting help.

35

After the Overnight Shift

The overnight shift at the Rock County Jail ends at 7 a.m., so the sun is about to rise on these fall mornings when Kristi Beyer walks out of the jail and into the parking lot. When she was first hired, Kristi rotated shifts—days, evenings, nights. Switching around her sleep didn't seem to bother her. Still, she found that she likes nighttime at the jail best. It is quieter. Besides, after Barb surprised her and quit almost a year ago, Kristi missed her, and two other correctional officers who have become her friends happen to work nights. When an opening came along, she applied. So Kristi works the overnight shift now, and it is 7:30 a.m., just daylight, by the time she reaches home.

The house is quiet at this hour. Her husband, Bob, has left already. Only her mother is up and about. Kristi likes an after-work smoke before she goes to bed, and Linda doesn't allow smoking in the house. So this is the hour when Linda gets her coffee and Kristi, still in her Sheriff's Department khakis, grabs her Newport 100s, and they head out onto their wide back deck and talk about everything.

Kristi enjoys this hour with her mom. The deck is nice for sitting outside and talking, even if the mornings have gotten cool. The wooden boards are covered with indoor-outdoor carpeting, and a metal overhang, with skylights to let through the early light, blocks the wind. This is the hour when Kristi entertains her mom with the stories from her night. About some stupid thing that a prisoner did. Or some prisoner needing to get sent to the hospital. Or officers needing to take TV privileges away, and what a prisoner had to say about that. She knows her mom loves these jail stories. Something different happens every night. Not like factory work.

Working at the jail is tough, though. Now and then, Kristi calls Barb and says she is unhappy there. Still, Kristi is proud that she has what it takes. And Linda is proud of her only daughter and happy that, at thirty-nine, Kristi has found a good job in a town with so many people who have not.

Most of their life, it seems, is settling down. Even for Bob, who started at Blackhawk later than Kristi, studied heating and air-conditioning installation and maintenance, and graduated in May. His unemployment was about to run out in September, no Janesville jobs in sight. His classmates have been having a hard time; one is planting soybeans to make some money, another is a store clerk. So Kristi felt Bob was fortunate when he was hired, at last, in August as a maintenance specialist at one of the state office buildings in Madison, which is why he needs to leave for work before Kristi gets home from her shift.

If Bob is working, finally, Kristi and her mother still have one big worry that they talk over on their back deck, along with the jail stories and their cigarettes and coffee. Kristi's only child, Josh, is twenty-two. When he graduated from Parker High School in 2007, months before the recession arrived, a year before GM and its suppliers started to shut down, Josh joined the National Guard. And now he has been shipped off to Iraq.

36

Late Night at Woodman's

Kayzia Whiteaker tiptoes over to the couch, where her mom, Tammy, is still up, as she often is now on weekend nights, working her scissors through a stack of coupons.

"Want to go grocery shopping?" Kayzia asks, gently as she can, trying to make it sound like it's no big deal, like it's the most ordinary thing in the world for a sixteen-year-old kid to offer to take her mom to Woodman's and pay.

She realizes, as she asks, that her childhood is slipping away. This is what growing up too fast looks like, and it has been creeping up on her for a while.

A child wouldn't notice that, the longer her dad, Jerad, works at the jail, the more depressed he seems. She can't remember the last time he made one of his dumb jokes that crack her up. She has noticed that her mom, plowing through her coupons while her dad is asleep, has become the chief worrier. Kayzia knows that stressed-out look that sometimes sneaks across her mother's face when she thinks no one is around. It's a look that Kayzia can't bear, and her mother knows it, so they have an unspoken agreement that Kayzia will pretend not to see.

Best not to talk about certain facts that were once surprising but now are old news. That after ten months at her first after-school job, at Culver's, home of the ButterBurger, she has more in her checking account than her parents have in theirs. That it isn't so rare anymore for one of her parents to ask her or Alyssa, very politely, whether they could lend a few dollars for groceries or gas. That her dad tries sarcasm—"We supported you the first half of your lives, you can support us the second half"—to hide that asking kills him, every time.

Kayzia and her parents may joke, but they don't talk about the stark facts. Even now that she knows about the Parker Closet, so she no longer has the impression that her family is alone in these problems, she doesn't talk about money with her friends. She doesn't talk about it even with her grandmother Lucille, her dad's mother and her biggest cheerleader on Facebook and in life—the one person Kayzia is pretty sure knows just how she feels, because one other fact she has noticed is that her grandmother is quietly sending her parents a little extra each month for the mortgage.

There is someone, however, with whom Kayzia talks about everything. Especially about this. Since eighth grade, Kayzia and Alyssa have continued to worry together, ever since they huddled on their beds in their basement bedroom, trying to figure out what it meant that their dad was home for breakfast.

Looking back, Kayzia now understands that those were innocent days, their anxieties those of kids. The reality is that her dad still doesn't have a job that can support them the way he once did, and there are no good jobs for him to find. Kayzia and Alyssa try to approach this problem in an optimistic and practical way. Kayzia will add a second job—working as a receptionist for a chiropractor in town. Still, once in a while, she and Alyssa let their minds drift further outward. What if a day comes when their parents can't pay the mortgage? How will they afford college? Can Alyssa achieve her dream of becoming an engineer? Kayzia's of becoming a general practitioner?

But that's for the future. It's now that's the immediate problem: the fridge is nearly empty again, and her parents are low again on cash. And that specific problem, not the future, pulls Kayzia to decide that tonight is the time to tiptoe over to the couch and ask her mom the grocery question that has been in her brain for a while but has not, before this night, come out of her mouth.

Her mom looks up from her scissors and her coupon stack. From her expression, Kayzia can tell she's used the right tone. Whew! Her little plan is going okay so far. It's a delicate matter, after all, this scheme to pay for the family groceries.

She finds Alyssa in the paneled family room, watching TV with Justin, her boyfriend. "Do you want to come with?" Kayzia asks, putting it that way because she doesn't want her sister to feel pressure to help. Alyssa has more obligations than she does, with the payments on the 2005 Chevy Impala she's just bought to get to work, and her car insurance, while Kayzia is still saving up to make sure she has enough money for a car. But Alyssa is in, of course. Justin, too, because, even if it hasn't been plain to him what's up, if Alyssa is going, he is, too.

Before they leave, Kayzia and her mom look through the coupons to see which ones would be useful. Her mom makes a grocery list. Then they are in the car, Tammy at the wheel and Kayzia in the front seat, with Alyssa and Justin in back, as if this thing they're doing isn't completely topsy-turvy. First stop is the Blackhawk Credit Union ATM, where Kayzia and Alyssa jump out and get $100 each, the maximum daily withdrawal from their accounts. Then they shoot off to the all-night Woodman's on the north side of town. By the time they arrive, it's almost midnight, the wide aisles nearly empty of shoppers.

Kayzia has worked out the details. Justin takes charge of the coupons, Alyssa works the calculator, and she pushes the cart and helps her mother load. They buy chicken because they've been having too much pasta. Lunch meat, because Kayzia is sick of pb&j. Cocoa Puffs and Cap'n Crunch for a change, instead of generic cereal. And then they come to an aisle so tempting but unnecessary that Kayzia lets herself walk down it only because it is, after all, her own money: the aisle with chocolate chip cookie dough Pop-Tarts.

The crucial part of the whole venture, the key to its success, is the checkout. They need to do it just right. No clue that her mom isn't buying the groceries the way mothers usually do. So, in line, with no one saying a word, the girls slip Tammy their crisp $20 bills. She takes them as easily as she does the coupons that Justin hands her.

On the ride home, groceries in the trunk, Kayzia relaxes. Sure she's tired, but the thought of Cocoa Puffs in the morning makes her as happy as the little girl she used to be. Funny she should think that, she tells herself, because, at this moment, she's feeling more grown up than ever in her life. Taking responsibility. There are times when she doesn't know how to think about what it means that she and Alyssa have more money in their accounts than their parents. With her bringing home $150 to $200, depending on her hours, from Culver's every two weeks, and trying to save $100 of it, as often as she can. Sometimes she resents the sacrifices and the responsibilities. But she reminds herself that she and Alyssa have been taught to be helping people since they were little. They donate to the National Honor Society blood drive and raise money for Parker High's Relay for Life. So why, really, when her parents need the help, should it be any different at home?

When they get to the house, and she puts away the groceries with her mom, Kayzia is feeling something besides happiness over the Cocoa Puffs: relief that her dad is asleep. All this time after his General Motors job went away, with him bumping in and out of other work that doesn't pay enough, she knows that he still isn't over the idea that he's supposed to provide for his family. He's so hard on himself, she thinks, not giving himself credit for trying as hard as he can, looking online all the time for better jobs. In the morning, she knows, he will not be happy to find the refrigerator filled by this midnight shopping adventure fueled by his daughters' checking accounts.

Part Five

★ 2012 ★

SHINE

Mary Willmer is in the audience of the Janesville City Council chambers, her son, Connor, at her side. It is 7 p.m. on the second Monday in February, and the third City Council meeting of 2012 is about to begin. Mary doesn't often come to watch her local government in action, and she certainly doesn't bring her kids. Tonight, the chambers are uncommonly full. Driving downtown to the Municipal Building, on Jackson Street just off Milwaukee Street, where the Labor Fest parade marches each year, Mary reminded Connor, her youngest and a Craig High School junior, that it was good for him to come because this is such a big night for the community.

In the car, Connor had asked whether she was nervous. "Scared to death," Mary admitted.

The source of Mary's anxiety, and the reason she is here, is item #1 under new business on the Council's agenda. The item is a pricey, $9 million proposal, two years in the making, to help what Mary—and the rest of the Rock County 5.0 economic development coalition—regard as a linchpin to Janesville's revival. It is called SHINE.

As linchpins go, this one isn't the sturdiest. SHINE Medical Technologies is a start-up company in Madison that has devised a novel method for producing a medical isotope from uranium. The isotope in question is needed in hospitals for stress tests to detect heart disease, bone scans to detect cancer metastases, and twenty-eight other diagnostic imaging purposes. The global supply of this isotope, molybdenum-99, is running low, and SHINE is one of four companies that have received $25 million, early-phase matching grants from the U.S. Department of Energy to try to develop commercially viable manufacturing methods to keep enough Moly-99 (or Mo-99), as it is known for short, flowing.

In an odd coincidence, another of the four companies, called North-Star, is planning to build its manufacturing plant down the road in Beloit; Diane Hendricks has become the main investor. In the past, these coinciding ambitions would have ignited rivalry. But now, with the government encouraging them both, the pair of start-ups is being welcomed in the spirit of regional collaboration that is Rock County 5.0's bedrock. Maybe the area can emerge as the nation's hub of medical isotope manufacturing. "A whole different halo on our Rock County brand," is how John Beckord, the president of the business alliance, Forward Janesville, is putting it.

At the moment, SHINE has just a dozen employees, insufficient investment capital, a never-before-used isotope-making process, and a considerable government obstacle in its path: rigorous, complex reviews by the federal Nuclear Regulatory Commission, which will evaluate whether what SHINE wants to do is safe and environmentally sound before deciding whether it deserves a federal license. No license, no manufacturing.

These hurdles notwithstanding, SHINE has been prominent on the radar screen of Janesville's business and political leaders. It has been there because of the vision of SHINE's founder and chief executive, Greg Piefer, a guy of thirty-five with floppy brown bangs, an easygoing manner, and a formidable intellect backed up by a University of Wisconsin PhD in nuclear engineering. Two years ago, a Madison business journal singled out Piefer as a "shining star" in its annual listing of forty local entrepreneurs under forty. That was around the time that he began shopping for a community as the site for a future manufacturing plant, if and when SHINE becomes ready to do any manufacturing.

From Mary's vantage point, SHINE looks like a perfect opportunity.

Ever since the assembly plant closed just over three years ago, she and local economic development officials have been working to court businesses that could lift up and diversify Janesville's sunken economy. Paul Ryan, too. From Capitol Hill and when he is back home, Paul has been making business recruitment calls anytime that Rock County's economic development manager, James Otterstein, sends him a lead and the name of a CEO to contact. Paul has learned that there is not a good pool of businesses to call because, even two and a half years after the recession officially ended, not many companies are looking to move or to expand. "In this economy? I'm not taking a risk," is the reply that Paul has heard from CEOs more times than he cares to remember.

Paul has spoken with Piefer four times. Paul has talked up Janesville— its community spirit, its geographic assets, its favorable cost of living. How you can have a really good life in Janesville. The basic spiel he makes to all the CEOs. He has even offered to take Piefer to dinner and, while Piefer has declined, Paul senses that he appreciates that the congressman is there for him. Mary and the rest at Rock County 5.0 have been working on Piefer, as well. And Janesville's economic development officials have been negotiating with Piefer and the SHINE team over a crucial piece of nitty-gritty: what it would require in dollars and cents as incentives to bring SHINE to town.

Finally, not quite three weeks ago, Piefer announced that he was very excited to call Janesville home and "to become part of the community as an employer and corporate citizen." He selected Janesville over two other Wisconsin communities that also had been competing to become SHINE's future manufacturing home.

After all this wooing and negotiating, after all the futile attempts by Paul and Rock County 5.0 to recruit other companies, the joy with which Mary has greeted SHINE's decision cannot be overstated. All along, the Rock County 5.0 philosophy—in contrast with that of the no-longer-auto-workers still hoping that the GM plant will come back to life—has been that Janesville needs to update its identity from an old auto town to a twenty-first-century center of advanced manufacturing. What a waste, Mary and the other 5.0'ers believe, that the University of

Wisconsin–Madison has a research park, just forty-four miles north-west of Janesville, filled with start-ups dreaming up entrepreneurial in-novations in the life sciences and other technologies, and none of the manufacturing spun off from these innovative ideas has ever come to Janesville. Mary and other 5.0'ers have toured the park and met with the people developing new technologies and explained how eager Janesville is to diversify and how especially eager it is for companies in the bio-sciences. And now, here comes SHINE, the first Madison-born high-tech venture to choose the town. SHINE would, Mary believes, be a game changer.

This joy is undimmed by certain facts. SHINE would not bring many jobs. Piefer has been saying that he'd need 125 employees—a tiny fraction of the jobs that went away. And the soonest those jobs would arrive is three years from now, and it could be later, unless all goes smoothly with investment capital and the federal reviews. And whenever he's been asked, Piefer has side-stepped the question of how many of those jobs could be filled by people from Janesville, instead of people from elsewhere with greater scientific expertise. "What are the skills he is looking for?" Bob Borremans, over at the Job Center, has been wondering. And if SHINE is going to need to import people with master's degrees and doctorates in nuclear engineering, Bob wonders, too, what makes Piefer so confident that he can attract those people to what has essentially been a blue-collar town?

Still the salaries Piefer has been talking about—$50,000 to $60,000 a year—have stirred hope across the city, when so many are working for so much less than their wages in the past. From her perch as vice president of learning at Blackhawk Technical College, Sharon Kennedy winces when she sees how this hope has welled up. A *Janesville Gazette* story saying that SHINE had chosen Janesville mentioned that Piefer was planning to meet soon with administrators at Blackhawk and another technical col-lege to discuss the possibility of creating a new program to train nuclear technicians. No jobs yet. No training yet. Yet Blackhawk's switchboard lit up right away. All over town, Sharon can see, people are still grabbing on to any shard of hope they can find.

There is another catch, too. The joy that Mary is carrying around, the hope stirred across town by the seductive idea of even just 125 well-paid jobs, have run smack into a sobering reality: Getting SHINE to come to Janesville would cost a lot of money. Exactly how much it would cost has only now become apparent because, though Mary and all the rest have been talking with Piefer and his team for a long time and giving city officials their advice, the negotiations have been conducted by the city's economic development director, who has disclosed the details to the public just a few days ago.

What details they are! As part of its economic incentives to get SHINE, the city government would donate an eighty-four-acre tract of land. The land, worth $1.5 million, would be on the south side of town, next to the airport, because Moly-99 degrades within hours, so being able to speed freshly made isotope to airports and then to hospitals around the country is vital. The land in question is adjacent to 224 acres of which Mary and Janesville's other economic development leaders are very proud, because it is intended for a business park, and Rock County 5.0 has paid a pair of consultants to certify it as shovel-ready, meaning that companies could build on it and move right in. This future business park and a smaller site in Beloit make Rock County the only county in Wisconsin with this kind of designated, certified, shovel-ready land for manufacturing or offices or distribution centers. For just over two years now, this has been a big piece of Rock 5.0's economic development marketing pitch. Except that so far, no businesses eager to build have shown up.

This dearth of interested businesses makes SHINE an especially big deal and is why Janesville, in addition to donating the land, is offering to cover the cost of extending utility lines and otherwise developing the site for the future Moly-99 plant. The city also is offering to guarantee a $4 million private loan that SHINE will need if it is to move forward. This money, nearly $9 million in all with incentives for land, utilities, and construction costs, would come in the form of relief from future property taxes—a much-debated public financing technique that has become popular around the country. Over the years, the idea is, SHINE would more than repay its loan in taxes. And the help would not come directly from Janesville's hurting city budget. But to put in perspective just how big the incentives are, this $9 million offer to SHINE compares with an entire city budget this year of $42 million. And this question of incentives to SHINE has arisen as, up in Madison, Governor Walker prodded the legislature to approve last summer, over the objections of Tim Cullen and every other Democrat, spending cuts that now have drained from Janesville fully 10 percent of the state aid it had a year ago.

For tonight's meeting, the city's economic development director has prepared a candid, detailed memo that lays out the specifics of this SHINE incentive package. It explains that, as Mary and Forward Janesville have urged, most of the incentives would be withheld until SHINE reached specific milestones. Among these milestones would be proof that its nuclear particle accelerator actually works, plus permission from the federal Nuclear Regulatory Commission to build the plant.

These milestones would be a kind of financial buffer for the city, a hedge against dumping a fortune into a bad investment. Even with this hedge, though, the economic development director admitted in his forty-page memo that risks to this investment exist. Among these risks, the memo says, is that neither SHINE, nor the NorthStar operation planned for Beloit, nor the other two isotope-making companies that also have been given the $25 million federal grants have so far "proven that their processes can work on a large scale." Besides, the memo says, the milestones in the deal that Janesville has negotiated with SHINE do not guarantee that SHINE's technology will be on such a "production scale" before it gets the money. "The challenges facing the company that could put a portion of the city's funding at risk include economics of the project, federal regulatory process, competition . . . from other countries, and providing a plan to manage any environmental issues."

SHINE, in other words, is no sure bet.

This, then, is the weak linchpin to Janesville's economic revival. And this is the deal—the $9 million economic incentive package—that is item #1 on the City Council's agenda and that has caused Mary to come sit in the audience, with Connor beside her to see a crucial moment of the city government in action.

To Mary, SHINE is such a no-brainer that she was surprised, at first, by the pushback from some in town. She is not surprised anymore. Driving downtown this evening with her son, Mary knows that the City Council is divided about the wisdom of this investment. The public is divided, too.

Still, it is disheartening to Mary and more fuel for her nervousness that, as ten citizens take turns speaking to the Council, only two are in favor of the project. Give SHINE a chance, the pair of proponents say, to make Janesville part of what one calls the nation's "biotech heartland." The eight citizens who speak out against SHINE warn of the financial risk to taxpayers, the lack of planning for nuclear storage and disposal, the possibility that other companies might not want to come to Janesville to be neighbors to a plant that uses uranium.

Nearly an hour into the meeting, Piefer moves from the back of the Council chambers, where he has been hanging out all this time, to the microphone. In addition to being a smart nuclear scientist, he is a good listener with a soothing manner. He is not surprised, he says, that there are a lot of questions about the agreement that city officials have reached with SHINE. The agreement has taken two years, he says, specifically because city officials have been so careful and brought in so many experts.

"If I were a Janesville citizen, which I look forward to becoming," Piefer says, "I would be proud that this is my City Council."

In fact, Piefer tells the Council, in a message calculated to delight Mary and everyone else who has been trying so hard to recruit companies to town, he already has begun spreading the word that Janesville is a good place with good leaders with whom to do business.

"SHINE is very much looking forward to building a future in Janesville," Piefer says. "It is an exciting company. It is the next big thing."

And yet, for all his geniality and his soothing touch, Piefer is tough enough not to let this moment slip away. One Council member asks what would happen if the vote were delayed a couple of weeks, so that the public could have a little more time to learn and ask questions about the deal.

"The probable result of an unknown delay," Piefer replies in a quiet tone, "is we will re-engage other sites." Janesville, in other words, might lose SHINE to somewhere else.

By the time the Council members take turns asking Piefer and members of the SHINE team their own questions, it is past 9 p.m.—more than two hours since the meeting began. They are about to vote. But first, two Council members deliver soliloquies. Their speeches frame the debate in a city that, for all its proud entrepreneurial history, never faced a decision this hard or divisive back when George S. Parker patented his first fountain pen, back when Joseph A. Craig persuaded General Motors' founder to take over the tractor factory he ran.

One speech is by Russ Steeber, who, in addition to being the Council's president, works as a captain in the Janesville Sheriff's Department. Russ begins with the very words that Mary often uses. A game changer is what SHINE will be.

His argument unfolds: "The city of Janesville, for almost 100 years, produced automobiles. . . . Unfortunately, those days are done, and that stream has dried up. Although we can hope that that plant someday opens its doors again, the reality is, we have to redefine what the city of Janesville is. This is one of those opportunities that can really take and define where we are for the next century. . . . And I truly believe that sometimes, when you look at making a decision like this, you have to be bold. I understand that the money the city of Janesville is about to possibly expend can be fairly extensive, but we are looking beyond SHINE. . . . We are looking at other technical type jobs that could come in, other medical research that could come in. We are looking at developing a region for the future."

The opposing view comes from Yuri Rashkin. Yuri is the Council's most colorful member—born in Moscow, emigrated with his parents as a teenager, and arrived in Janesville eight years ago. He is a musician, a Russian interpreter, and a talk radio host. He already was a Council member four years ago when a man in town was arrested—and eventually sent to prison—for a foiled contract murder plot against Yuri and a Ukrainian woman he was dating who was the man's estranged wife.

Yuri takes his Council work seriously, and he has concluded that the cost of the SHINE opportunity is too steep, the gamble too big, and the opportunity for public input too slim. The core of Yuri's soliloquy is a long metaphor: "I feel like we maybe are looking to cross a river that we really need to cross, because we need the economic development, and we have a great company with people I've been really impressed with, who are looking to build a bridge, and they got an awesome plan, because we really need to get across the river . . . but this material has never been used, and the bridge has never been built with this stuff."

By the time the Council members vote, two hours and twenty-one minutes have passed. Mary is fearful. But four vote yes, one abstains, and Yuri alone votes against SHINE.

Mary stands up and rushes out the Council chambers door and into the hall, where a celebration already has begun. In a few minutes, she and the SHINE team and everyone else who worked for two years on this deal will gather for a toast at O'Riley and Conway's, the Irish pub on Milwaukee, a block from the Municipal Building, whose booths display old photos of Paul Ryan's ancestors and the rest of Janesville's Irish mafia.

For now, Mary is just starting to taste relief. If the vote had gone against SHINE, she would have felt like a failure, shot down not just for the future home of an isotope-making plant but for Rock County 5.0's vision. General Motors to Moly-99. Such a long way to have come.

And with that thought, Mary finds Piefer in the midst of the party breaking out in the hallway and gives the founder of SHINE a hug.

★ 38 ★

Janesville Gypsies

The gypsies from Janesville, scattered among General Motors plants across the Midwest and the South, are now staying in touch with each other and with what is happening back home through a Facebook group, Janesville Wisconsin GM Transfers. It has 535 members, including Matt Wopat.

Posted February 18: "Seems like everyone thinks their new plant is full of idiots—we had our share at home too. It was just better cuz we WERE HOME."

Posted March 29: "Today in Fort Wayne, I talked to somebody from Arlington that heard from someone in Lordstown that heard from someone in Wentzville that is related to someone in Lansing that heard about a psychic in Detroit that contacted Elvis, and Elvis said that he heard from a 'good source that is high up' that the day Hell freezes over, GM is going to reopen the Janesville plant. Probably just a rumor."

A Charity Gap

Ann Forbeck, the Janesville school system's homeless student liaison, often is out around town. But her base is at Edison Middle School, in a hideaway on the second floor with pale cinder block walls papered with posters. On the wall behind her desk: "Dream lofty dreams and, as you dream, so you should become." On a side wall: "Do you know where you will do your homework?" And a lime green bumper sticker on her file cabinet: "End child poverty 2020WI.org." Ann happens to be in this small office when she gets a call from the director of the YWCA of Rock County. It is late on a Monday morning, one week after the City Council has approved the $9 million for SHINE.

Ann's days are unpredictable, each trilling of her cell phone bringing a fresh challenge to her formidable problem-solving skills, often requiring her to rush down the stairwell across from her hideaway, past the school's main office, out the back door, and into her ten-year-old Mazda, with its bumper stickers for Project 16:49 and public unions, so that she can deal with the latest emergency involving a teenager with nowhere steady to live. The call from the YWCA's director, Allison Hokinson, sets Ann in motion once again. This time, the drive is quick. The Y is just a few blocks from Edison.

When she arrives, Ann learns from Allison the particulars of this emergency: A woman drove up to the Y in a car with no license plates and got out with two teenagers—a girl and a boy. Her grandkids. The grandmother walked with them into the Y and announced to the staff, "I can't keep these kids."

Their mother, her daughter, had just left Wisconsin with a younger child, after depositing the older two with her. With a tiny one-bedroom apartment and not much money, she was willing to let the kids stay with her for two days, but that's it.

At this point, Allison did something she had never done before. She walked into her office to get her purse, opened her wallet, and handed the girl and the boy each a $10 bill. And then, of course, she called Ann to say that she had on her hands a pair of teenagers two days from becoming abandoned.

Handing kids her own cash, Allison was aware even as she did it, wasn't the best idea. A slippery slope. Not a solution. She did it this time because the sister and brother weren't the only ones traumatized by a mother who had left the state and a grandmother about to ditch them. Allison was traumatized, too. This wasn't the first time she had come face-to-face with homeless youngsters without relatives with the means to keep them. But the timing today couldn't be worse.

This pair are exactly the kind of unaccompanied homeless teenagers that Project 16:49, Ann's project, is supposed to help someday with a shelter for girls and one for boys. The YWCA has a big stake in the project. Eleven months ago, the Y's governing board had voted to become its fiscal agent and parent organization. Yet tonight, just hours from now, the board is going to vote again—this time, on a recommendation from Allison that the Y jettison responsibility for Project 16:49.

Allison hates that she has reached this conclusion. And she hates that she needs to tell Ann.

When the Y took on the project, it was a half year after the debut of *Sixteen Forty-Nine*, the documentary that exposed the lives of its three homeless kid stars and began to wake up Janesville to the surprising fact of homeless teenagers in town. Since then, the film has been shown at venues around the county. Fundraising has picked up. The first big event was a benefit concert, "It's not Fine—16:49," with five bands on a Saturday night and so many people who came out that some were turned away at the door. The benefit concert raised more than $10,000. Then came a pancake breakfast by the young adult ministry of Faith Community Church and a downtown pub crawl and a nice donation by the local builders association. Even a raffle of a red antique Chevy hot rod, whose owner donated it for the cause.

Ann is feeling good that consciousness about Project 16:49 has sparked around town. But it's not nearly enough yet. And now, late this morning of February 20, Allison knows that, when Ann arrives in a few minutes to figure out a plan for this about-to-be-abandoned sister and brother, she will need to hand Ann some very bad news.

Allison's recommendation to the Y's board is a reflection of what has been happening with philanthropy all over town ever since General Motors shut down. The Janesville tradition of generosity has been colliding with the limits of what the city now can do. This is no longer the same Janesville in which Joseph A. Craig endowed the YWCA with a mansion. He bought the place on Courthouse Hill that had once belonged to a man, A. P. Lovejoy, who had given Craig his start in business. In 1953, at the age of eighty-six, Craig bought the Lovejoy mansion from the estate of Lovejoy's widow for the express purpose of presenting it to the YWCA as its headquarters. Craig paid to remodel the mansion and a few years later for an addition, and it remained the Y's headquarters until it outgrew it a half century later and moved to its current site. This was just one, late example of the philanthropic acts that Craig performed for Janesville over his ninety-one-year life. He promoted 4-H clubs locally and nationally. And back during the Great Depression, he bought the entire Rock County Fairgrounds to prevent the then-destitute county fair—Wisconsin's oldest—from fading from existence.

Where is today's Joseph A. Craig? Where is today's George S. Parker, who was another one-man philanthropic hurricane and, beyond his support for the Parker Pen Band, donated an entire fleet of the latest hospital beds to the wards of Mercy Hospital and contributed to the building of the Salvation Army temple and gave monthly awards to outstanding high school students and gifts to the Janesville police department and the fire department? Where are these moneyed, philanthropic industrialists now that Janesville so needs the help?

The big generosity is gone, and so is even the next layer down, since Parker Pen ceased to have its corporate headquarters in town a few decades ago, and now the GM'ers—plant managers and workers alike—are gone, too. Like lots of nonprofits, the YWCA has lost board members who were GM'ers. And while fundraisers for some good cause or other still go on nearly every week of the year, Allison notices that nonprofits are all competing harder for a shrunken pool of dollars. And she notices that the compassion level is lower now and that certain segments in town even have started to say out loud that, if only people looked harder, they would find a job. As if it were that easy.

Of all the philanthropy hits that Janesville has taken, perhaps none has been as far-reaching as over at the United Way of North Rock County. In 2009, the year after the assembly plant closed, the United Way cut its grants to community groups by one fourth. Although annual giving fell even more the two years after that, the United Way was able to avoid further cuts because of the remarkable gift and raffle of the last Tahoe— which rolled off the assembly line with all the cheering and hugging and weeping among the losing-their-jobs workers and the nostalgic retirees. Now, the United Way's goal for this year—$1.3 million—is a million dollars less than a decade ago. And the United Way of North Rock County is planning to merge with an adjacent chapter. More efficient, sure, but some of its own staff are about to lose their jobs.

As a result of this charity gap, the YWCA has taken a $10,000 cut in United Way funding for its housing program for women transitioning from violent relationships to independent lives. The Y is getting less money donated for the gas cards it has handed out—a lifeline for women who otherwise couldn't afford the gasoline for their cars to look for a job, to get to a job. And all this is happening as the Y is starting to see more first-generation poverty than ever before—young women who are poor but did not grow up poor, who have a dad or a mom, or both, who worked at GM.

All this is what has compelled Allison to take a hard look that she'd prefer not to have taken at what the Y can afford to do. Better to continue what it is doing already, as best it can? Or to take on the big Project 16:49 mission of housing some teenagers with nowhere steady to live?

When Ann arrives at the Y to talk to the staff about this soon-to-be-homeless brother and sister, she is surprised that Allison first asks if she has a minute to step into her office.

It is midday. Once the door is closed, Ann is stunned because Allison starts bawling. Allison is crying so hard that she can barely get out the words to tell Ann that, at tonight's meeting, the Y's board is going to kick out Project 16:49.

Ann's first reaction is anger. She is mad. Very mad. The number of homeless teenagers in Janesville is growing year by year, and she spends her days—and sometimes her nights—patching together not-good-enough solutions for them, especially the ones who have been abandoned and are on their own, as this brother and sister are about to become. And Project 16:49 is a better solution, and she has poured her heart into it since the two shelters she is planning to build were just a glimmer of an idea nearly four years ago. And now, after the film showings and the fundraisers have been going so well, but not yet well enough, it suddenly seems as if maybe Project 16:49 can't happen, after all.

Now Ann is crying, too. Stinging tears of betrayal.

After a few minutes, Ann stops crying.

She throws her arms around Allison and gives her a huge hug, because the thought has just come to Ann that the two of them are in the exact same boat.

"We will find another way," is what is running through Ann's mind.

It will not take long for Ann and Robin Stuht, her 16:49 partner in Beloit, to approach other organizations in town for help—and be turned down. If their shelter for girls and shelter for boys are going to materialize, they will have to do it on their own. They are social workers. They have no idea how to form their own nonprofit. They will need to learn.

Gypsy Kids

At five-foot-eight, Bria Wopat is a starter on the freshman girls' basketball team at Milton High, just over the Janesville line. Games are Monday and Friday nights, times when her dad, Matt, is in Fort Wayne. She gets lots of playing time and, when she is in possession of the ball, dribbling down the court or shooting a basket, Bria's mind is, of course, on the game. But sometimes, when she's made a basket and glances up into the bleachers and sees her mom sitting by herself, clapping, that's when, for a flicker of time, it hits her how much she misses her dad.

It's not the same to have her dad call just before 10 p.m., when he's gotten off work, and listen to her mom tell him how well she did on the court that night, and then, when it's her turn on the phone, have him tell her how proud he is of her, sweetie. There is less to talk about, because he wasn't at the game.

She remembers Friday nights when she was younger and her dad was working second shift right in Janesville. Fridays were the nights, about once a month, when she and her mom and her older sister, Brooke, would go down to the assembly plant, stopping on the way at Taco Bell or Subway or maybe packing up leftovers if they'd had something for supper that her dad especially liked. And her dad would come outside on his supper break, and they would all sit in the parking lot and talk until he had to go back to work. Back in seventh grade—two years ago—was the last time they could do that.

Spring is coming, and it will be time soon for Bria to start to do the mowing again and clear the weeds. Even though she knows her dad wishes he were around more to do the lawn and other chores, she and Brooke figure the weekend should be his time to relax and, besides, he also has his apartment in Indiana to take care of.

Bria can tell that her dad says to her and Brooke all the things he thinks will make them feel as good as they can about him being away: If he were still working second shift at home, it's not as if he would be around anyway when they get home from school or for dinner. And if he hadn't taken the GM transfer, who knows how much time he really would have had with them, if he'd ended up with a job in town that didn't pay enough so he had to take a second job on weekends, like some kids' parents are doing. Even as a fourteen-year-old freshman, Bria knows that what they need to do is just do the best they can. And that's what they do.

Twice now, she and Brooke have gone down to Fort Wayne to see their father's life there. Once was with their mom. The other time, she and Brooke spent a week. On Monday morning, they drove with their dad the four and a half hours to Indiana, leaving early enough to be sure he would get there in time for his shift that afternoon.

Mornings that week, the three of them went golfing at the course where he kills time with other GM gypsies. While he was at work, Bria and Brooke watched movies. They walked to the public library down the street from his apartment in the Willows of Coventry. They were going to all drive home when he got out of work on Friday night, except that he got called in for Saturday overtime and, then again, for Sunday overtime. Her dad didn't want to let Brooke, who hasn't had her license that long, drive back with Bria on their own, going through all that Chicago traffic without him. So they all drove home late Sunday night, and her father got a couple of hours of sleep and then got picked up for his car pool at 8:15 a.m. on Monday.

On weekends, they spend as much time together as they can. Brooke, a junior now, doesn't hang out much with her friends on weekend nights when they get together at someone's house or go to a movie or, in the summer, have a bonfire. Her friends aren't surprised anymore when she says that maybe they can do something after supper one night during the week, if there's not too much homework, because she doesn't like to go out weekends when her dad is home.

Bria and Brooke don't watch their favorite TV shows during the week, like *Ghost Hunters*. Instead, they record the show so they can all watch together on Sundays. The good thing is that another favorite, *Finding Bigfoot*, is on Sundays anyway, so they can just squeeze, all four of them, on the couch and watch it when it's on. Sunday has been family day for her family, since even before her dad started working far away. Except now he gets to pick what he wants for dinner on Sunday nights, because he is not around to pick during the week. Making fajitas is a favorite.

Then Monday morning comes again, and the car pool takes her dad away, and it is back to fifteen minutes on the phone when he gets off work. Brooke has come up with something that she doesn't start to say after Monday night phone calls, but waits until Wednesday nights. "Two more sleeps until he gets to come home," she says once the number has gotten small enough to be comforting. Then the next night, it's down to "One more sleep." And in the middle of the night after that, hours after Bria and Brooke have gone to bed, their dad will walk in the house. And he will go into their rooms and wake them up with a kiss to tell them he is home. Even if they almost never remember by daylight that he woke them, they ask him to let them know.

Recall

Milton Avenue widens to six lanes with a median where it crosses U.S. Route 14 on the north side of town. It is Janesville's busiest intersection, with a Kmart and fast food places and three cell phone stores. Late this afternoon, the intersection is the site, too, of unmistakable evidence that the incendiary politics that began up in Madison seventeen months ago, with Governor Walker's bill to weaken public workers' union rights, have tarnished the civility on which Janesville has prided itself.

Today is June 5, the day on which Wisconsin voters are deciding whether Scott Walker will become the third governor in U.S. history to be ejected from office through a recall election. The mass protests at Capitol Square have billowed into a crusade by Walker's opponents to pry him from the statehouse, matched by a counter-crusade to keep him in office. The recall fight is venomous, backed by twice as much campaign spending as any Wisconsin election ever before. It is white-hot. It is in the glare of national news. And on Milton Avenue, it is prompting drivers, as they come to Route 14, to honk or jeer at campaign signs that partisans are waving on opposite corners of the intersection.

The governor has had his troubles in Janesville, which is still, in spirit if no longer as much in fact, a union town. Last winter, a manufacturing association that supports him began to erect billboards around the state that said, "Governor Scott Walker—Creating Jobs for Wisconsin." The signs listed the phone number to the governor's office so that citizens could call to thank him. Somehow, no one realized that it might be awkward to place the first of these billboards directly across from the silent General Motors assembly plant. The sign immediately became a laughingstock in town. It was soon gone.

Even so, the governor has his enthusiasts among Janesville's citizens. One of them is a husky young man with a crew cut who is standing at the intersection's southwest corner, holding aloft a sign that says, WE STAND WITH WALKER. The young man, Kirk Henry, is a business student at the University of Wisconsin–Whitewater and the only Republican in his family. As he holds up his sign, not everyone driving by in Milton Avenue's southbound lanes shouts friendly sentiments. But Kirk is pleased when a young woman in a white SUV shouts out her window, "Walker for president!" and a man in a green Corvette honks his horn three times, opens his window and yells, "Thank you. Thank you. We are keeping Wisconsin today!"

Kirk Henry leaves his spot at the intersection moments before Dave Vaughn, Mike's father, arrives on the northeast corner. Dave begins waving to passersby with one hand as, with the other, he grasps a long stick to which is attached a red and white sign that says, VOTE TODAY. Mike has, by now, been working nights for a year on the management side of human resources for Seneca Foods. In his retirement from GM, Dave has become the chairman of the Rock County Democratic Party, as well as the vice president of UAW Local 95. The local's president, Dave's old friend Mike Marcks, stands next to him at the intersection, holding up a sign that says, BARRETT. Last month, Milwaukee's mayor, Tom Barrett, won a primary election to face Walker in the recall. His victory turned the recall election into a rematch, because Barrett lost the governor's race to Walker nineteen months ago. This time, Barrett was not the top choice of most of the unions, which have invested so much in trying to pry Walker from office. But Barrett is the Democrats' candidate, so it is natural that Dave and

Mike are holding up their VOTE TODAY and BARRETT signs for the benefit of the northbound drivers along Milton Avenue.

What is more surprising is that, as rush hour is building, these two old friends are the only UAW Local 95 guys standing with campaign signs on a street corner anywhere in town. Even though the impetus for the recall began with the goal of protecting union rights. Even though "boots on the ground," as Dave still likes to say, has always been the local's way of operating. For decades, Rock County's Republicans have outspent Democrats in elections—just as, throughout Wisconsin and far beyond, Walker's supporters have donated nearly $59 million to try to repel the recall crusade, two and a half times the amount that the anti-Walker forces have raised. In Janesville, while the GOP has traditionally had the edge in money, the Democrats, aligned with the unions in town, have had the edge in ground troops to get out the vote.

Except that today, Dave and Mike are the only remnants of these boots on the ground. Two retirees leading an emaciated UAW local.

On this anti-Walker side of the recall fight, the biggest boots on the ground in Janesville are imported. The boots are over at the Union Labor Temple, on Center Avenue, across the street and a block up from the Job Center. Commanding this operation is a woman hired and dispatched to Janesville by the national office of the AFL-CIO, the federation of fifty-six unions in the United States, including the autoworkers. She arrived in town six weeks ago. On the walls of a workroom at the labor temple that is serving as the command post are lists of all the union locals in the vicinity and the strength of their membership. For the once mighty UAW Local 95, which had more than 7,000 active members just over a decade ago, the list shows 438 active members and 4,900 retirees.

The ground troops being coordinated from the Labor Temple include reinforcements from out of town. Union locals from Illinois and further away have sent members into Janesville and elsewhere in Wisconsin to canvass, give rides to polling places, and perform other necessities for getting out the vote.

As these imports knock on the doors of those houses that match the addresses on lists of known Democrats, the rivalries in the recall fight are in plain view. Even in Janesville, which has prided itself on its harmony. Dueling lawn signs hint at neighbors no longer on speaking terms.

In Dave's own family, his wife, Judy, has banned a nephew from her Facebook page. At sixty, Judy Vaughn is a retired schoolteacher and as ardent a Democrat as Dave. The Facebook trouble began when, to the surprise of no one who knows Judy, she began to post her views about Walker, which boil down to a belief, stronger than she has ever felt about any other politician, that the governor is evil. A couple of relatives didn't take that too well, including the nephew who eventually posted a reply, asking Judy to please do her politicking on a separate Facebook page because he was sick of her posts and, besides, she wasn't going to change his mind. Judy posted that she would not create a separate page. Then the nephew had a birthday party and didn't invite her and Dave. Still, she didn't unfriend him from Facebook until the day that he posted, "I am sick of my retarded friends and relatives and my union whiners." That did it.

Ordinarily, while Dave was standing with his VOTE TODAY sign on Milton Avenue, Judy would have been at the Democratic recall headquarters, a rented storefront on Milwaukee Street at which volunteers have been staffing a phone bank and coordinating door knocking. She has volunteered there, all day every day, in recent weeks. But she hadn't been feeling well. It turned out to be serious—blood clots in both lungs. So the day of the vote, she is in a bed on the third floor of Mercy Hospital, having arrived by ambulance a few days ago in a gray "Recall Scott Walker" T-shirt.

Judy is supposed to be taking it easy, but she is furious that she is cooped up in the hospital on recall day. So she has done the best she can, turning her hospital room into a field office of the recall crusade. A recall T-shirt is draped over a chair next to the IV pole that is dripping blood thinner into her veins. Two signs for Barrett are tacked up on the wall across from her bed, just beneath the board listing Judy's nurses on duty and the time of her medication doses. On the wall directly across from her room's door is a hand-lettered sign that says VOTE TODAY ★ MAKE IT COUNT ★ BARRETT. Judy insists on keeping the door ajar so that anyone walking down the hall can see the sign if they glance in.

It is just before 7:15 p.m.—forty-five minutes before the polls will close—when Dave arrives for a visit, fresh from his waving and sign-holding stint on Milton Avenue. Judy is pleased—she feels responsible for four anti-Walker votes today, just from talking down the governor to the staff on her hospital unit, including a nurse whose husband hadn't realized that he could register to vote on the spot. And Judy has combed through every number stored on her phone and called everyone she thought might not have voted yet, omitting the ones she did not consider a reliable vote in favor of the recall. Minutes after Dave arrives, her phone rings, as it has been doing all day. Another field report. "What time did you vote today?" Judy asks this latest caller. "Were they lined up? Really? Wow. Wow. Wonderful."

She hangs up. "Good will prevail," she tells Dave. "It will be a long night."

*

The expectation of a long night of vote counting around Wisconsin is common wisdom on both sides of the recall fight. Perhaps even a recount. Public opinion polls this spring have suggested a close race. As of a few weeks ago, Walker and Barrett were within one percentage point, though the governor seemed to have pulled ahead by a few points in the most recent polls. So a cliffhanger is what both sides are anticipating as Janesville's most active Democrats and most active Republicans converge on their respective gathering spots to watch the election returns.

The Democrats, including Dave and Mike, are packing into Steve and Holly's Restaurant, a long, narrow joint just off Milwaukee Street, with a television perched high over the bar. The Republicans are at the Speakeasy Lounge and Restaurant, a spiffier place with a patio that is lovely on spring nights like this one.

The restaurants are two and a half blocks apart, separated by Janesville's police headquarters and a Presbyterian church that has stood on this spot since before the Civil War. Though they are close together, the two gatherings symbolize the rift that has appeared in once unified Janesville since General Motors' announcement that the assembly plant would close—four years and two days from this recall night.

At Steve and Holly's, not much more than an hour has passed since the polls closed when Fred Yoss starts to yell at the television overhead. Fred worked today as a polling official at another church in town that is Janesville's largest voting site. At the moment, he is on a bar stool, a few seats away from where Dave and Mike are chatting. "NBC—how can they project that already?" Fred yells, alarmed that the network is forecasting a win for Walker. "I am going to go with the presumption that they still don't know what they are talking about."

A few minutes later, at a table on the Speakeasy's patio, Jay Mielke is breaking out a cigar. Jay is a broadcast engineer in town and Dave's counterpart: the chairman of the Rock County Republican Party. Before 9:30 p.m., the major television networks have called the race for Walker. Instead of becoming the third U.S. governor ejected from office in a recall election, Scott Walker has just become the first U.S. governor ever to survive a recall vote.

Jay is beaming as Mary Willmer walks onto the patio. Rock County 5.0 is nonpartisan in its economic development work, but it is public knowledge that Mary's co-chair, Diane Hendricks, has given $510,000 to Walker's campaign—the single largest donation by any individual. Mary is smiling as broadly as Jay as she high-fives him and the other Republicans seated around this patio table.

For Mary, who has been striving so hard to rebuild the city's economy, this decisive victory—*no one* expected that it would be over this fast—is the best news Janesville could get. Jay sees it the same way. Businesses, he is saying as he turns philosophical, have been wary of coming into Wisconsin while a dagger has hung over the future of a pro-business governor. The dagger removed tonight, the governor solidly in office, Janesville—all of Wisconsin, really—is poised for a surge in jobs. What a night.

Back at Steve and Holly's, the mood feels like a funeral. People are leaving early. Dave is standing near the end of the bar, hands on his hips. "What a bummer," he says quietly. "I'm devastated."

"I am just amazed," Mike says. And then he glances up at the television. "Here comes stupid."

It is not quite 10:30 p.m., and few of the other Democrats left in the restaurant are paying attention when Walker appears on the screen over the bar to claim his victory. On the stage of the Waukesha County Expo Center west of Milwaukee, before a cheering throng, the governor-who-will-stay-governor is hugging his wife and two sons and thanking God for his abundant grace. "Voters really do want leaders who stand up and make the tough decision," Walker says. And then he glides toward a conciliatory tone. "Tomorrow is the day after the election. And tomorrow we are no longer opponents. Tomorrow, we are one as Wisconsinites, so together we can move Wisconsin forward."

Dave and Mike are skeptical about Janesville moving forward with Walker still in office. Statewide, the governor may have won, with 53 percent to 46 percent for Barrett. But not in Rock County. Rock is one of just twelve of Wisconsin's seventy-two counties that voted in favor of recalling the governor. "Now this governor knows we don't like him," Mike is saying to Dave. During his original campaign for governor, Walker pledged to add 250,000 jobs across Wisconsin during his first term; a year and a half since his swearing in, jobs are up by fewer than 30,000.

Mike is thinking out loud. If General Motors ever considered coming back to town, with Janesville and the county having voted for the recall, would Walker ever lift a finger to help?

Dave is quiet. He walks alone to the back of Steve and Holly's, takes a white paper plate and a hot dog roll and spreads some ketchup. He opens a metal vat and, with tongs, pulls out a bratwurst. Wisconsin food. The same food that Walker will serve to the state's legislators, Republican and Democrat alike, when he invites them over to the governor's mansion in a gesture of reconciliation.

Dave walks back over to Mike, two stunned union veterans in a thinning crowd. "We lost the battle," Dave says, trying to cheer them both up. "We haven't lost the war."

"You can't say we didn't pull all the pins," Mike says.

"We did pull all the pins," Dave agrees.

A Rough Summer

One of the basic lessons students are taught in Blackhawk's criminal justice program is not to let themselves be manipulated by jail inmates. It is common knowledge that some inmates try to prey on guards who they sense are personally vulnerable. And by this summer, correctional officer Kristi Beyer, heralded in the Job Center's newsletter two years ago for turning hardship into victory, is in a season of vulnerability.

Her son, Josh, is home from Iraq. Home with an honorable discharge after five years in the National Guard. Home, having managed not to be wounded or worse. But something is wrong. He began running out into the backyard, waving knives, hiding behind trees. The police have come a few times to try to calm him down. It hasn't helped. So, even though she needs sleep during the day after her overnight shift, Kristi has been driving her son to a veterans hospital in Madison for post-traumatic stress treatment.

She and her husband, Bob, aren't getting along. They don't see each other much, with her working third shift and him first shift, leaving before dawn to commute to his job as a maintenance specialist in a state office building. Lately, she has been talking about a separation. He tells her they can work things out.

An inmate in the Rock County Jail on a probation violation expresses interest in Kristi. She is receptive. The affair begins in July. She brings him food. She brings him marijuana. She arranges for money to be transferred into his jail account to help him buy snacks and toiletries from the commissary.

The next month, he is out of jail. They continue to see each other. He wants Kristi to buy him a car. He threatens to tell her husband about their relationship if she doesn't.

Kristi does not share any of this with her mother. But one August morning, when she gets home from another overnight shift, she settles in on the covered back deck with her Newport 100s for their daily chat.

"I got something to tell you," Kristi says to her mother.

"Oh, gosh. *What?*" her mother, Linda, replies.

Her mother has known the tones of Kristi's voice her entire life, and something in this particular tone gives her the impression that, whatever Kristi needs to tell, it is not going to be just another quirky story about what happened last night at the jail. It is not going to be good.

A rough summer, Linda has been thinking lately. Very rough, with Josh still in treatment for his PTSD and the iffy future of Kristi and Bob's marriage. Now she tries to steel herself.

"I met a guy," Kristi says.

Her mother hasn't seen that coming. The first thing she thinks of to say is: "Kristi, please don't tell me it was a prisoner."

"It is a prisoner," Kristi says.

Her mother typically sides with Kristi, and she wants to now. But she can't. Instead, she says: "You better try to break that off."

⋆ 43 ⋆

The Candidate

At 9:28 a.m., swelling, majestic music—the soundtrack to the movie *Air Force One*—fills the air as Paul Ryan emerges onto the deck of the USS *Wisconsin* and strides down the ramp toward a cheering, flag-waving crowd below. The retired battleship is a museum on the Norfolk, Virginia, waterfront. On this Saturday morning, August 11, it is draped in bunting—a perfect political prop. Paul is waving his long arms, his grin huge, as he walks a roped-off path through the crowd, then steps onto a stage, at which point he reaches out to grip the outstretched hand of Mitt Romney, the 2012 Republican candidate for president.

They lean into a hug, then walk around a podium to face the cheering flag wavers, after an awkward instant during which Paul figures out where to stand. Romney has just announced that Paul is his vice presidential running mate, and they have never, before this moment, appeared together on the campaign trail.

Two tall, handsome, dark-haired men, they stand side by side until Romney pats Paul's arm, steps away, and walks down a few steps off the back of the stage. The movie music fades, then stops.

Paul is alone on the stage. He is about to utter his first words as candidate for vice president. He is still grinning and, for a heartbeat, looks

just a bit overwhelmed as he turns and stretches his right arm toward the
bunting-draped battleship and says: "Wow! Hey. And right in front of the
U.S.S. *Wisconsin*, huh? Man!"

The Norfolk crowd roars.

Back in Janesville, it has been four and a half years since Barack Obama
arrived at the General Motors plant on a winter morning, running for the
Democratic presidential nomination in the first months of the recession.
Now, jobs and good pay are still too scarce, not just in Janesville, but in
enough places that the issue is dominating 2012 presidential politics. Republicans have been blaming the economy's slow recovery on policies of
the Democratic administration in the White House, calculating that the
blame will deny Obama a second term. In introducing Paul, Romney has
just called him "an intellectual leader" of the Republican Party. He has his
chairmanship of the House Budget Committee. He has his "roadmap" for
cutting federal spending, curbing the federal deficit, and reconfiguring
the government's main entitlement programs. Among various Republicans whose names have surfaced over the months as possible running
mates, Paul has been regarded as a bold, conservative option for a Romney campaign that has not been defined by boldness.

With this unexpected choice, Romney already is drawing attention
to his running mate's hometown. "Paul Ryan works in Washington, but
his beliefs remain firmly rooted in Janesville, Wisconsin," Romney said,
moments before Paul's appearance on the battleship deck. "He combines a
profound sense of responsibility for what we owe the next generation with
an unbounded optimism in America's future and an understanding of all
the wonderful things the American people can do." The GOP presidential
candidate was describing Janesville's can-do spirit in a nutshell.

Paul was, in fact, home as recently as yesterday afternoon when he was
spirited away to this spot in Virginia's Tidewater through a clandestine
plan to keep Romney's decision secret so that the battleship-and-bunting
theatrics would remain unspoiled. After attending a memorial service
yesterday, Paul walked in the front door of his house on Courthouse Hill
and out his back door. He sneaked through the small woods in which he
had played as a boy, past the spot where he had built a wooden fort as a

kid, and onto the driveway of the house in which he had grown up. In the driveway, a car driven by the nineteen-year-old son of a Romney campaign aide was idling, ready to take him to a small chartered plane that was waiting for him at a suburban Chicago airfield, along with his wife, Janna, and the kids, Liza, Charlie, and Sam.

★

Less than twenty-four hours after this covert departure, television crews from the major networks already are on Main Street. Their arrival, and the televised image of Paul striding down the battleship ramp, are elating Janesville. They are salve for bruised political feelings. They narrow the fissures that have been widening since the assembly plant closed, culminating in the recall election two months ago. Who wouldn't be proud to have a native son of Janesville on a presidential ticket?

Well, not quite everyone is proud. Over at the Job Center, Bob Borremans is uncertain that having Paul in the White House would be helpful. During the nine years that Bob has been the Job Center's director, he has invited the congressman to come take a look, to see what the needs are and see how the center is doing at helping people try to get back on their feet. He has asked Paul's staff so many times whether the congressman could come take a look that he has stopped bothering to ask.

But with the TV crews on Main Street and the theatrics in Norfolk, such skepticism is a minority view. Even among people who dislike Paul's fiscal and social conservatism, his appearance on the battleship is stirring hope in Janesville that his candidacy will lift the city's fortunes. Tim Cullen, the state senator who is one of the last surviving moderates in the legislature in Madison, doesn't share Paul's pure faith in the private sector, in private charity to solve social problems. Still, Tim has begun to say around town: "It can't possibly hurt to have the vice president of the United States come from Janesville." Paul is, Tim has begun to point out, the first Wisconsinite ever to become a vice presidential candidate for a major political party. Tim has begun to say such things as he is having political troubles of his own, even within the State Senate's Democratic caucus. Less than a month ago, he quit the caucus in protest for a few days, saying that perhaps he would become an independent because the State Senate's Democratic leader had just punished him for his bipartisan leanings by denying him the chairmanship of any meaningful Senate committee. The two resolved their spat, but for Tim the episode was another depressing sign of the polarization that has seized Wisconsin's politics.

Of course, delight over Paul's ascension is greatest among those who have been trying hard to bring new jobs to town, marketing Janesville as a good place to do business. John Beckord, an ally of Mary Willmer's as the leader of the business association, Forward Janesville, is delighted. Last night, when the rumors started to filter across town and the first TV crews arrived, his delight was mixed with a realization that he would need to handle Paul's candidacy with delicacy. Forward Janesville is apolitical. It does not endorse candidates, even if the businessmen and businesswomen who attend its meetings tend to share Paul's views in favor of the private sector and against government deficits. Still, John is ecstatic that Janesville is becoming a household name. "It doesn't hurt," he is telling people, "to maybe have a favorable connection in the minds of people as they think of Janesville as an opportunity for investment. 'Oh yes, that's the home of Paul Ryan.' We couldn't buy this kind of public relations."

⋆

As for Paul himself? After fourteen years as a congressman, he is forty-two years old and, at this moment, standing in a dark suit and white open-collared shirt with the gray battleship behind him, eight minutes into his first speech as a candidate for vice president. He has just condemned "a record of failure" by the Obama White House. "We are in a different and dangerous moment," he says.

"I have seen and heard from a lot of families, from a lot of those who are running small businesses, and from people who are in need. But what I've heard lately, that's what troubles me the most. There is something different in their voice, in their words. What I hear from them are diminished dreams, lowered expectations, uncertain futures.

"I hear some people say, this is just the new normal." And now his voice crescendos, his right hand jabbing at air. "Higher unemployment, declining incomes, and crushing debt is not a new normal!"

Though he does not say so, Paul could be trying to comfort his hometown.

Thirty hours later, early Sunday evening, he arrives with Romney for what the campaign is billing as Paul's homecoming rally.

It is an emotional scene. Governor Walker has the microphone onstage and has just whipped up the crowd. "Isn't it great to have a Cheesehead on the ballot?" the governor yells out as he introduces "America's comeback team." The majestic *Air Force One* movie music swells again, and Paul weaves through the crowd, shaking hands, greeting people he knows, Romney a few paces behind. By the time he bounds onto the stage, Paul's hands are on his cheeks, wiping away tears. He and the governor share a long hug. He blows kisses from the stage. His wife, Janna, standing near the podium with their three kids, points out someone in the crowd. And so, as the movie music subsides, Paul leans into the microphone, and the first words he says are: "Hi, Mom!"

Walker is standing center-stage, right behind him, as Paul thanks the crowd and says, "It is good to be home. Oh, oh, I tell you, I love Wisconsin!"

It is a beautiful homecoming, and Romney is beaming at the Wisconsin Republicans' adulation for a native son.

Except that, for Paul's hometown, there is just one catch. This rally is not taking place in Janesville. It is taking place at the Waukesha County Expo Center, the site of Walker's recall election victory speech forty-seven nights ago. The Expo Center is a few miles beyond the northern boundary of Paul's congressional district, in a district represented by another Republican congressman, Jim Sensenbrenner. Waukesha is not like Janesville. Waukesha is one of the most reliable, solid Republican parts of the state.

Sure, Janesville is home. Two weeks from now, as Paul prepares to leave for the GOP presidential nominating convention in Tampa, Florida, he will be introduced by his older brother, Tobin, at a send-off rally in the gym of Craig High School, their alma mater, and Tobin will say that the values and people of Janesville have forged this candidate. Paul's seven-year-old, Sam, will be wearing a Cheesehead hat, orange foam and shaped like a wedge of cheddar. But none of that counts for much today. This is presidential politics, with its narrow margin of error. And so when it comes to homecoming rallies, after the heckling that Paul endured from pro-union agitators at last year's Labor Fest parade, and elsewhere around his district since then, the Romney-Ryan campaign organization is not taking any chances.

44

Labor Fest 2012

"We're about ten minutes from parade step-off," WCLO radio DJ Tim Bremer booms into his microphone from the reviewing stand along Main Street, across from the grassy swell of Courthouse Park. "Getting ready to start the Labor Fest parade here in Janesville."

The clowns, as always, are first to bend from Milwaukee Street onto Main, tossing hard candies toward the kids scrambling off the laps of parents, who have brought their lawn chairs to the sidewalks that, on this day, September 3, are radiating a steamy heat.

This Labor Day is a shimmery scorcher. Compared with the old days, when as many as fifty thousand pressed together on these sidewalks for the parade, a few more storefronts than usual are sporting "For Rent" signs, and there is more room between the lawn chairs on the sidewalks. None of that dims the festive feeling that lives on—at once homey and electric.

The clowns give way to a phalanx of motorcycle-revving police in bright yellow shirts and navy shorts. Next comes the Janesville Patriotic Society, founded back in 1930, when the assembly plant already had been turning out its Chevrolets for seven years. And then comes the 2012 parade marshal, Pam Weadge, who worked at the plant for thirty years until it closed and now spends her time running karaoke at the VFW hall.

The Labor Fest parade connects Janesville with its past, even as it exposes what has changed. "The Parade of Champions" the celebration's crowning event was called from the 1950s to the 1970s, when the UAW local, the Central Labor Council, and the town's business owners all came together for the planning. During those years, workers from the local gathered down at the union hall, setting aside the labor of assembling Chevys to assemble parade floats, each year's seeming more elaborate than the last. One year illustrated the benefits that unions conferred on working men and women, with a family on a simulated fishing trip atop a float with a fake stream. Another year, the parade set a world record for a hitched team, with a three-hundred-foot extravaganza—eight ponies and sixty-four llamas towing a wagon. Labor Fest, as the celebration has been called in more recent years, pulled in enough donations to hire the nation's top-rated fife and drum corps.

Three years ago, the first Labor Fest after General Motors left town, the parade still had 152 units, marching from Five Corners through downtown to just below the reviewing stand. Today, Bremer, the DJ with his folksy style and radio-rich baritone, is announcing just eighty-three parade units. With Labor Fest no longer drawing enough donations to bring in bands, the only fife and drum corps coming down Main Street is Janesville's own, formed for the 1976 U.S. Bicentennial. The only marching bands are from the city's two high schools: the Parker Vikings in their emerald green and gold uniforms and the Craig Cougars in their royal blue.

As for the autoworkers who for so many decades were the parade's chief sponsors and backbone, not only does Local 95 no longer have a float, no unit of autoworkers is marching today at all. Just two old guys in black T-shirts and union caps, each holding up one end of a dowel from which hangs a square banner that says, "UAW Local 95 Retirees."

Yet there is an aspect of the parade even more surprising than the absence of autoworkers. The surprise is riding down Main Street in a borrowed white carriage with crimson lining. The carriage is just behind the marshal and just in front of the local fifers and drummers who are faint reminders of the parade's more affluent days.

"Goodwill Ambassador Ann Forbeck," the radio DJ announces, introducing the social worker who has been trying to knit together the frayed lives of the city's growing crop of homeless kids. As Ann holds up her goodwill plaque, Kayla and Cory, two of the students from the film *Sixteen Forty-Nine*, are sitting across from her. They ride backward on the carriage's red velvet seats, smiling and waving like any teenagers would in a spiffy parade carriage, and not like kids who at times haven't had a safe place to sleep at night.

As the DJ is booming out thanks to Ann for her "dedication to our community," no one in the crowd reacts, other than with polite applause, to what would once have been the unthinkable sight of a Labor Fest parade unit bearing homeless kids right down Main Street.

45

Pill Bottles

L ate in the summer, Rock County sheriff Bob Spoden gets a report from the commander who oversees the jail: One of the correctional officers was having an improper relationship with an inmate. Other inmates were talking about it.

The silver-haired sheriff is genial, but he also is no-nonsense. He grew up in Janesville, the son of a sheriff's deputy, so that a Spoden has been in law enforcement in town for a half century. Bob was the department's chief deputy before he was first elected sheriff six years ago. Now he does what a sheriff under these circumstances is supposed to do. He opens an investigation into correctional officer Kristi Beyer.

The improper relationship hasn't been going on long—about two months—but the report is lengthy. It documents the allegations of the affair, the food, the drugs, and more. Kristi could be fired. She could face criminal charges because, under Wisconsin law, it is illegal for a correctional officer to have sexual contact with an inmate, no matter who initiates it, because the law regards inmates as unable to give consent.

So far, the sheriff and his staff have not told Kristi about the investigation. At 10:30 p.m. on Monday, September 17, when Kristi reports for her overnight shift, the sheriff's chief deputy summons her. The chief deputy tells her that she is under investigation. She tells Kristi that she is on paid administrative leave. She tells her to surrender her jail keys. She tells her to return for an investigational interview at 1:30 p.m. on September 19. A commander escorts her out the door.

Kristi tells her mother what has happened. She does not want to go through questioning. She thinks that she is going to be fired, that she might even get some jail time herself.

"Well, let's go then," her mother says to her. "Let's leave. What do we got here? Nothing. I will go wherever you want."

*

Kristi's suspension begins five days before her fortieth birthday. Since she was a girl, Kristi has liked people making a fuss over her birthday. This past Friday, she asked her mother to go with her on an early birthday shopping trip to Johnson Creek, the outlet stores forty minutes away, between Madison and Milwaukee.

Kristi was in a good shopping mood. She had been dieting, and her five-foot-five frame fit into size 8 jeans. She bought a pair.

Her mother, Linda, was surprised that Kristi talked so much about her new guy. Her mother let her talk.

"Give him a chance," Kristi said.

He was out of jail now, but that, in her mother's view, didn't make it any better. "I don't approve of you going with a prisoner," she told Kristi.

On their way home, they stopped at Olive Garden, the same one where Kristi and Barb and their families had celebrated on the spring day more than two years ago when they graduated with honors with their criminal justice degrees from Blackhawk Tech.

That evening, Kristi went out and got a tattoo on her right foot—an infinity symbol, shaped like a sideways figure eight. Inside one loop of the symbol was "Josh," her son. Inside the other was "Ty," the guy from the jail. She went home and showed off her fresh tattoo to her mother.

★

Kristi and her husband, Bob, have been sleeping lately in separate bedrooms, hers on the left at the end of the hall, his on the right. At 5:20 a.m. on Wednesday, before he leaves the house for his commute to the state office building in Madison, Bob steps into her room to say goodbye. Normally, Kristi wouldn't be home yet from her overnight shift, but this is the second morning of her suspension. When he steps in, she is wearing a gray T-shirt and white leggings with two silver pendant necklaces—an angel and a cross. She is on her left side with an arm hanging over the bed's edge. She does not seem to be breathing.

Kristi's mother is jolted from sleep by Bob screaming, "Kristi, wake up! Kristi, wake up!" Kristi's son, Josh, sleeping in the finished basement, awakes from the commotion, too. He sprints upstairs, notices an empty pill bottle, calls 911, and starts chest compressions on his mother until an ambulance arrives.

★

On April 28, 2008, five weeks before General Motors announced that it intended to close the assembly plant, the company said that it planned to end the plant's second shift. That day, a sixty-year-old worker on that shift for twenty-seven years took his own life.

Since then, suicides in Rock County have doubled, from fifteen in 2008 to thirty-two last year. The county's crisis hotline has been getting more calls. A volunteer in the county coroner's office has been speaking out lately about suicide prevention to any community group willing to listen.

This has not been happening just in Janesville. Across the United States, the suicide rate has spiked. The rate is not as high as it was during the Great Depression of the 1930s. Still, compared with the few years before, the rate increased four-fold during the couple of years after the recession began.

In Rock County, Kate Flanagan manages a shrinking supply of public mental health services. She can see that, when a community is under stress, some people have less hope. People who were barely managing their addictions, their depression—their fragilities, no matter the form—sometimes lose their grip when they lose a job.

Running the Parker Closet, Deri Wahlert sees the stress and its effects. Last year alone, seven of her Closet kids threatened suicide—a few even attempted it. She notices that her Closet kids who have grown up poor, always been poor, tend to be tougher, better at coping with it. The fragile ones are new to being poor, with parents fighting about how to live without the money they used to have.

With her brood of homeless teenagers, Ann Forbeck, the school social worker, sees the stress, too. One girl's mother—distressed that her daughter was pregnant and time was running out at the shelter where they were staying—confided to Ann that she was thinking about killing herself by driving her car into a tree. Ann tried to line up psychiatric help. She contacted the motor vehicle department and made sure that a boot was put on the woman's car, so that she couldn't drive until the situation calmed down. Not long after, the family left Wisconsin. Ann never did hear how things turned out.

*

The ambulance arrives and speeds Kristi to Mercy Hospital. She is wheeled into the emergency room at 5:50 a.m., a half hour after Bob found her. A medical team tries to revive her, even though she arrived without a heartbeat. At 6:32 a.m., the team stops trying.

Seven minutes later, Rock County's coroner, Jenifer Keach, hears her pager go off, telling her to come to Mercy. Another suicide.

*

The coroner's autopsy finds that Kristi died by taking a muscle relaxant her doctor had prescribed for back pain. She took more than ten times the daily amount safe for an adult. And she took nearly twenty times the safe amount of Benadryl.

Kristi's mother had been thinking about throwing out the bottle of muscle relaxants. Kristi didn't like to take them, because they made her sleepy. And her mother didn't want Josh, on his medicine to treat his PTSD, to be tempted. But her mother hadn't gotten around to it, so she feels guilty. She feels guilty for having come up with the idea that maybe Kristi, with her love of TV crime shows, should study criminal justice.

Beyond the pill bottles and the crime shows, her mother sees that everything ran downhill from jobs in town going away. If the recession hadn't come, she figures, Kristi still would be at Lear, with a little market for the work aprons she designed. She wouldn't have been at the jail, and she wouldn't have met her new guy. Just one big spiraling down until her daughter—her best friend—is gone.

*

Over at the Job Center, Bob Borremans is shocked when word reaches him that a client has killed herself. Not just any client but one the center singled out in its publicity as a success story. This makes Bob think hard about a fact that he already knows: It isn't simple to take someone with a high school degree and a factory job and to help lead them into new work.

*

Late on this Wednesday afternoon, Barb's cell phone rings while she is at the group home where her disabled client lives. The call is from a woman she had worked with at Lear who had also gone to Blackhawk.

She isn't sure, the woman tells Barb, but she heard from someone else that Kristi might have committed suicide.

"What????" Barb says into the phone.

It seems impossible. Lately, they haven't been talking too often. The last few times, Barb urged Kristi to go back to school for her bachelor's degree, as Barb has done, as Kristi said she wanted to do. Barb has had the impression that Kristi is hooked on the pay at the jail, always bringing up something that she needed to buy.

But suicide?

Less than five minutes later, her phone rings again. This time, she can see, it is her husband, Mike. Mike never calls her at work.

She answers. At first, he doesn't say a word.

From his silence, Barb knows it's true.

Then Mike starts to tell her that Kristi's son, Josh, couldn't find Barb's phone number but found his. Barb is having trouble listening. Right now, she just loses it.

As soon as she gets off work, she goes over to be with Kristi's mother, Linda.

For much of their friendship, since their first nerve-racking days at Blackhawk, Barb accepted that Kristi was a few steps ahead of her. Edging her out on grades. Getting hired first at the jail. Barb was okay with that. She accepted that Kristi was the smarter one, the stronger one. Except maybe, Barb is realizing tonight, she wasn't.

Kristi's mother is beginning to think that, after losing one job, she couldn't deal with the idea of losing another one—getting fired, this time. Her mother can understand that. What she can't understand is why her daughter worked so hard for a second opportunity and then threw it away.

More than anything else, what she can't understand is why Kristi didn't tell her she was thinking of killing herself. She would have stayed up with her all night. Kristi was such a planner. They told each other everything, she always thought, so it seems totally unlike her not to have left a note. She and Josh will hunt and hunt, but one never turns up. Linda can't believe that, either.

The next Monday, a few hundred people turn out for Kristi's funeral. On the way from Schneider's funeral home to the Maple Hill Cemetery, off Route 14 in the little town of Evansville, northwest of Janesville, Linda notices that they drive past the County Jail. She wishes they had gone a different way.

Kristi is laid to rest in a casket that Josh picked out. Her mother has chosen her burial clothes—the new, size 8 jeans she was proud to fit into—with a Green Bay Packers blanket wrapped around her.

★ 46 ★

Circle of Women

The Holiday Inn Express banquet room is transformed this evening into a glittering space. Fifty-three round tables have been adorned elaborately, each with a different centerpiece and place settings in a competition for best decorations. In the center of the room, a long buffet table is laden with mounds of strawberries, grapes, and fresh pineapple; bowls of crudités and dips; platters with dill sprigs surrounding whole smoked salmon.

This is the Circle of Women, the biennial gala and a main fundraiser for the YWCA of Rock County. "Celebrating the giving spirit of women," its motto goes, "and the ways in which they lift up other women in our community." The Y may be getting less help now from the United Way. It may be unable to afford to sponsor Project 16:49 for homeless teens. But none of that means that the Y is not trying hard to keep its programs going. And if there were any doubt that Janesville's philanthropic heart is still pumping as best it can, proof lies in the 450 women from across Rock County who have dressed up to mingle and admire the table decorations and donate to the Y on this Thursday evening, the 1st of November.

The goal tonight: $50,000. The Circle of Women will come close.

Filling this festive space are Janesville's professional women and its do-gooders. The Y's staff is here, of course, including its director, Allison Hokinson. So is Ann Forbeck, the school social worker whose disappointment with Allison over Project 16:49 is now in the past. Each table has a captain, and each captain's job was to have invited eight women to share her table. Of these fifty-three tables, one toward the front, on the right side of the podium, has as its centerpiece an oversized glass vase filled with silver and gold balls. The little balls are scattered, too, across an ecru tablecloth set with golden plates and matching fabric seat covers. This is the table at which Mary Willmer is captain, because BMO Harris Bank is one of the Circle of Women's corporate sponsors.

The bank that Mary leads in town has a new name. Four weekends ago, the signs on all of M&I's banks were replaced, the Marshall & Ilsley name originating in Wisconsin and dating back to the middle of the nineteenth century suddenly gone. The signs on all the banks, including the one on Main Street, were changed to BMO Harris, for the Canadian-based Bank of Montreal and the Chicago-based Harris. Last year, BMO took over M&I, because, during the recession and afterward, M&I, Wisconsin's largest bank, suffered three straight years of financial losses. The losses were mainly because of ill-advised real estate and construction loans it had made, many of them in Arizona and Florida. When BMO took it over, M&I still owed the federal government $1.7 billion for having bailed it out. Now, some employees of the old M&I are uncertain whether their bank branches or their jobs will continue. Mary, however, has come out of this fine, with an expanded role as regional market manager as well as community bank president for BMO Harris.

Tonight, she is looking lovely, in a lacy black blouse and black skirt. With several of her employees of what is now BMO Harris, she sits through this evening's video depicting the good that the Y does in the community—for children who have been neglected or abused, for women struggling back onto their feet after domestic violence, for immigrants who need someone to reach out to them. She sits through the presentation to tonight's honorees: two charity-minded women who formed a business selling keepsake lockets to help remember loved ones who have died. Finally, Mary rises and walks the short distance to the podium.

In her many leadership roles with nonprofits in town, Mary often talks up Janesville's virtues—the strength and character of its people, the community's generosity, the hard times it has been through with General Motors, the way it has endured. She begins tonight, too, with these themes. And yet tonight is different. It is the day after her fifty-second birthday, and, standing at the podium, looking out at the sea of table decorations and well-dressed women, Mary reaches back to grasp her past. She tells the Circle of Women about having been a scared girl with a widowed mother who had a piece of a farm and not enough to live on. It is part of her fund-raising pitch, a tool for touching the Circle of Women's empathy, an illustration that you never know who might need help, so generosity is the best policy. It also is a revelation. Mary has never talked of this part of her girlhood in public before.

★ 47 ★

First Vote

Before she goes to sleep on Monday night, November 5, Kayzia Whiteaker posts a message on her Facebook page: "Off to bed when I wake up I will be 18!"

The next morning, the first day that she and Alyssa are old enough to vote, happens to be Election Day. By now, they both have used Chevrolets that they are paying for themselves—Alyssa's a white Impala and Kayzia's a red Aveo. They begin their birthday by climbing into their cars. They need to drive separately to get to classes that they each take at U-Rock some afternoons of this, their senior year at Parker High, and to get to their jobs. But before their school day begins, they first meet a mile from their house at Madison Elementary School. This is their neighborhood's polling place.

When they arrive at 8 a.m., Madison has a line out the door—a big turnout, because of the presidential election. They get in the line. When they finally are handed ballots to fill out with black markers, they vote for the reelection of President Obama and for every other Democrat on the list, none of whom they have ever heard of before, including a Democrat named Rob Zerban from Kenosha who is challenging Paul Ryan for his seat in Congress. Their parents vote for Democrats, Kayzia figures. And this year, watching the presidential debates and being old enough to understand, Alyssa decided that Obama sounded more for the working class than the Republican, Mitt Romney. Besides, no way they are voting for anyone who has anything to do with Scott Walker's viewpoint on unions, since their parents used to be union members, or with the cuts the governor has made to money for public schools, which have caused Parker to have bigger class sizes now and not as many Advanced Placement courses.

After filling out their paper ballots, Kayzia is nervous about whether they are feeding them into the machine the right way for their votes to be counted. They manage to get the thick paper fed properly. It is a big moment on the day that they come of age. Alyssa remembers that their parents have taught them that people can't complain about any outcome if they haven't done their part. They have now done their part. Kayzia updates her Facebook page: "Only took a half-hour to vote today. A great way to start this chapter of my life!"

They have completed this first rite of adulthood before 8:45 a.m., the time when, two miles east of Madison Elementary, a caravan of shiny black SUVs pulls up to the curb alongside Hedberg Public Library on Main Street. Secret Service officers emerge and scout the sidewalk. And then, from the third of the SUVs, Paul Ryan hops out in a dark suit and pale silver tie and helps his three kids step down to the ground. Paul, with Janna and the kids and the Secret Service in tow, shakes a few hands and greets reporters and camera crews waiting inside the library entrance. This little entourage Paul is leading walks past the line of people waiting to vote that snakes through the library's first floor. The entourage walks right up to the front, and the Secret Service hangs back a few yards, scanning the crowd for anything untoward, in the unlikely event that anything untoward would happen inside the public library in downtown Janesville, while Paul and Janna give their names to poll workers and are handed their ballots. Two of Paul's children lean in toward the voting booth with him. When he is done, he points on the ballot to Liza, his eldest, who is wearing a butterfly headband and smiles at the sight of his name. Then, the entourage walks through a door, where the press corps is waiting, and one of the reporters asks: "How do you feel today?"

"I feel great today," Paul replies. "It is a great tradition. It is Election Day, so I'm really excited to be here. I've been voting here for a long time. It felt good waking up in my hometown. This is the neighborhood I grew up in. I went to junior high about 60 yards that way." He points with his index finger to the right. Paul's past still meshing seamlessly with his present.

He is already on the move when a reporter shouts out: "Are you going to get a win today?" Paul turns his head back and nods. "I think we are."

★

Paul is not spending much of today in his home state, much less his hometown. He is heading to Cleveland and then to Richmond—cities in swing states with more electoral votes than Wisconsin—before joining up with Romney in Boston tonight.

Still, Wisconsin is one of nine swing states in this 2012 presidential election. And the closeness of the contest has drawn Obama yesterday to a stage forty miles away from Janesville, in front of Madison's City Hall—and drawn eighteen thousand people to see the president and his warm-up act, Bruce Springsteen. Springsteen came on holding his guitar and, when he reached center stage, slipped his harmonica over his head. He wore jeans and a vest over a gray shirt with the sleeves rolled up past his elbows despite the 42-degree temperature. Working-class clothes. He had a view of the statehouse with Scott Walker's office inside just one and a half blocks up the hill. He sang a campaign anthem he had written and debuted a couple of weeks ago, playing off Obama's 2012 reelection slogan—"Forward," same as the Wisconsin state motto—and filled with rhymes that the Boss admitted were pretty strained. And then he could have been talking straight to Janesville, when he said that his dad had worked on a Ford assembly line. "For the last thirty years, I've been writing music about the distance between the American Dream and the American reality," Springsteen said, punctuating the end of that thought with a guitar strum. "I am troubled by thirty years of increasing disparity in the wealth between our best-off citizens and everyday Americans. That is a disparity that threatens to divide us into two distinct and separate nations. We have to be better than that." Another guitar strum.

"Finally, I am here today because I have lived long enough to know that the future is seldom a tide rushing in. It is often a slow march, inch by inch." Strum. "Day by long day." Strum. "We're in the midst of one of those long days right now."

And then Springsteen sang "Land of Hope and Dreams" before he introduced Obama, and the troubadour and the beaming president hugged, clapping each other on the back.

And after the president called his opening act "an American treasure," who "tells the story of what our country is, and what it should be," Obama settled into his speech for this last day of his final campaign. He ticked off victories from his four years in office—among them that "the American auto industry is back on top." Words that would have been hard to say in Janesville.

★

Whether it is faith that this president can lead Janesville's once sturdy middle class back to its heyday, whether it is the tradition of unionism and Democrats that Kayzia and Alyssa have inherited on the first day they are eighteen, the voters of Janesville by tonight choose Obama over the Republican ticket of their native son.

It has been five months and a day since the spring evening the city's Republicans sat outside on the Speakeasy patio, celebrating that Wisconsin's voters—if not Janesville's—had repelled the drive to recall Walker from the governorship. Tonight is the Democrats' turn to celebrate, over at the UAW Local 95 union hall that Mike Vaughn's grandfather, Tom, the first of the union Vaughns, helped to plan.

The voters of Rock County have been emphatic. Six out of ten have voted to give the president a second term. It has not been a good night for Paul. Even in his own ward, his neighbors have voted for Obama. Paul has won an eighth congressional term, but his victory margin is narrower than in the past. Janesville—and his ward within it—have favored his opponent.

As this election night wears on, the mood sinks inside the Holiday Inn Express banquet room, where the Circle of Women gathered a few evenings ago and where, tonight, hundreds of Republicans have gathered for what is becoming clear is not a victory party. It is after midnight in Boston, but still Tuesday in Janesville, by the time the giant screen at one end of the banquet hall televises Romney on a stage with sixteen eagle-topped American flags as he says that he has called the president to congratulate him. Most of the Rock County Republicans have left the banquet room when, at the end of Romney's compact concession speech, Paul walks out onto this Boston stage, his lips pulled tight, in the same suit and silver tie that he was wearing this morning when he voted at the library.

Others may have gone home by the time the native son walks out on the stage, 1,100 miles away near the Boston waterfront, but Jay Mielke is sticking around. The county's GOP chairman has been hanging out in the back of the banquet hall, and he watches Paul on the screen across the room. Jay is savvy. Tonight, he is pensive. He knows that Janesville, even missing so many of its union jobs, is still a Democratic union town at heart. A native son on the GOP ticket, Jay muses, was not enough. The other side, he has to admit, spoke more to the middle class.

HealthNet

In the election yesterday, Janesville's voters chose a new representative to the Wisconsin State Assembly. Like Tim Cullen in the State Senate, Debra Kolste is a Democrat and a former school board member. She works as a lab technician at Mercy Hospital, and once a week she volunteers at HealthNet of Rock County. HealthNet is a shoestring operation, a free medical clinic downtown that, for nearly two decades, has been treating as many people as it can without health insurance or much money. On this afternoon after the citizens of Assembly District #44 have voted her into the state legislature, Deb is at the clinic, because today is a Wednesday, and Wednesdays are the day on which, for two hours, HealthNet accepts new and reenrolling patients.

This chance at free health care begins at 1:30 p.m., and the session has been in progress for just over a half hour when Deb opens the door to the clinic's waiting room.

"Number eight," she calls out.

Sue Olmsted hadn't been sure how early she needed to arrive at a back door behind Milwaukee Street and climb the staircase that leads to the narrow hallway outside the clinic's entrance so that she could stake out a good spot in line. A spot good enough that she can get inside the clinic and not be sent away to come back another week and try again.

Sue had been in line for nearly an hour by 1:25 p.m. when a strapping young man in a polo shirt named Ryan Messinger came out into the hallway, as he does every week moments before the enrollment session begins, a clipboard under his arm. Ryan is HealthNet's clinical operations director, and he sports a perpetually cheerful demeanor that gives no hint that he is working fifteen-hour days to help keep this overwhelmed nonprofit clinic running.

Ryan looked up and down this week's line of people hoping to become patients, including Sue, seated in metal folding chairs and, after the chairs run out, standing or sprawling on the linoleum floor as the hallway bends around a corner and out of sight. HealthNet used to take thirty new and renewing patients each week. Not lately. "Today, we are only able to take thirteen people," Ryan said in a tone, at once apologetic and firm, that he has perfected while giving some version of this prologue to each Wednesday afternoon session for months. "Just because of our budget constraint. And our funding has been cut again."

Sue was in time, it turns out, to receive a small slip of paper with #8 on it. Finally, Sue tells herself when she hears her number called a half hour later. Her lucky day. She could use one.

Sue worked for nineteen years at SSI Technologies, a company on the north side of town that manufactures automotive and industrial parts from powdered metal. By the time she was laid off in 2009, two months before the recession's official end, Sue was performing quality audits and being paid $15.50 an hour, making her one of SSI's highest paid workers on the production floor. Her job was eliminated. In the three and a half years since then, the only work she has found was three weeks at a temp agency.

She is fifty-three and has been divorced for ten years. Like so many others in town, when she couldn't find another job, she went back to school, starting at Blackhawk a year ago to study medical administration. Her studies haven't been going well. She has had to miss a lot of classes because of medical problems, so she is debating whether to withdraw from school, rather than having failing grades on her record. Of her medical problems, the biggest is in her lungs. All those years around powdered metal, she suspects. Whatever it was, she hasn't had health insurance since SSI got rid of her job, which was particularly unfortunate when she landed at Mercy with recurrent pneumonia. She explained to the hospital that she didn't have insurance, hoping for a discount, but she was charged full price and, though it killed her to do it, finally pulled out $15,000 from her 401(k) to make a dent in what she owes. Her lungs still aren't in great shape. Plus, among other ailments, she has arthritis in one foot that makes it hard to stand too long. She is pretty sure she has a touch of depression, and she needs medicine to help her sleep. Being #8 right now at HealthNet is a piece of rare good news.

When Deb calls out her number, Sue follows this wiry woman with short blond hair into the clinic's inner sanctum. "I'm Deb, I'm a volunteer here," she says, once they are settled in the first of the clinic's two small exam rooms and Deb has pulled the door closed. No mention that she has just been elected to represent Janesville in the statehouse; even though Sue voted for her yesterday, she does not recognize Deb in person.

Deb makes clear that the examination about to play out in this little room is not about Sue's lung troubles but about the stack of documents that Sue has been careful to tuck into a manila folder whose contents will determine whether she is eligible for the lifeline of free care that Health-Net provides people who qualify.

"I do believe I have everything," Sue says, seated on the room's one chair. She has a heart-shaped face and chin-length straight brown hair. She is wearing a purple sweatshirt, black jeans, and black sneakers with hot pink trim.

Deb begins the routine of screening questions. "Who lives in your household?"

The question isn't as easy as Sue wishes it were. When she and her husband split up a decade ago, she got the house and, once their two kids were out of high school, was supposed to sell it, pay off the mortgage, and give him half of whatever was left. But the house's value dropped so much that, with what she still owed on the mortgage, she couldn't afford

to sell it. So she has stayed. More than a year ago, when her ex-husband
lost where he was living and asked whether he could stay for a while, she
let him in, figuring that, even though they don't get along at all, a four-
bedroom house was big enough that they could stay out of each other's
way. Her unemployment benefits were running out. He made a mortgage
payment, and then another and another.

"I live with my ex-husband," Sue tells Deb. "It's for economic reasons
only."

Deb asks Sue for the tax forms she has brought and, after scanning
them, looks up with a quizzical expression. "So, you have no means of
income?"

"Last year, I got unemployment," Sue says. "I am a full-time student. I
have a little bit of money from school."

"And your BadgerCare denial letter?" Deb asks.

This is a topsy-turvy aspect of screening would-be HealthNet patients.
The state has handed volunteers like Deb a charade that they must play.
HealthNet accepts patients only if they are ineligible for BadgerCare—
Wisconsin's name for Medicaid. Three years ago, Wisconsin created a new
part, called BadgerCare Plus Core, that is, in theory, more generous than
in most states. The idea is to provide stripped-down health benefits to
adults who aren't raising children at home—people like Sue. Except that
BadgerCare Plus Core opened in July 2009 and stopped accepting applications three months later. Ever since, anyone who signs up is put on a
waiting list. When Sue applied in September 2010, one and a half years
after her job was eliminated, she received a letter from the state saying
that she is eligible and that she is #48,874 in line. She has not moved up
on the list.

Deb looks at the letter and is fine with Sue being #48,874 on a mo-
tionless waiting list. But she keeps looking back over the federal tax
forms. Something isn't right. She tells Sue that she'll be back in a minute.
One of Sue's feet, in its black and hot pink sneaker, begins to swing ner-
vously.

Deb is looking grim as she walks out of the exam room and finds
Ryan in a back room, near a bulletin board on which a sign is posted that

says: "Life is not about waiting for storms to pass. It's about learning how to dance in the rain."

She thrusts the tax forms in Ryan's face—the one for Sue and the one for her living-under-the-same-roof ex that Sue brought because HealthNet's instructions had said to bring proof of all household income. The clinic accepts people if their income leaves them at less than 185 percent of the federal poverty level.

Ryan looks at the form and considers the dilemma: Even if Sue has no income, can she become a patient if her ex's wages at a Beloit engine-making factory were covering the mortgage payments and were the only reason she hadn't lost the house? Ryan squints at the forms for a long time before he says, "I think we need to count it as income."

"I am not liking this today," Deb tells him. "The people who need help are not being helped."

Ryan does not try to sugarcoat what's happening. "We have some people falling through the cracks," he agrees. He doesn't like this business of turning people down. He wishes he could let everyone in.

Except that for HealthNet, this is not a time for bending rules. With grants cut and donations down, even as the clinic is holding more fundraisers, Ryan and his boss, the clinic's executive director, wrote a plan a few months ago to carve $54,000 from the clinic budget this year. They cut expenditures on medicine from $35,000 last year to $9,000, hoping that some of their patients can qualify for drug companies' private assistance programs for the poor. They have stopped paying for X-rays, hoping that Mercy and another hospital that opened in town early this year, St. Mary's, will step up and do their part. And under a new rule written by the clinic's medical director, another volunteer who happens to be Deb's husband, doctors can order just two lab tests for a patient. If they want any more, Ryan—even though he is a health education specialist and not an MD—combs through the patient's medical records for evidence of whether further tests are crucial.

Last year, HealthNet provided nearly nine thousand visits for medical or dental care. The wait for a doctor's appointment, no matter how urgent the problem, is now running about three months.

As Deb walks back to the exam room where Sue is waiting, she passes the bulletin board again. Next to the sign about dancing in the rain is another: "Did you know HealthNet donations from patients are at an all-time low, and the number of patients served is at an all-time high?" it says. "HealthNet survives off of the contributions and donations from everyone. HAVE you donated today?"

Not a time for bending eligibility rules.

Deb hates what she is about to have to tell Sue once she opens the exam room door.

"Well, Susan," she says as gently as she can, "you have no means of self-sufficiency, but your ex-husband makes a lot of money." Sue can see where this is heading. She is beginning to look upset.

"He isn't legally responsible for me," Sue points out. "I'm just sponging off him. That's all I'm doing. I own half of a house that isn't worth anything. I have thyroid, restless legs, and a lot of pneumonia the last three years—a lot of respiratory illnesses."

Deb is starting to look as upset as Sue. "I will just ask Ryan to clarify," she says, before she ducks out the door again.

This time, Deb finds Ryan in the back area where, even if HealthNet is buying fewer drugs, it still stores a lot of medicine, including donated pills originally prescribed for people who died or were released from prison before they finished taking the drugs, because, as a free clinic, HealthNet is allowed to collect and dispense any medicine that it can scrounge.

"Just one more time," Deb says to Ryan, a pleading tone creeping into her voice. "I know I am just putting it off on you."

"I can take it," Ryan says, no crack showing in his geniality. "The only thing we can say is, if he kicks her out, she qualifies."

Deb returns to break the news. "I am so sorry, honey."

Sue doesn't speak. She looks down at her lap. She folds her eyeglasses and puts them into a case. She takes back the tax forms and replaces them in her manila folder. When she looks up, her eyes are reddened.

"If something changes in your life . . ." Deb says. Apologizing for not having a tissue for Sue, she tears off a paper towel from a roll on the wall. Deb walks Sue to the clinic's rear door, patting her on the back.

Sue is gone by the time Deb rips up the enrollment form she had begun to fill out.

She walks back to the waiting room door, opens it and calls out number eleven. "I'm Deb, I'm a volunteer here," she says to a woman, holding the number eleven slip of paper, who runs a struggling bed-and-breakfast on Courthouse Hill, three blocks from Paul Ryan's home. The new woman, it turns out, is collecting FoodShare, Wisconsin's food stamps program. That pushes her income, too, over HealthNet's limit.

Deb ushers number eleven out the back door. "I am batting 1,000 today—NOT!" she mutters to another volunteer. The volunteer is in a celebratory mood because of Deb's election victory. Not Deb.

Governor Walker, she knows, has decided not to spend most of the $37 million that the last governor, Doyle, accepted from the federal government to help pioneer a new insurance marketplace under the Affordable Care Act, the big, new national health care law.

Standing in the clinic, on this afternoon after her victory, she wonders what one new legislator in Madison will be able to do.

Out of a Job Again

Deri Wahlert is no longer a novice at running the Parker Closet. This is her fifth year, and now she has two hundred teenagers darting in and out for used clothes and canned food and toothpaste. In these years, Deri has learned quite a few things about how to spot when a Closet kid is hurting, one of which is that it's a good idea to keep an eye on kids' Facebook pages. Yesterday, she noticed on Kayzia Whiteaker's page, near a smiling photo of Kayzia with her best friend and a query about whether anyone could recommend a cheap haircut, a post that sounded glum, burdened. Deri sent Kayzia a note, asking if she could stop by.

Kayzia is ahead in calculus, so she has just gotten permission from her math teacher to miss class. At the moment on this Wednesday afternoon, December 12, she is in Deri's social studies classroom for a heart-to-heart. Deri waits until the two of them are seated at facing desks in the middle of her room before she asks Kayzia, point-blank, "What happened?"

Her dad is unemployed again, Kayzia explains. "We haven't even made the house payment," she says, as if this were somehow her responsibility, too.

"Gotcha," Deri says.

It's been a rough couple of months. Since Kayzia's dad was laid off from

GM, he has been careful never to leave a job until he had lined up another one. He stayed at his job at the jail, even though his anxiety worsened into full-fledged claustrophobia and panic attacks in the locked spaces. He was prescribed anti-anxiety pills, but they didn't always work, and his supervisor called Kayzia's mom late one night last summer to come pick him up and take him home before the end of his shift. Her mom had to sit outside with her dad for a half hour before he could get into the car and, when they got home at midnight, she had to walk the streets of Janesville with him for more than an hour to help him calm down. A sergeant at the jail told her dad that he thought, as a friend and not as his boss, he needed to get out of there.

He'd been searching for another job for a year when he finally got an offer. He left the jail in early September and began to work, for less pay, at United Alloy, a manufacturer of fuel tanks and other metal objects. He worked at United Alloy for one week. He got laid off. Another week went by, and he was called back for some training. He soon noticed that his hands started tingling and going numb—overuse syndrome, a doctor told him. So United Alloy put him on light duty for two weeks but, after that, sent him home. Her dad was trying to get workers' comp, but the company wasn't making it easy. So he managed to line up another offer pretty fast—in a distribution center for Grainger Industrial Supply. He gave notice at United Alloy. He'd already had his final day and was supposed to start at Grainger last Thursday. Instead, Grainger told him that they didn't need him yet. Didn't know when they would.

Her dad can't even collect unemployment because he wasn't laid off.

Kayzia and Alyssa are doing everything they can to help out. At the start of the school year, Kayzia sent a note to the teacher who coaches the Parker debate team that she's loved. After three years on the team and making it to state, she told him she would not be able to participate this year. "I have family things and school that I need to focus on," she wrote, thanking him "for everything you have taught me in the last few years."

What Kayzia didn't say in her note was that, in addition to her AP classes and her course at U-Rock, she is working two jobs. She is a receptionist for a chiropractor after school every day, and she does office work at a car dealer.

The dealer is in the same family of dealerships as the one at which her mom started working in the fall, processing paperwork for car deals at $13.50 an hour—a full-time job, at last, even if it means that her mom misses being a teacher's aide. Alyssa is working three jobs—at the same car dealer as their mom and as a lifeguard for Parker's swim teams, plus she has started selling Tupperware. Alyssa wants her to sell Tupperware, too, Kayzia tells Deri, but she isn't sure. The good news is that the chiropractor has decided to let her work a sixth day, on Saturdays, for the next couple of months.

Deri hears a lot of stories like this. She knows what she can suggest, and it is never enough.

"Have you guys been to ECHO?" she asks.

At the mention of ECHO, the main food pantry in town, Kayzia starts to cry. Her mom tried ECHO before and was furious when she was told that her family wasn't quite poor enough to qualify. ECHO is so strapped that it is limiting food these days to the first forty people in line when the doors open, and only if you haven't been there in at least a month. Last spring, ECHO was so short of money that it had to stop handing out emergency gas cards and bus tokens. For part of last summer, it cut its staff's hours, so that for the first time since it opened in 1969 it wasn't distributing food on Fridays. Strapped or not, ECHO had made her mom so mad, telling her that her family was just over the income limit, that, when Kayzia and Alyssa were collecting donations for ECHO with the National Honor Society, they didn't tell their mom where the seven hundred pounds of food that the society collected were going.

Kayzia doesn't explain all that. She just says to Deri, "They won't give us food."

Deri stands up. As she often does during conversations like this, she walks over to her desk, picks up the telephone, and calls the school social worker. Parker used to have two social workers, but that was before budget cuts. It's down to one, even though nearly half of the 1,400 kids now come from families with incomes low enough that the federal government pays for their school lunches—almost twice as many as before the assembly plant closed.

Deri calls the social worker because she knows she should, even though, after this much time with the Parker Closet, she often feels as if she has become a social worker herself. Kayzia can hear Deri's end of the phone conversation. "He can't get unemployment insurance because he quit. . . . Yeah, if you hear anything, pass it along."

Deri comes back over to Kayzia and hands her a small card with ECHO's phone number on it. "They'll pay your rent one time," Deri tells her. "It depends on how much funds they have."

Kayzia may still be in high school, but she knows what's going on enough to remind Deri that ECHO, even when it has funds, does not help people make mortgage payments. Before GM went away, who would have thought that families that own their homes would have needed ECHO? Deri tells Kayzia that at least she can give her a few donated cards for free groceries at Sentry Foods.

For the past two years, the Whiteakers have gotten Bags of Hope—groceries to tide them over to New Year's. Not this time. Each Janesville school has a quota on how many families it can sign up for Bags of Hope. The school system has exceeded its target, raising $46,000 this year, but more schools are doing Bags of Hope now, so Parker got a lower quota than before. "There are so many families and only thirty-five spots," Deri tells Kayzia. She doesn't tell Kayzia that at least fifty Parker High families that really need the groceries will not be getting any, or that she and the social worker she just called sat down a few weeks ago with the whole long list and had to make awful decisions. That they tried to reach as many families as possible by coordinating, when they could, with schools that have younger brothers or sisters. That they felt they should give preference to families that hadn't gotten Bags of Hope before. Or that the families lucky to have been chosen will be getting less than the two weeks of groceries that Bags of Hope has handed out in the past.

All that Deri tells Kayzia is that she has managed to get another private donation so she can provide gift cards to some families for Christmas dinners. "So don't you worry about that," Deri says.

Kayzia smiles.

Kayzia says that her mom just bought toilet paper, so they are okay with that. And a neighbor has given them a pot roast, so Kayzia is going to make it with some potatoes. And they are not having Christmas lights this year, to save on the electricity. And her grandmother is coming for Christmas and will help out.

"You are doing everything right," Deri tells her. The problem, she says, is the economy, and it's not their fault.

Deri pauses for a moment. And then she asks: "How are you and your sister doing with all of this?"

"It's really, really hard."

"Do you feel guilty," Deri asks, "for going off to college next year?"

Kayzia nods three times. "Just because I help my parents so much, even though they don't ask for anything." And she worries about Noah, who is in eighth grade—the same grade she and Alyssa were going into when the assembly plant was shutting down. Her parents don't have the $6 to give to Noah for middle school recreation nights, so Kayzia gives him the cash. "I won't be there for him," she says. "He's my little brother. I want six or seven dollars to be there for him. I don't want him to miss out on everything."

"You have each other," Deri says. "It's cheesy, but it's true."

Kayzia writes this down in her notebook.

"My dad filled out three applications this morning, before I even went to school," she says, "so he is trying." And he has signed up with BioLife, just past the Interstate, to donate plasma, because, even though he is scared to death of needles, it's $60 a week if you go twice.

"I was going to donate plasma," Kayzia tells Deri. "I asked him what do I have to do, do I need to make an appointment? He got mad at me.

"We'll get through it," Kayzia says. "We already do."

Deri stands up and wraps Kayzia in a hug. And Kayzia walks out of the social studies classroom and into the hall that is filling with kids because the bell for the next class has just rung.

★

Friday afternoon. Christmas miracles.

Tammy Whiteaker plans to go to the food-bagging operation tomorrow morning for the Bags of Hope. She will be taking along Jerad and Noah, but not the girls. Kayzia will be working at the chiropractor's. Alyssa will be doing her own volunteer work, making fruit baskets for Rotary Gardens through DECA, a school club that is helping her build skills in marketing and entrepreneurship and is, in fact, making her quite a good Tupperware saleswoman, even though she is just starting out.

Bagging food and not taking any of it home will not be easy. Still, it hasn't occurred to Tammy not to go. Bags of Hope have arrived at her home in the past. She needs to give back.

Tomorrow will be December 15, the day a mortgage payment is due, and they still can't afford to send it. But today, Blackhawk Credit Union has finally, *finally* decided to let Tammy and Jerad refinance their mortgage. Their new mortgage rate will be just 3.75 percent. Tammy figures this will save them nearly $250 a month.

So she already is in a good mood when she gets a call. Deri is on the phone. A family has dropped out. No longer wants to accept donated food. The Whiteakers will be getting Bags of Hope, after all.

★

Saturday morning is gray, the rain cold and driving. By 7:30 a.m., inside a big distribution facility on the south side of town, next to a bay of new John Deere lawn and garden tractors, 150 volunteers are milling about, next to row after row of long tables stacked with groceries. Among the volunteers is a smattering of UAW Local 95 members, GM retirees who still come as a reminder of all the years when the assembly plant's management and the union came together for the holiday food drive. Now, most of the volunteers are teachers, parents, and kids.

At 8 a.m., the volunteers gather in a large circle around Jim Reif, a Craig High School math teacher who gives the morning's pep talk that Marv Wopat delivered for twenty-five Christmas seasons before the plant shut down. The teacher's message is low-key. The 350 families around Janesville that will be getting groceries "are all going to be appreciative when we are done, because they are going to have enough food to get through the Christmas break.

"We are early," he says. "Go slow, and be perfect."

Jerad is one of the bag runners, walking up and down the aisles with one Woodman's-donated paper bag at a time, starting out with it empty and feeling it grow heavy with the food that volunteers place inside. Tammy is stationed halfway down row #5, two rows over from the lawn and garden tractors. When each bag runner comes along, including Jerad, she puts inside Saltines, Stove Top Stuffing Mix, and Swiss Miss cocoa powder. "I like this," she says, as the stacks before her dwindle, background music of sleigh bells playing over the public address system. "It makes me feel good."

Next to her is a Parker teacher. "I loved your daughters," she tells Tammy. "They are the sweetest girls."

By 8:45 a.m., all the food is in the bags, and the bags are laid out in neat rows on the concrete floor for the next phase of the operation: delivery. Some of the bag stuffers are about to be the drivers, and the organizers are handing them slips of paper with the names and addresses of families to which deliveries are to be made. Tammy has talked with an organizer ahead of time. No point in having a driver bring food to her house if she and Jerad and Noah already are right here. So Tammy picks up a slip with her own address on it.

The three of them are about to head out into the rain. They will run through the puddled parking lot to their car, and drive around to the back of the distribution center and get into a long line of cars. And when it is their turn, a man standing in the rain in a red vest will ask how many families they are delivering for, and Tammy will reply "one," never hinting that the one is her own. And the man and another in a red vest will load six bags of groceries into their car's trunk—half as many as in the past. Some Bags of Hope, though, are better than none.

But before they run through the parking lot in the downpour, while Tammy and Noah continue crossing the concrete expanse toward the door, Jerad stops for a moment. Behind a yellow cord, roping off some John Deere tractors, he has noticed a security guard. The guard's shirt has an "Allied Barton" patch on the sleeve.

"How do you get hired by this company?" Jerad asks the guard. "I've applied multiple times and didn't hear a word."

The guard is kind. "I'll tell my officer to keep an eye out," he says.

Jerad thanks the guard, and keeps walking to join Tammy and Noah near the exit.

Part Six

★ 2013 ★

★ 50 ★

Two Janesvilles

A s the fifth year without the General Motors plant arrives, the ways that time and economic misfortune can rend even a re-silient community—a community determined not to lie down and give up—are now plain to see. The city on the Rock River is now two Janesvilles.

In one Janesville, Mary Willmer is in a whirlwind. She is in good spir-its. The initial work of converting her corner of M&I bank into BMO Harris is starting to ease, even as her responsibilities at the bank are about to expand. Next month, she will become BMO Harris's manager in charge of developing teams of "premier bankers" and financial advisors through a swath of Wisconsin that stretches nearly two hundred miles from Green Bay down through Madison and Janesville and into Beloit. Premier bank-ing is offered to BMO Harris customers "in the mass affluent sector," with savings in the range of $250,000 to $1 million. "At BMO Harris, we believe a higher level of financial achievement demands a higher level of atten-tion," the bank's marketing material says. In her work, Mary will be striv-ing to improve service to the well-off.

In town, she remains at the apex of the business community, pursuing her considerable volunteer work for nonprofits, attending charity events, continuing Rock County 5.0's regionally minded efforts to rebuild the local economy. She sees progress. Leaving aside GM's 4.8 million square feet of emptiness, the vacancy rate for the county's industrial space has fallen from 13 percent three years ago to just over 7 percent. Rock County 5.0 was conceived of as a five-year project, and it will begin its fifth year in the fall, but, even after that, it will persevere, with Mary and her co-chair, Diane Hendricks, at the helm.

Toward the end of January, Mary attends Forward Janesville's awards luncheon, at which she introduces the 2013 recipient of the organization's lifetime achievement award. The businessman she introduces is Mark Cullen, the chairman of JP Cullen & Sons, Inc., a fifth-generation, family-owned construction business whose patriarch, like Paul Ryan's ancestors, created a branch of Janesville's Irish mafia. The construction industry, in Janesville and across the United States, suffered during the recession, but JP Cullen & Sons is well entrenched, with big contracts over the decades at the University of Wisconsin and other major institutions, even if its long-standing contracts with General Motors in Janesville ended when the assembly line went silent. Five years later, as today's achievement award attests, Mark Cullen has emerged unscathed. As Mary is unscathed.

Mary's life is evolving. She is falling in love. Her long marriage to a mortgage banker has ended, and she has just met a new guy, an architect in Madison. She recently was asking her Facebook friends to recommend their favorite all-inclusive resorts for a January trip to Mexico, and they are planning a week in California's Napa Valley later in the year.

"Couldn't be happier," Mary posts on Facebook the day that she helps her youngest, Connor, celebrate his eighteenth birthday—and that she books the wine country trip.

*

The same week as the Forward Janesville luncheon, the Whiteakers get some help. Jerad, still out of work, has gone online to apply for FoodShare, Wisconsin's version of food stamps. On Monday, three days before the luncheon, a woman from the state government calls him for an interview. The next day, Jerad is notified that his family has been approved to receive

$160 toward groceries per month. The amount is less than Tammy used to spend on groceries for the five of them each week. It is less than Food-Share would be sending if it hadn't insisted on counting Alyssa's and Kayzia's incomes because they are now eighteen. Not right, Tammy thinks, that the state expects kids in high school to be propping up families' incomes. Still, $160 will be a big help.

The Whiteakers live in the other Janesville. This year, 41,000 families in Rock County will get FoodShare, twice as many as the year before the assembly plant shut down. The Whiteakers are not the worst off in town. They have not lost their home, though Tammy still wonders sometimes whether they should be looking for a needle-in-a-haystack buyer who wants a nice house with a backyard pool—and find a cheaper place to rent. They have not been out of work all this time; they are just bumping in and out of jobs that don't pay enough. With their good grades and their AP courses, the twins now have acceptance letters from the University of Wisconsin–Platteville, a campus about a hundred miles west of Janesville that is good for Alyssa's interest in engineering and Kayzia's in medicine. The girls are pretty confident that they will find a way to afford it, even if they aren't sure how. No, the Whiteakers aren't the worst off. They are just part of a broad tumbling downhill as a result of which, for many families in town, life is not what they'd expected.

To bring in extra money, Tammy has started selling Norwex—a line of cleaning products she likes because they are made without damaging chemicals. After coming home from the car dealership, she has begun to do Norwex-selling parties, hosted by relatives and friends, in the same way that Alyssa is doing Tupperware parties.

And Alyssa has just discovered a way to work more hours. One of her teachers at Parker mentioned something called Virtual Academy, a state program in which the Janesville schools take part. It allows students to study independently, taking their classes online. The main teacher who oversees Virtual Academy in town is Dave Parr, who is still leading the Janesville Education Association, even after the predawn Walmart episode in which another shopper wouldn't stop yelling at him about how good teachers have it.

When Virtual Academy started a year before the GM plant went away, most of its students had trouble learning in a traditional classroom, or were drawn by the wider array of Advanced Placement courses available online. Dave has watched the changes among the city's teenagers. The cars in the parking lots at the two high schools, Parker and Craig, have gone from new ones bought by parents to old, used ones that students are paying for with what they earn at their own jobs. Just as Kayzia and Alyssa are doing. For making car payments or helping out with families' bills, Virtual Academy has a benefit: Its students are exempt from Wisconsin's limits on how many hours teenagers are allowed to work. The online courses available seven days a week, day or night, its students are trusted to get their studies done on their own schedule and work as much as they want. This has become the main draw.

Alyssa figured that maybe she can bump up the hours at one of her three jobs—the one at the same car dealer as her mom—from fifteen hours a week to twenty-four, if she can go in at 1 p.m. a couple of weekdays. So, earlier this month, she took a test to assess whether she would be a good fit for Virtual Academy. The results showed that she is self-motivated, efficient at time management, hardworking, optimistic. Quite a good fit.

So at 8:30 a.m. on Thursday, January 24, mere hours before Mary will introduce Forward Janesville's 2013 lifetime achievement winner, Alyssa is not at Parker. She is sitting on the living room couch at home, with a black ASUS laptop that she bought herself. Rocky, their miniature pinscher, is quiet at her side. Alyssa is doing Marine Science, module 1.07. "What makes the ocean a nice place to live?" She read this module last night but wants to review it before taking the quiz.

This month already, she has completed six of forty-five assignments in Marine Science. She is on pace to complete the course on time, though she is hoping to get ahead. For one of the assignments, she has made a PowerPoint presentation for the lesson "What is a stream?" She went down to the Rock River to make her January observations—birds and animals, slope of embankment, texture of the shore. No green algae, she noted. No geese present. And she made her set of predictions for her next observation, at the same time of day, to be faithful to scientific principles by holding constant as many variables as she can.

Her PowerPoint so far ends with an image of the river in winter and the words that Alyssa has typed: "What is to come?"

★

On Monday, February 4, Jerad starts a new job. It is one that he applied for after Tammy's boss heard that he was having a hard time finding work and put in a good word with a cousin who runs a local branch of a company that delivers reconditioned auto parts to repair shops.

Jerad's route is more than two hundred miles a day. He needs to punch in at 6:30 a.m., drive a truck filled with parts to body shops in Chicago's western exurbs, drive the truck back to Janesville, and, if all goes smoothly, clock out ten and a half hours later. It does not take more than a month before the Interstate traffic in Illinois, heading toward Chicago, begins to stoke Jerad's anxiety. Not as bad as the claustrophobia and panic attacks back at the County Jail, but bad enough that he sometimes calls Tammy at *her* job to vent about the bad drivers on the road, about the body shop owners who don't always find the parts acceptable, about the GPS telling him for miles in advance to turn right when he *knows* he needs to turn right.

Tammy recognizes that these calls help Jerad with his stress, even if they increase hers. And she wonders how they ended up like this. She never was someone with big plans for their lives. Just wanted them to be comfortable. These days, she tells Alyssa and Kayzia—and even Noah, though he is younger—that they are ahead in the game of life. They already know how to live without enough money.

Jerad's newest job comes with a trade-off. It pays $12 an hour—not enough to live on, but enough, with what Tammy and the girls earn, so that their FoodShare goes away. But it is a job, Jerad figures, and it almost pays the bills.

Night Drive

"Come on, get the hell out of here!" a guy shouts as he bursts out the door and speed-walks across the terra-cotta-tiled lobby, barely slowing to slide his ID card through the punch clock. Friday night at the Fort Wayne Assembly Plant. The end of the workweek. The end of second shift—a nine-hour shift today, with a lucky hour's overtime, so that it is 11:45 p.m. as this guy is shouting, one guy among 1,100 GM'ers pouring off the factory floor to start their weekend.

Amid this horde, Matt Wopat reaches the lobby at 11:47 p.m., wearing a knit cap, a backpack slung over one shoulder. He is not running, but he, too, is walking very, very fast. A Friday night ritual. He reaches the chilly night air, and a co-worker wishes him a safe drive tonight. He stops for an instant at the '97 Saturn, which he parks in the same part of the vast lot every Friday—in a middle row under a street lamp—so that he won't have to think about where he's left his car when he returns on Monday. He pulls his duffel from the trunk and continues walking very, very fast over to a nearby 2003 Pontiac Grand Prix, already idling. In the driver's seat is Chris Aldrich. In the backseat, his coat scrunched up between him and the door, is Paul Sheridan. Janesville GM gypsies, both. Chris pops the trunk for Matt to toss his duffel inside and slam the trunk shut before he gets in on the passenger side. Matt's door is barely closed when Chris guns the engine and roars off.

Two hundred eighty miles to go. Four hours and thirty-five minutes, speeding just a little where they are pretty sure they will not get caught. Matt pulls out his phone, calls Darcy to tell her they are leaving. Same as he does every week.

When Chris guns the engine, it is 11:54 p.m. in Fort Wayne, except that Matt is not the only one who stays on Janesville time, so the dashboard clock on the Grand Prix says 10:54. Chris started working at Fort Wayne on August 17, 2009, seven months before Matt. Chris will never forget that day. His wife and kids along to help him move, except that he doesn't like to say he has "moved," so he says that he "stays" in Fort Wayne. Anyhow, his family left on Monday morning when he went to the plant for orientation, which was during first shift, so he was back in this new apartment by 3:30 that afternoon, and he sat on a chair from a cheap dinette set they'd just gotten, staring at a wall. Alone. His wife and kids already back in Janesville. One of the worst feelings of his life.

That was three and a half years ago. The Grand Prix had 47,000 miles on it. Now it has 134,407.

On this night, they are not yet ten minutes from the plant, about to turn onto Route 114, when Matt says in his quiet way, "This is my three-year anniversary."

Chris doesn't miss a beat. "We aren't going to celebrate *that*," he shoots back.

Matt already texted Darcy before going to work: "Happy anniversary to me. 3 years."

And the reply came back: "Has it been 3 years? Seems a lot longer." Darcy had added a sad-face emoticon.

Three years, even with GM vacations factored in, is a lot of Fridays, hurtling through the night to get home. This week, it snowed ten inches in Fort Wayne, but then it thawed, and today was sunny. Tonight is clear, so the stars are bright on the drive through the Indiana farmland, so much flatter than Wisconsin's.

"Think we'll get lucky and get a double raccoon tonight?" Chris asks.

Last summer on this stretch of Route 114, with exquisite timing, one raccoon ran into the road from the left and another from the right, and the Grand Prix struck them both, one with a front tire and one with a rear.

You don't get *that* every week.

But they do get the house alongside the road whose occupants have a flair for decorating. Tonight, it's lit up like Christmas but in green and gold with shamrocks for St. Patrick's Day coming up.

And now the bend north for a few miles and then west onto U.S. 30, four lanes divided, which Chris and Paul and Matt agree is a better way to go than the Indiana Toll Road further north that some of the other Janesville gypsies take on Friday nights.

U.S. 30 gives them the chance in the summer to try to guess what's playing at the drive-in movie theater just off the road—not Chris or whoever's turn it is to drive, but the passengers craning their necks to get a quick peek at the screen at an angle. And one time, they drove through a giant thunderstorm, with lightning bolts that, along this flat land of long views, they could see shooting straight down into the fields.

No matter the season, there is always the Bourbon Bible Church, with its weird, larger-than-life David and Goliath diorama that you can see as you drive by.

Matt's phone rings. It's Bria, his youngest, calling past her bedtime. "In Indiana," he says. "About three hours probably. Okay, sweetie. I'll let you go. I love you, too."

And now they are in Valparaiso, where they stop, as always, at the truck stop called the Pilot Travel Center. Some of the Janesville gypsies wait until the next fast food stop, the last one before the Illinois line, but Chris and Paul and Matt like this one for its good snacks and multiple bathrooms. They are back in the car soon with their snacks—teriyaki beef jerky for Chris, regular jerky for Paul, and Smartfood popcorn for Matt along with a bag of chewy Sour Patch Kids that he is saving for Bria and Brooke.

Then it is north onto Highway 49 and west onto the Toll Road.

"You are going under the speed limit," says Paul, who has mostly been sleeping, curled up against his coat.

"Fuck you," Chris says. "You want the tire to wobble off?"

"You know how to change a tire," Paul says.

Matt jumps in. "You are doing a good job, Chris."

"Thanks," Chris says. "You are very supportive."

And now they are whizzing past Gary, with what remains of its steel mills on the right. Lights sparkling. Gray smoke plumes dissolving into the sky. A flicker of flames. Gary was known as "Magic City," when U.S. Steel arrived in 1906 to build the mills on Lake Michigan's southern shore. Now its population of 78,000 is less than half of what it was in its heyday of 1960, nearly one fourth less than even in 2000. Four in ten of the people left are living in poverty. Gary is a perfect specimen of what the Rust Belt looks like and what Janesville is striving not to become. Chris drives on.

It is almost 1:30 a.m. Janesville time when the Grand Prix glides through a tollbooth with an EZPass and enters Illinois—the Skyway and then the Dan Ryan Expressway, which gets clogged even with its fourteen lanes. The Dan Ryan is easy to cruise along tonight because, with the extra hour at the plant, the overtime, they are later than usual, and most of the city of big shoulders, as Carl Sandburg christened it for the toil of piling job on job, is asleep.

The downtown skyline comes into view.

Just north of Chicago, a red car passes with four guys inside. "Tom is driving," Chris notes. "Almost looks like O'Leary in back."

More Janesville gypsies.

Matt dozes off for a few minutes, joining Paul in his slumber. Chris doesn't like the silence. "You are supposed to be doing color commentaries," he teases Matt when he wakes up.

Good thing Matt is awake when, a little after 2 a.m., a text arrives on his phone. It's from yet another car filled with Janesville gypsies, up ahead. "Mile marker 28 or so, cop in the median." Chris slows. Nine minutes later, Matt spots the cop. "No likey tickets," Chris says. "Can't afford to."

The one time Matt got pulled over, the summer before last, he told the officer the truth: that he works in Fort Wayne during the week and was driving home, and he guessed he was just a little bit excited to get there and see his family. The cop said he could understand and let Matt off.

They pass the Belvidere Chrysler plant, the one that wasn't hiring when the assembly plant shut down. When they get to Rockford, Chris says, "The home stretch. We'll have Paul in his driveway in twenty minutes."

"Holy shit, we are nearly home," Matt says.

Paul continues his gentle snores.

And at this hour—2:41 a.m. Janesville time—Chris gets philosophical about spending his workweeks in Fort Wayne. "Funny how we count time," he says. "I count how many Christmases I have to spend there. Three more Christmases."

He's coming up on twenty-seven years since he became a GM'er on August 17, 1986, part of a big hiring wave that came right after Janesville survived one of its near-death experiences. When the last day really came—December 23, 2008—Chris was down at the plant, shooting video with a digital camera. His anniversary date means that Chris has three years and seven months until he can retire. Matt has twelve years and seven months.

"When I retire," Chris says, "I don't want to leave you guys there. I want everyone home. Maybe that'll be my business after I retire. I'll be a shuttle guy and bring you guys home."

Paul wakes up as the Grand Prix pulls off the Interstate at exit 177. "Cool your jets," Chris says to Paul. "I'll have you home in a heartbeat."

It is just after 3 a.m., Janesville time because this is Janesville, when Chris pulls into Paul's driveway. After dropping him off, Chris drives up Center Avenue, crossing the Rock River near where the assembly plant still stands vacant, up Centerway Street and then up Milton Avenue to Matt's nice house on the north edge of town that he and Darcy have managed to keep because he is a gypsy. It is a straight shot up through town. But sometimes they go through town different ways, just because it's nice to be home, nice to see Janesville's streets.

At 3:20 a.m., Chris pulls into the driveway of the beige house with its dark red front door. Darcy hasn't remembered to turn on the outside light, but she has left the light on in the laundry room—just inside the garage door where she and the girls once cried as Matt was leaving for Fort Wayne the first time—to welcome him home.

Matt hands Chris a $20 bill for gas and oil changes, when the Grand Prix needs them. "What time you going to be here Monday morning?" Matt asks just before pulling his duffel out of the trunk.

"Probably 8:10, 8:15," Chris says. "The usual."

The Ebb and Flow of Work

U nion or not union, no job is forever. No guarantees. Nearly two years since he began to work in the human resources department of Seneca Foods, Mike Vaughn understands this in a way he did not back when it had seemed that being a UAW representative, his family legacy, was his life. Sure, serving as shop chairman for the union brothers and sisters of Lear Seating had shaped who he was. Yet it wasn't, it turns out, his only opportunity.

Mike notices the ebb and flow of work, in particular, because of the burst of seasonal hiring each year for the production months at Seneca. The 1.1-million-square-foot processing plant has about four hundred full-time workers, adding two to three hundred more during peak processing times. There is a rhythm to the crops that ripen, most of them on Wisconsin farm fields, and come through the plant: peas from June until late July, corn until early fall with potatoes running alongside, then mixed vegetables and a time of potatoes again. Mike puts people through orientation, enters them into the personnel system, knowing that they will be gone once the last potatoes have been processed by Christmastime.

Though he is a year-round employee and not a seasonal one, these crop rhythms affect Mike's work. Off-season, his shift is 3:30 p.m. to midnight. During the canning season, he works overnight. And during this production season, there is opportunity for overtime. Mike volunteers to be available for overtime seven days a week. Sometimes, he gets six days. Sometimes, all seven.

Mike grabs this overtime because there is extra personnel work to be done, and overtime is a way of making sure that he does not fall behind. Plus, working overnight makes days off complicated for his body clock, so he might as well be working, instead of at home, awake during the dead of night. His biggest reason for grabbing as much overtime as he can is financial. Mike has gotten raises since he started at Seneca, but his wages still aren't what they were at Lear. Adding in all the production season overtime, though, he does pretty well. He and Barb have developed a money rhythm: they put aside some of what Mike earns in the summer and fall, and they spend down some of it during the lean, cold months—like a larder. This is how they have propped up their standard of living close to what it was before they lost their Lear jobs.

He and Barb always have tried to save, but he is aware that putting money aside seems more crucial than in the past. Having lost a job once, it's always in the back of his head; he can't rule out its happening again.

And if it happens a second time, Mike has a faith in himself and in the nature of opportunity that he did not have before. If he puts his mind to it, he can turn a negative event into a positive outcome. This was, he realizes, the very advice that he gave out when he met with small groups of union brothers and sisters on the Lear factory floor: that they needed to make the best of the situation and formulate a new plan.

When he was dispensing that advice, over and over again, he knew that it was true. But it was in his head—abstract. He did not see what seizing opportunity looked like, really see it up close, until he watched Barb rush back to school, watched her study as she had never studied in her life. He followed her lead.

Barb is moving along in her new work. Last June, Creative Community Living Services promoted her from residential coordinator/community protection to a position called program manager/supervisor. The pay is just a little more, climbing toward $13 an hour. But she is now dividing her time between administrative work and the work she loves most—the direct help to clients.

To her surprise, Barb believes that Lear's closing was the best thing that could have happened. Its closing taught her that she is a survivor. It taught her that work exists that is worth doing, not for the wages, but because you feel good doing it. Working with developmentally disabled adults, who depend on her and call her day and night, often does not even seem like a job. It is a way of life. Barb has promised herself that, after the injuries to her shoulder and wrist on the Lear assembly line, after her brief and depressing stint at the County Jail, she will never again stay working anywhere that she is not happy. She does not look back at Lear. She looks forward to how her clients are growing and, with her help, becoming as independent as they can be.

Project 16:49

The premiere of *Sixteen Forty-Nine* seems to Ann Forbeck a long time ago. Nearly two and a half years have gone by since that first showing. She and Robin Stuht, the Beloit school social worker who is her partner in the project, now laugh at their naïveté to have ever thought that they could open a shelter for girls and one for boys within twelve months.

Still, fundraising for Project 16:49 is coming along. In a community once shocked by the very idea of homeless kids in its midst, the project is being embraced. On June 1, a thirty-six-year-old Janesville insurance agent, who had a homeless spell himself as a boy, will begin to ride his bicycle around town every day for thirty days, with the goal of riding 1,649 miles as a magnet for donations. He will complete those miles and, in the process, collect $16,000.

Since last spring, when the YWCA made its painful decision to sever ties with the project, Ann and Robin have learned more than they ever dreamed they could about the incorporation of nonprofits. Project 16:49 is now a 501(c)(3), with its own board of directors, the directors including a pair of homeless kids. The board is about to begin a search for an executive director.

Project 16:49 has been leading Ann places that she never imagined a school social worker would go. Today, she arrives at another new place: Room 411 South, a gold-painted committee room, three floors above Governor Walker's office, in the Wisconsin State Capitol. It is mid-March, six months since Ann was riding in a carriage down Main Street with two of her crop of homeless teens in the Labor Fest parade. It is early afternoon, and she is here to testify at Wisconsin's first Homeless Youth Symposium. Deb Kolste, three months into her first term as Janesville's Assembly member and no longer a volunteer on Wednesdays at HealthNet, is sitting at the perimeter of desks surrounding the oak witness table at which Ann and Robin are taking their seats. Of all the professionals in Wisconsin who cross paths with homeless students, Ann and Robin have been chosen as two of the symposium's four "voices from the community."

Ann has never testified anywhere before, but her delivery is solid. She tells Deb and the other lawmakers in the golden room that the Janesville school system has counted 968 students this year who do not have a fixed place to sleep at night. Of those students, 170 are on their own, without an adult. These, she says, are the students that Project 16:49 is trying to help.

"Mostly, kids end up couch surfing," Ann testifies. "We see in our kids a lot of depression, a lot of anxiety. We want to make sure kids have a future."

Ann and Robin show clips from the documentary, ending with the scene of Brandon sitting on a step in a school stairwell, saying that his mother won't come to his graduation. Some of the lawmakers are looking as weepy as the first audience that saw the film.

Ann has done her homework. When the film clips end, she says, as if she lobbies in the statehouse all the time, "We want to put together some legislative fixes."

Getting help for her kids would be easier, she says, if state law allowed those who are sixteen or seventeen to sign up for housing assistance or BadgerCare by themselves, if a parent is not around to give consent. She has brought a model statute from Oregon that she found. A legislator from Beloit tells Ann that she would be happy to look into the Oregon law. It isn't a guarantee, but perhaps it's a start.

Glass More than Half Full

Another spring weekend, and Paul Ryan is home, as usual, from Capitol Hill. Tonight, he is looking out from a small stage at 750 well-heeled Janesville citizens packed into the Holiday Inn Express banquet room—the room where Mary Willmer revealed her poor girlhood to the Circle of Women, where Rock County's Republicans gathered to watch their native son lose a chance at the White House.

Paul's experience on the vice presidential campaign trail happens to be the subject of the remarks he is making tonight—remarks that are personal, whimsical, sentimental, moored in love for his hometown. The occasion on this last Friday of April is the annual dinner of Forward Janesville, the business alliance hell-bent on reviving the city's economy. The members of Forward Janesville, the city's business people and civic leaders, are seated at round tables squeezed close together tonight because, with Paul as the keynote speaker, the 2013 annual dinner has a record draw. Tickets sold out weeks ago.

Each table is covered with a heavy sand-colored tablecloth, and at each place setting is prime rib with hollandaise and, as a party favor, a clear tumbler with green printing that says, "We See the Glass More than Half Full."

While some in town scoffed at the slogan that Mary came up with early in Janesville's economic crisis—that everyone needs to become ambassadors of optimism—Forward Janesville embraced it. Exuding optimism has become central to Forward Janesville's credo and its strategy. The organization now has a cadre of volunteer "good-will ambassadors," who attend ribbon cuttings and visit every Forward Janesville member at work at least once a year.

To begin this evening's program, before Paul speaks, John Beckord, Forward Janesville's president, takes the stage and introduces a video. The video was made for this occasion, and its purpose is to deride what John calls "um, a pervasive, negative attitude in the community, especially anonymous online commentators."

"The Crabby Bloggers" is the video's title. It juxtaposes upbeat statistics about Janesville's economy with a cartoon that features furious typing and grumbling by blogging nay-sayers. It celebrates "a resurgence in employment opportunities," showing that 1,924 jobs have been created in Rock County by forty-one companies since the start of 2010.

At a table toward the back of the banquet room, Bob Borremans, head of the Job Center, murmurs his sympathy with the bloggers, "That's my perspective." As a civic leader, Bob is attending tonight's dinner, but he doesn't share this crowd's prevailing view of the glass as more than half full.

Nearly two thousand new jobs are not trivial, but neither the video nor John mentions that the county still has 4,500 fewer jobs than when GM announced it was closing the plant. And when the video highlights the opening this month of the Janesville Innovation Center, built with a federal grant and city money to provide office and manufacturing space to nurture start-ups, it gives no hint of the scant interest so far among fledgling companies in renting space in the center.

When the video ends, John is back at the microphone, talking up the most recent issue of Forward Janesville's magazine, with its cover article, "Thirty-three Reasons to Be Optimistic About the Future of Janesville, Rock County and Wisconsin." He reminds the audience about the billboards "advancing this notion that we can all become ambassadors of optimism and be part of the comeback story that we're experiencing right now." And then John introduces Mary, who he says is a thirty-fourth reason to be optimistic about Janesville's future.

Mary walks onto the stage in an elegant black dress and recalls this very dinner three years ago, when she and Diane Hendricks "stood up on this stage and really looked out at an audience that was probably in a bit of shock. . . . We had all been through some really tough times." Since then, Mary says, "we've gone from feeling sorry for ourselves as a community to having hope and inspiration and motivation."

If John and the "Crabby Bloggers" video and Mary herself attest to certain headway in Janesville since the depths of the Great Recession, they attest to something else, too: an optimism gap that divides these crusaders for economic development with the experiences of many other people in town.

The two Janesvilles are still trying hard to pull themselves—and their community—back up. They haven't forsaken the old can-do. And yet, by this spring, if you ask people in Rock County whether the economy has recovered, nearly six in ten will tell you that it has not. Not surprisingly, among people who have lost a job since the recession began—or live with someone who has lost a job—two thirds will tell you that the economy has not recovered.

And here is another glimpse at the gap between Mary and her fellow optimists versus the rest of town: a survey has shown that nearly six in ten people think that Rock County will never again be a place in which workers feel secure in their jobs, or in which good jobs at good pay are available for people who want to work. Most of the rest think that returning to such a place will take many years. Just one in fifty believes that Rock County has returned to the job security—or to the good jobs at good pay—that it used to provide.

Overall, just over half say that their household's financial situation is worse than when the recession began. Yet among people who lost a job—or live with someone who did—nearly three fourths now say that they are worse off. And of those who found a different job, two thirds are being paid less than before—compared with slightly more than half overall.

These, then, are the two Janesvilles—some spared harm, some hurting still, no matter how vigorously they have clung to the old can-do.

Tonight, the job losers and the pay losers are not in the banquet room, tucking into tulip glasses of strawberry and chocolate mousse for dessert as Mary is onstage, saying that, since the dark, stunning days right after the plant closed, sales tax receipts have been rising and industrial vacancy rates falling. The progress this community has made, she says, is phenomenal.

Then Paul bounds onto the stage to a standing ovation so echoing and sustained that it is almost enough to make you forget that Janesville—that his very own ward—voted against him both for vice president and for Congress just five months ago. If Forward Janesville's members are Mary's brand of optimists, they are Paul's people, too. They adore his vignettes from the campaign trail—an experience he describes as "kind of like you get stuffed into a cannon and shot out into the country" on a campaign plane dubbed the Flying Badger in honor of Wisconsin's state animal. And they adore the Valentine he is delivering tonight to Janesville. The hard-bitten national press corps who tailed him everywhere, discovering his favorite Wisconsin supper club, the Buckhorn. And seeing his old high school teacher and Stan Milam, the veteran newsman, on national TV, explaining what Paul and what Janesville are all about. And the homesickness that crept up on him in hotel rooms with his family back home. "Well, technically you're not alone. You've got about twenty Secret Service agents with you, some with machine guns, outside your door. You got staff and you got law enforcement and all these other people. But I would lay in bed at night, thinking about this place, this place where I grew up in."

They adore his ode to flying back from Washington into Milwaukee, as he did just hours ago, and the drive home, passing the spot where he bow hunts; passing Ryan, Inc., where he mowed the lawn as a kid; passing the funeral home where he washed cars in high school; passing St. John Vianney, where he went to church as a boy and he goes with his own family now. Every time, he says, "I get the same feeling—the stress of DC literally just rolls off of me as I . . . come into town. It's a feeling of comfort that you really can't describe that you have living here. It's a feeling of belonging to something, of belonging to some place, that you live in a community that is bigger than yourself."

Paul now reaches for a broader point, a point that adds up to "the American Idea," a catchphrase he has devised lately that fuses his fiscal conservatism with a newer identity he is carving out as author of a Republican approach to poverty. The American Idea is Paul's new way of expressing his belief that people who need help in their lives should look, not to government as the New Deal and the Great Society encouraged, but to generosity and resources within their own communities. Janesville is, he says, "a community that . . . [has] so many dedicated people; it's a community where we think about, you know, HealthNet, ECHO."

Paul does not mention that the need is so great and the charity on which Janesville still prides itself so strained that HealthNet has had to cut back the number of new patients it can take each Wednesday, or that ECHO has people lining up outside two hours before the doors open, hoping to be one of the first forty in line before the food pantry has to cut off the line for the day. Paul is still deep into his Valentine. "It's an amazing community. It's a community that is second to none to raise your family. And when I come home every weekend, I think about how special it is. And I look around this city, and I see people who have been here literally for generations of families. The social scientists, they call this civil society. I call it Janesville, Wisconsin."

Paul is winding down, and the 750 business people and civic leaders are sated on their prime rib and mousse and the words of their native son. "The point is," Paul is saying, "there's a reason why we have all these generations of families that stay in this town. You can't put your finger on it. But if there's anything that Janna and I learned during this campaign, in this town—a Democratic town, and believe me, I'm a Republican—it's the absolute warmth, the hospitality, the community, the 'we're in it together' kind of spirit we have here. That's what makes this town so great. That's what makes it home."

The members of Forward Janesville are on their feet, and this standing ovation makes the one they gave Paul when he first stepped onto the stage sound like just a warm-up act. They are thrilled by his message. And Paul is thrilled to be surrounded by his fellow optimists. Instead of heading out into the soft air of this April night, Paul sticks around. He stands with his wife, Janna, and older brother Tobin and sister-in-law Oakleigh. They are standing toward the front of the banquet hall, greeting old friends, many of whom he has not seen since the campaign.

Like Paul, Bob Borremans is in no hurry to leave. His wife, Dyann, is away for the weekend. When the speeches end, he wanders into a hallway linking the banquet room with the hotel lobby, and settles into a wingback chair. After this weekend, he will go back to his latest project, trying to launch an innovative way to teach out-of-a-job people new skills by leaning on local companies for help. Bob knows that the upbeat talk of John Beckord and Mary and Paul and their fellow optimists packed into the banquet room doesn't match what he sees, still sees, coming through the Job Center's doors.

By this night, April 26, 2013, four years, four months, and three days have gone by since General Motors pulled out of town. "I was optimistic we would be farther along," Bob reflects. "I believe we've done the best we can do, given the circumstances. Have we recovered? No way."

The Forward Janesville crowd, as Bob sees it, believes that sugarcoating reality might make Janesville more appealing to new businesses. And yet, as he thinks about the situation, the truth is that a lot of people are still hurting, still can't afford their mortgage or their rent. "To sit and say things are back to normal is bogus," he muses. "I have a problem with people not accepting reality."

Bob gave up a few years ago on trying to persuade Paul to visit the Job Center, to see the work the center does and the people who, after all this time, still need a decent job. But what the hell? Bob gets up and walks back into the banquet hall, where, at the other end of the room, Paul is still shaking hands and giving hugs and autographs. Bob stands at the edge of the crowd. Finally, as the crowd thins, as some Forward Janesville members are taking their "We See the Glass More than Half Full" tumblers and heading into the Holiday Inn Express parking lot, Bob and Paul are face-to-face.

Bob introduces himself to his congressman, hands him his business card. Bob tells Paul that he should stop by the Job Center. Paul is in an expansive mood. Sure, he says. Happy to visit.

Bob walks away, wondering on this optimism-drenched night whether Paul will ever come to glimpse the Janesville that he knows.

Graduation Weekend

It is early June—five years to the week since General Motors announced that it would close the assembly plant. Graduation season has arrived.

Matt Wopat has been worrying whether his sixteen-year-old Saturn will get him back for Brooke's commencement. The car hasn't been as reliable lately as he wished. Last month, three nights before a rare Thursday solo drive home for his stepdaughter Brittany's wedding, Matt had just left the Fort Wayne Assembly Plant and was on the phone with Darcy, as usual, when trouble cropped up. "There are no lights," he told Darcy. No headlights or rear lights or dashboard lights as he turned north onto I-69 for the five-mile stretch toward his apartment at the Willows of Coventry. Then, as he was easing over to the Interstate's shoulder, the car died.

Luckily, another GM'er from Wisconsin was behind him. Not a guy he knew well, but someone with an apartment at the Willows of Coventry. The guy stopped and gave him a lift.

The culprit turned out to be the alternator. It cost Matt $210 to have it replaced, plus the towing, and he ended up being late to work the next day. All this reminded him that needing to keep an extra car in Fort Wayne is more expensive than living at home would be, and he can't afford to go buy a new car. In fact, he and Darcy had tried to persuade Brittany to wait another year, until she was a little older than twenty-one and the wedding expenses wouldn't hit so close to the graduation party for Brooke and a cousin finishing high school, too. But Brittany was eager to marry her boyfriend. And the Saturn, with its new alternator, held up on the drive back for the May 4 wedding—Star Wars Day, with Han Solo and Princess Leia on the cake. Matt's dad, Marv, who was ordained as a minister over the Internet and already had performed weddings for three cousins, officiated.

The Saturn also held up, thank goodness, on the drive home for Brooke's graduation weekend. So now it is a muggy Sunday afternoon, and the skies are threatening around 1 p.m., an hour before the ceremony is to begin. A decision is made to move the commencement indoors, from the Milton High School football field to the school gym. This means that there are not enough tickets for the best bleacher seats. Matt is sitting on one side, in the good seats, with Darcy and Bria. Across the way, on an upper row toward the back of the gym, are Brittany and her new husband; Matt's sister, Janice, and her husband; Matt's nephew; Darcy's dad; Darcy's sister and brother-in-law; and, of course, Marv, who has ridden his Harley to the graduation. Marv is still on the Rock County Board of Supervisors even though he is now dividing his time in retirement between Janesville and Florida, where he has a lady friend. Most of the family together, where they belong. Home.

The Milton High class of 2013 is filing into the gym, the girls in crimson caps and gowns, the boys in black.

Matt is clutching his Samsung camcorder, Darcy is holding a camera, and Bria has a camera on her cell phone—small trappings of the middle-class life that GM is still supporting, even if it does cost more to live in two places. Matt waits to start videoing until his daughter appears in the gym's back door and walks to her seat to the cadence of "Fanfare," the processional being played by the school band. "Brookie," Darcy shouts out when, near the end of the alphabet, Brooke finally emerges in the doorway, a big "B" in sparkly silver glitter decorating the top of her mortarboard.

Inside the program listing the 235 graduates is the class motto:

"Things turn out for the best for the people who make the best of the way things are."

Brooke has decided that the way to make the best of the way things are, at least for now, is to stay in town. Keep living at home. She has thought about becoming a physical therapist but is enrolling in the fall in a more general program at U-Rock. With her dad not home much, she doesn't want to move away and see even less of him than during most of her high school years.

At 2:02 p.m., the school band stops playing, and the senior class president rises to address his fellow graduates. "After today, we enter the real world where the possibilities are endless. We can be whatever we want to be if we work hard enough." Then come speeches by the two honor graduates and the school principal, none of them hinting that possibilities around Janesville are less endless than they used to be.

The school choir sings Garth Brook's "The River"—chancing the rapids and dancing the tide and not sitting on the shoreline.

It is a little after 3 p.m. by the time Brooke crosses the stage to receive her diploma, as a Wopat near the bottom of the alphabet, the sixth graduate from the end. Matt and Darcy are beaming, clapping hard. Helped by Marv's thundering voice, a loud cheer for Brooke arises from her family on both sides of the bleachers.

*

Tammy Whiteaker is walking up the bleacher steps of Monterey Stadium, where Parker High's graduation will begin in three and a half hours. The stadium has stood since 1931, when the city of Janesville and its school system, in trademark, good-government fashion, joined forces to win a federal grant to build a track and football field and bleachers in one of the many parks for which Janesville is known. This particular park, Monterey, leads down to the Rock River at the spot where it narrows, just across from the hulking General Motors Assembly plant, which had been producing Chevrolets for eight years already when the stadium was built.

Tammy is here early, like no small number of other parents, to save good seats for tonight's ceremony by spreading blankets over a little section of the concrete bleachers. Everything else is pretty much ready. Her parents are providing most of what is needed for the girls' graduation party tomorrow afternoon, her mother having made two hundred meatballs, with Kayzia helping. An older cousin of Jerad's, who is close to his mother, has made other food, including the chicken and stuffing sandwiches that everyone loves. Tammy offered to pay her back but knew the cousin wouldn't accept, which is a good thing.

In these hours before commencement, one thing that isn't settled is how Alyssa and Kayzia will afford the University of Wisconsin–Platteville, which sent each of them an acceptance letter in October. Over the winter, they wrote essay after essay, applying for every scholarship they could find, as well as filling out federal financial aid forms. Kayzia is concerned about their financial aid packages, whose contents they are still waiting to learn. She and Alyssa were required to list their incomes—hers is $8,000 this year, a lot for a student—along with their parents' earnings, creating the illusion that her family can afford college better than they can.

With their good grades, AP courses, and U-Rock classes, they are graduating near the top of their class. Alyssa has a 4.15 grade-point average, putting her twelfth among the 324 Parker graduating seniors; Kayzia has a 3.7 GPA and is thirty-third. So they were not surprised—but excited, still—when invitations arrived last month to Parker's Senior Awards Ceremony. At least, they'd be getting something.

The ceremony was disappointing. Scholarships from the community these days are not abundant. Alyssa and Kayzia each won $1,000 from the Noon Rotary and a $100 scholarship named for a teacher at their elementary school. Plus, Alyssa won $1,000 from the Janesville Community Foundation and will be allowed to renew it if her college grades are good. All very nice as far as it goes, but not much of a dent in the nearly $15,000 it will cost each of them for their courses, plus living on campus, their freshman year alone.

As it turns out, they also will get $500 each their first year for having signed the Wisconsin Covenant back in eighth grade, pledging to maintain at least a B average and do volunteer work. It's not much money, but they feel lucky they were in eighth grade when they were; Governor

Walker closed the program so that no new students are able to sign the covenant.

Beyond these scholarships, they will work as many hours as they can, Kayzia holding two jobs in Platteville and Alyssa coming home every other weekend to keep her job at the car dealership where her mom works. And it still will not be enough. One July day, after she takes out an $8,000 private loan that she will need to repay with 11 percent interest, Alyssa will post on her Facebook page: "That moment when you feel like the people who are in charge of education don't want you to receive one. I hate working my butt off to have to figure out a way to get the education I deserve."

That moment will come in a month. This afternoon, Alyssa and Kayzia are focused on getting ready for commencement, curling their hair into corkscrews and putting on their Kelly green caps and gowns. When the time comes, the Whiteakers need a few cars to get everyone to the stadium, but Tammy has spread enough blankets for them all: Noah, who is fourteen now, and his girlfriend; Alyssa's boyfriend, Justin; Kayzia's boyfriend, Phil; both sets of their grandparents; Jerad and her.

They have just sat down on the blankets when a guy says "hi" to Jerad. Someone he knows from the assembly plant but hasn't kept up with. He hasn't kept up with most people from General Motors.

Down in front, on the track at the edge of the football field, Deri Wahlert is working commencement this year, giving hugs and helping kids and parents with questions, making sure things go smoothly. Last year, she organized a graduation party for her Parker Closet kids, a luncheon with balloons and gifts and school administrators and a motivational speaker. Unlike the Whiteakers, some of her Closet kids, she figured, wouldn't have parties at home. This year, she went smaller: a marble cake with strawberry frosting. Thirty-two of her forty graduating Closet kids came, along with Amy Venuti, the AP psychology teacher who helps Deri and introduced Kayzia to the Closet. A few of the kids couldn't come because they had to work.

At 7 p.m., the evening is perfect, sunny and in the low 70s with a light breeze, as "Pomp and Circumstance" begins and the Parker class of 2013 walks, double-file, to white folding chairs on the track. Alyssa and Kayzia are among the first, because they have been selected as part of the class leadership team, which walks up a ramp and takes seats on a small stage at the field's edge, festooned with Kelly green ribbons.

The theme of Parker's 2013 commencement is "Carpe Diem." The principal, Chris Laue, tells of the importance of controlling the present, because the future is unforeseen. He tells of students who, each in their own way, have seized the day, including a girl who worked two jobs to support herself and her family and came to school every day. He wasn't talking about Alyssa or Kayzia, though he could have been.

A math teacher, Joe Dye, who was Parker's head football coach and now has coached track and field, borrows the school team name for a riff on resilience. "You are Vikings," he tells the graduates. "When there are challenges, Vikings battle them. When there are storms, Vikings weather them. When there is no wind at your back, when there are storms, Vikings know how to row."

The Janesville school system itself, buffeted lately by revenue cuts and an enrollment dip, has been pulling a Viking-like maneuver. This year, the school superintendent has traveled to China to form relationships there through which the school system will invite Chinese students to attend Janesville schools—for a yearly fee of $24,000 each. A flicker of Janesville's old entrepreneurial spirit.

It is just before 8 p.m. when the principal instructs the graduates: "At this time, prepare to receive your diplomas." He calls the names of the class leadership team members, Alyssa and Kayzia among them, who take turns handing diploma cases to the principal as each Parker student crosses the stage. It is just after 8:30 when Alyssa and Kayzia are handed their own diplomas, a few minutes before fireworks are shot off along the Rock River's bank.

As the girls' names are called, the slanting evening sunlight throws a golden glow on the vacant assembly plant across the river. Neither their grandfathers, with their good pensions after thirty years, nor their dad, cast out after thirteen years, look over to notice.

Epilogue

O n the Wednesday before Halloween of 2015, the people of Janesville awoke to a front-page headline in the *Gazette*. "It's Over." Seven years after the last Tahoe came off the assembly line, four years after Janesville became the only assembly plant in the entire General Motors Corp. assigned to the limbo of "standby," the company and the United Auto Workers had just agreed to a new contract that would shift the empty behemoth to a different category: permanently closed. In recent years, as the city was splitting into its two Janesvilles, separated by political outlook and economic circumstance, opinions on what to do about the closed plant had become a bright dividing line. Business people and economic development leaders had been urging GM to designate the plant as officially closed, so that its site could be sold off and reused for a new purpose. On that morning, they celebrated. Many of its former workers, however, had been hoping all this time that the plant would someday reopen. For them, the morning's news, particularly as the U.S. auto industry was reaching record sales, was like a death knell.

Even a small city wrenched by the worst of what a mighty recession metes out does not have a single fate. With broad outside forces—the federal government and the state, industry and labor—unable to lift back up its once prosperous middle class, Janesville has been left to rely to a considerable extent on its own resources. Fortunately, those resources include more generosity and ingenuity—and less bitterness—than in many communities that have been economically injured. Still, over time, some people prosper. Some grieve. Some get by.

This way of understanding what has happened in Janesville fails to align with the common wisdom following the 2016 presidential election, which ended in one of the most astonishing upsets of U.S. history when Donald Trump defeated Hillary Clinton. The common wisdom is that an unorthodox Republican (uneasy in his relationship with Paul Ryan and many other leaders of the GOP) became an improbable symbol of hope for the white working class, the fallen middle class, and other people who had accumulated grievances against a government they felt did not understand their pain and resentment. Certainly, the economic catastrophe that befell Janesville is the kind of reversal of fortune that fueled such grievances. And Janesville today has aspects of the polarization that epitomized this election. Unexpectedly, Wisconsin went Republican in 2016 for the first time in thirty-two years. And yet, despite all that the city has been through, Janesville's Democratic identity held. Fifty-two percent of Rock County's voters supported Clinton. That was nearly 10 percentage points less than the margin for Obama four years earlier, but the difference was mostly that fewer people turned out to vote for the Democrat and not that so many more voted Republican.

So, seven and a half years after the Great Recession technically ended, how is Janesville faring? Surprisingly well, or not, depending on how you measure. By the most recent count, unemployment in Rock County has slid remarkably to just under 4 percent, the lowest level since the start of the century. As many people are working now as just before the Great Recession; distribution centers have arrived, Beloit plants such as ones for Frito-Lay and Hormel Foods have been hiring, and some people are working further away. Good news. But not everyone who now has a job is earning enough for the comfortable life they expected. Real wages in the county have fallen since the assembly plant shut down. And while factory jobs have been appearing lately in some parts of the United States, Rock

County is not one of those places. The county had about 9,500 manufacturing jobs in 2015—almost one fourth fewer than in 2008 and nearly 45 percent fewer than in 1990.

As for the results of Janesville's vigorous economic development efforts, SHINE Medical Technologies, the medical isotope start-up for which the city agreed to provide $9 million in financing, has passed tough regulatory hurdles and won a construction permit from the Nuclear Regulatory Commission. It is behind schedule. Having hoped to start manufacturing in 2015, it is aiming now for late 2019. Yet in a tangible step, SHINE has just moved its corporate headquarters from outside Madison to downtown Janesville, with still more financial help from the city—another nearly $400,000 in incentives to renovate office space two blocks from where Parker Pen's global headquarters once stood. SHINE expects to employ 150 people. For the moment, the big job news is that Dollar General has decided to put a distribution center on the south side of town. The city government is providing an $11.5 million package of economic incentives—a new Janesville record. The workforce that Dollar General says it will need—about 300 at first and perhaps 550 eventually—will bring the biggest hiring spurt in years. Most of the jobs will pay $15 or $16 per hour—far below the $28 wage GM'ers were being paid when the plant closed, but decent enough money in town these days. In a sign of a lingering hunger for work or better pay, when Dollar General held a recent job fair, three thousand people showed up.

The once mighty UAW Local 95 is a shadow of what it was, with a few hundred members and, with not many to pay dues, a perpetual effort to make money by renting out the union hall that Mike Vaughn's grandfather helped to plan. In 2014, Labor Fest shrank from its usual three days to just two. The next year, it was canceled altogether on short notice, so the sidewalks of Main and Milwaukee streets were empty when the parade should have been marching by. There was no official explanation, but many believed that the holiday weekend festival had become difficult to sustain with labor's role so diminished. In 2016, partly with money not spent the year before, Labor Fest managed to resume.

As for the assembly plant itself, it is unclear how long it will sit alongside the Rock River as an abandoned cathedral of industry. Early in 2016, Janesville's city manager sent General Motors a letter, asking for a $25 million "legacy fund" to benefit the community. The letter pointed out that a similar act of philanthropy by Parker Pen during World War II had led to the creation of the Janesville Foundation. So far, GM has not answered. Meanwhile, Wisconsin officials have told the company that it is responsible for cleaning up elevated levels of contaminants—not severe enough to harm public health—that have been found in sediment of the riverbed next to the plant. While this jockeying goes on, General Motors has begun trying to sell the 250-acre site. GM has identified as potential buyers four companies that specialize in the redevelopment of obsolete industrial property.

The trajectories of the politicians who helped shape Janesville in recent years have diverged. On October 29, 2015, the day after the *Gazette* headline announcing that the assembly plant would be permanently closed, Paul Ryan was sworn in as speaker of the U.S. House of Representatives. When his predecessor, John Boehner of Ohio, abruptly resigned, Paul insisted at first that he did not want the job. And even as pressure mounted on him from the party's elders, the people who know him in Janesville believed he wouldn't trade away the House Ways and Means chairmanship that he had attained just ten months before—his budget-wonk dream. But he did. Ryan remains the nation's fifty-fourth House speaker, second in line of succession to the presidency.

Scott Walker is still Wisconsin's governor, after a brief foray into the most recent Republican presidential primary. He was reelected in 2014, his promise to create 250,000 private sector jobs during his first term unfulfilled.

State senator Tim Cullen decided not to seek reelection that year, saying that Wisconsin politics had become too polarized and too unfocused on the issues he cares about most. In 2015, he published a book, *Ringside Seat: Wisconsin Politics, the 1970s to Scott Walker.* Tim devotes time to two local foundations that he created years ago and is considering a run for governor in 2018.

Sharon Kennedy has retired from Blackhawk Tech and moved to

Michigan. She has published a book on her research into technical colleges' retraining of unemployed Midwestern factory workers, *Classroom at the End of the 'Line,'* and is teaching doctoral students who want to become community college leaders.

Bob Borremans retired from the Job Center after successful treatment for tongue cancer. He is consulting to two workforce development projects that he is unsure will get off the ground, serves on the boards of two local nonprofits, and has just been recruited to join Wisconsin's Aging Advisory Council.

Mary Willmer continues to work at BMO Harris Bank. She has remarried and moved to a Madison suburb. She remains involved in Rock County 5.0 and other volunteer activities, including the YWCA's Circle of Women fundraiser.

Diane Hendricks remains chairman of ABC Supply and a major Republican donor. She gave $1.9 million to support Trump's candidacy and $8 million to a Wisconsin super PAC that paid for negative advertising against Clinton toward the end of the 2016 campaign. She was rewarded with a spot on Trump's inaugural committee.

In the Janesville school system, Ann Forbeck, who cofounded Project 16:49 for homeless teens, has changed jobs and is now a social worker at Craig High School. Early in 2014, Project 16:49 opened its housing for girls, called Robin House after Ann's partner, Robin Stuht, in Beloit. So far, it has sheltered thirty-seven girls, up to seven at a time, including one girl with learning disabilities whose parents had worked at General Motors and left her behind when they moved to GM jobs in Indiana. Planning and fundraising continue for the house for boys.

Deri Wahlert still teaches social studies at Parker High and runs the Parker Closet. She has married her longtime partner and become Deri Eastman. She is specializing now in teaching at-risk students and has begun to keep donated food in her classroom for times when her students don't have enough to eat at home. For the 2016–17 school year, the Closet has about two hundred students—as many as ever.

Among the former autoworkers, Barb Vaughn continues to work with adults with developmental disabilities. Since 2015, Barb, the former high school dropout, has been a member of the governing board for Rock County's Aging and Disability Resource Center. Mike changed jobs the summer of 2016 and is a human resources generalist for United Alloy. He is working days.

The late Kristi Beyer's husband, Bob, continues to do maintenance work at a state office building in Madison. Her son Josh is married, has a toddler son, and lives in Ohio, where he is working full-time as an auto mechanic and studying automotive technology at night at a local community college.

In the Whiteaker family, Jerad has found a job as a forklift driver at a Sub-Zero warehouse just south of Madison. Tammy is still processing auto deals but has switched to working for Tom Peck Ford, where she started out at $15 an hour, a dollar more than at her old employer. Their son, Noah, is a high school senior who works at Culver's, as his sisters did, and plans to enter the army when he graduates. As for the twins, Alyssa is a senior at the University of Wisconsin–Platteville, where she is majoring in engineering with a minor in business administration. She worked for a semester as a manufacturing engineering co-op student in Madison so will need a fifth year before she graduates. She is working two jobs, has scholarships, and takes out $17,000 a year in student loans. Kayzia finished her psychology degree at Platteville in three years, in part to save on tuition. At times, she worked three jobs. Over the summer, she married her longtime boyfriend. While working to start paying off student loans, she began studying this fall toward a master's degree in social work at St. Ambrose University in Davenport, Iowa. She hopes to work eventually with military veterans or people who are homeless.

In the Wopat family, Marv is enjoying retirement, dividing his time between home and Pensacola, Florida, with his lady friend and a rented condo on the beach. He still helps people into treatment and in recovery for addictions. His daughter-in-law, Darcy, continues to work for an appraisal company. For the first time, two of the Wopats' daughters were old enough to vote for president in 2016, and the entire family is now frustrated and confused that Clinton did not become the nation's first female president. As for Matt, he is in his seventh year of commuting to the Fort Wayne Assembly Plant, leaving home every Monday morning and returning late every Friday night. He remains a second-shift team leader, making about $30 an hour. He has eight and a half years until he will be eligible to retire with a GM pension.

Acknowledgments

This book is the story of a community. It also is the product of communities of people without whom the book simply would not exist.

My first thanks go to the people of Janesville who welcomed an inquisitive stranger into their midst. Many of their names appear in these pages but still deserve special mention. Stan Milam was the first person I met when I arrived in town; to the end, he was game to lend his considerable reporting skills to run down a stray fact or make sure I was current on goings-on. The staff of the *Janesville Gazette* was helpful and hospitable. I quickly learned to trust Jim Leute's knowledge of local business matters; Marcia Nelesen and Frank Schultz are terrific journalists and dinner companions. Paul Ryan made time for interviews in his Capitol Hill office; his staff, particularly Kevin Seifert, helped fill in details. Bob Borremans clued me in to the pleasures of a Wisconsin supper club. Deri Eastman's big heart made room for me. Ann Forbeck, a writer's spouse, made sure I knew she understood what working on a book was like. The staff of the Hedberg Public Library, with its excellent Janesville Room and local history database, and the Rock County Historical Society pointed me toward treasures in their files. Other generous local tour guides included Karen Schulte, superintendent of the Janesville Public Schools; Bob Spoden, the Rock County sheriff; Jenifer Keach, the former Rock County coroner; and Kristin Koeffler, director of the county's domestic violence intervention program. My greatest appreciation, of course, is reserved for the families at the heart of this story, the Whiteakers, Wopats, and Vaughns; I treasure your generosity, patience, and trust.

This book also would not have been possible without the support of *The Washington Post*, my professional home for the past three decades. *Post* editors allowed me more time to pursue this passion than any employee has reason to expect. Former executive editor Marcus Brauchli let me extend a one-year leave into two. And executive editor Marty Baron, who so deserves his reputation as the best leader of any American newspaper today, unexpectedly granted me another year to write. My thanks go, too, to managing editor Cameron Barr, national editor Scott Wilson, and my immediate editors, Laurie McGinley, Laura Helmuth, and Susan Levine, each of whom has been beyond understanding about my years-long juggling act.

While away from my newsroom, I was exceptionally fortunate to be harbored by universities and think tanks in stages throughout this project. I am especially indebted to Harvard University's Radcliffe Institute for Advanced Study, where Lizabeth Cohen, Judy Vichniac, and the late Lindy Hess were unfailingly supportive. Elsewhere on campus, economist Lawrence Katz and sociologists Robert Sampson and Bruce Western lent good ideas and encouragement early on. And across the country, David Grusky, director of Stanford University's Center on Poverty and Inequality, provided a first tutorial on recession effects.

I appreciated stints at the Woodrow Wilson International Center for Scholars. And I am grateful to Timothy Smeeding for inviting me to the University of Wisconsin–Madison's Institute for Research on Poverty, sharing his wisdom about public policy and income distribution, and helping in many other ways while I was there. Back in D.C., Kathy Courrier wangled office space for me at the American Institutes for Research and then extended my visit. At Georgetown University, I will always hold dear the crew at the Kalmanovitz Initiative for Labor and the Working Poor, with special thanks to labor historian Joseph McCartin, who took me in when I needed a space to draft the manuscript and was always available as a sounding board. Thanks, too, at Georgetown to Ed Montgomery, a dean who knows more than a little about hurting U.S. auto communities and, early on, welcomed me at what has become the McCourt School of Public Policy; Anthony Carnevale, who directs the Georgetown University Center on Education and the Workforce; and economist Harry Holzer, an expert in the low-wage labor market and a good lunch companion.

Along the way, I benefited from the intelligence, diligence, and friendship of wonderful research assistants. They are (in the order in which we worked together) Stephanie Garlock and Tara Merrigan at Harvard, Daniel Boger at the

Wilson Center, and Alyssa Russell at Georgetown. All went above and beyond—and are now on paths to make contributions of their own.

The survey of Rock County was possible because of the generosity of the Annie E. Casey Foundation. It would not have happened unless the University of Wisconsin Survey Center—and especially Nathan Jones—had been open to collaborating. Across campus, sociologist Gary Green was invaluable for his brainstorming, insights into Wisconsin's politics, economy, and public opinion, and indulgence of my myriad questions during the data analysis. Thanks, too, to Rutgers University's Carl Van Horn for big help on survey questions.

For the job-retraining analysis, I am grateful for the support of the Joyce Foundation, where Whitney Smith gave expert advice and was graceful when our findings didn't show the benefit for which she'd hoped from retraining around Janesville. Matías Scaglione was a determined and enthusiastic partner in prying unemployment and wage data from the Wisconsin Department of Workforce Development—and much more. At Blackhawk Technical College, Sharon Kennedy opened doors and became a friend. Mike Gagner provided institutional data and his expert knowledge of it. I am indebted for data analysis and stellar guidance to labor economists Laura Dresser at the University of Wisconsin's Center on Wisconsin Strategy and Kevin Hollenbeck of the W. E. Upjohn Institute for Employment Research.

This book has benefited greatly from friends and colleagues who, at various stages, critiqued what I was writing. John Russo and Sherry Linkon, the real experts on the working class, read an early draft and have supplied guidance and cheerleading. Laurie Hertzel, Tom Shroder, and Patsy Sims—gifted narrative editors all—made important contributions.

I am fortunate to have a passel of talented, seasoned author friends who have been indispensable for their advice and sympathetic ears. They include (in alphabetical order) Pamela Constable, Darcy Frey, Steve Luxenberg, Diane McWhorter, Amy Nutt, and Larry Tye. My friend Rochelle Sharpe, a topflight journalist, has listened to practically every twist and turn and offered steady support. So has Beth Glasser, who lent her proficiency at making charts to create the ones in the appendices. Renie Schapiro made Madison feel like a home and still does. They are a few among the many good friends on whom I have leaned.

Every writer should be as fortunate as I have been in editors. I cannot overstate my gratitude to Richard Todd, who began by helping me improve the manuscript and ended up providing a seemingly inexhaustible supply of wise counsel, wry humor, and steadfast encouragement. Paul Steiger, the founding editor-in-chief of ProPublica, took an interest in Janesville and what I was dis-covering about job retraining and made a home for an early article.

From the moment I called them out of the blue from Madison, Susan Rabiner and Sydelle Kramer have proven why they are known as the hardest-working and most tenacious literary agents in the business, coaching me on how to shape the story and hone the narrative, and standing alongside me to the end.

At Simon & Schuster, my editor Priscilla Painton's enthusiasm for "going to Janesville" was matched by her passion for pulling the best from the story. And I so appreciate the contributions of a great team, including the talented Megan Hogan who oversaw the final stages with remarkable efficiency, Fred Chase for deft copyediting, Cat Boyd for her work on publicity, and Elisa Rivlin for a thoughtful legal review. I owe special thanks to president and publisher Jonathan Karp, who believed that Janesville was an essential story for our times.

Most of all, I treasure the devotion and patience of my family throughout this book's gestation: my parents, Cynthia and Robert Goldstein, still my best role models for civic leadership and an enduring thirst to learn; my caring aunt Judy Berg; and David, Laura, Miranda, and Olivia. I love you all.

Appendix 1:

Explanation and Results of the Survey of Rock County

A book can contain only so many characters, and I was eager to go beyond their anecdotal experiences to explore more broadly the economic circumstances and attitudes of people who live nearby. For that reason, I undertook a survey of Rock County, the part of southern Wisconsin for which Janesville is the county seat.

The survey was conducted in collaboration with the University of Wisconsin Survey Center. Several social scientists contributed ideas. Gary Green, professor of community and environmental sociology at the University of Wisconsin–Madison, was most centrally involved in developing the questionnaire with me and analyzing the findings.

We conducted the survey during the late winter and spring of 2013, almost five years after the Great Recession officially ended and more than four years after the Janesville Assembly Plant shut down. The survey instrument was a questionnaire sent by mail to a demographically representative, randomly selected sample of 2,000 residential addresses in Rock County. The overall response rate was high: 59.7 percent.

Most of the questions were intended for everyone who received the survey, while some questions focused on the experiences only of people who had lost a job since the recession began or lived in a household with someone who had been laid off. Some of the latter questions were patterned after items in the few national surveys that have measured how people were affected by losing a job during the recession, so that we could compare the results.

Overall, the findings documented the breadth of job losses in Rock County. More than one in three who responded had lost work or lived with someone who had. They showed the diminished wages and economic pessimism that lingered years after the recession itself. The findings also displayed a decline in labor union membership and sharply divided attitudes toward unions. And they attested to the financial and emotional pain—half had trouble paying for food, nearly two thirds reported strain in family relationships—that losing work caused people in this part of southern Wisconsin.

Here are some of the main findings:

Three quarters of the people who responded said that the U.S. economy in 2013 was still in a recession.

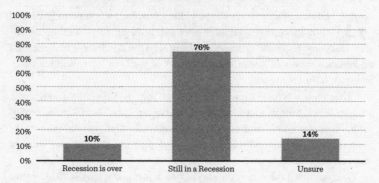

Do you think that the country's economic recession is over, or do you think the economy is still in a recession?

Overall, slightly more than half said their financial situation was worse than before the recession. And here is a glimpse into the two Janesvilles: People who had lost a job or lived with someone who had were far more likely to say that they were in worse shape than those without a layoff in their household.

Thinking about your household's current financial shape, are you in better shape or worse shape now than you were five years ago?

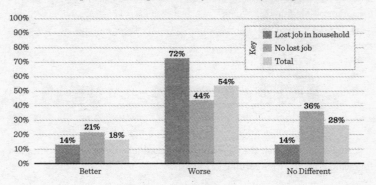

Over one third lost a job for economic reasons or lived with someone who had.

At any time during the past five years, have you or has anyone in your household lost a job because of business closing, lack of work, or elimination of positions?

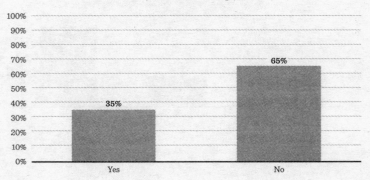

A drop in housing values was widespread.

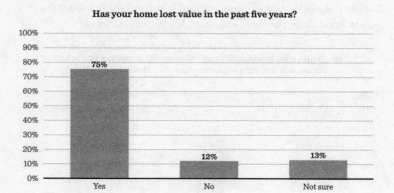

Has your home lost value in the past five years?

And more than half the people who switched jobs for any reason—not just following a layoff—were earning less money.

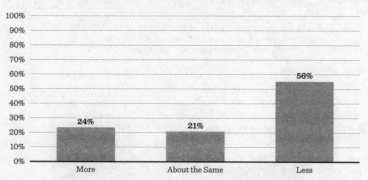

If you have taken a new job in the past five years, are you earning more, about the same, or less than in the job you had before?

Pessimism about the economic future was widespread.

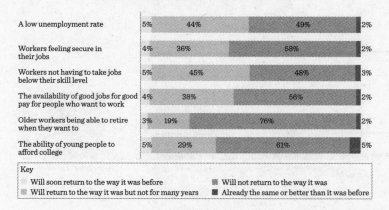

**Thinking about Rock County, please indicate
what you think will happen in the following areas.**

Overall, about one third said the government should be doing more to help people who had lost a job. Among those with a layoff at home, more wanted greater government help, but still not a majority.

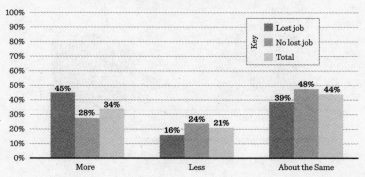

How much should government help people out of work?

About half had been in a labor union, but most of those were former members.

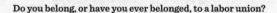

Do you belong, or have you ever belonged, to a labor union?

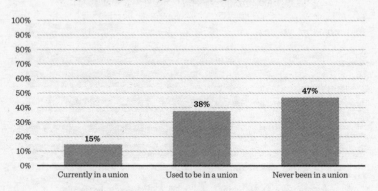

Opinions about unions were closely divided.

**Overall, do you think labor unions mostly help or
mostly hurt the U.S. economy in general?**

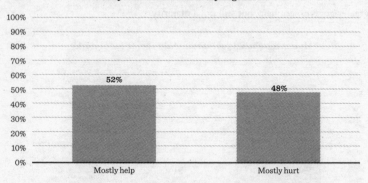

Many of those who lost a job, or lived with someone who did, took steps to try to cope financially. Here is the percentage who said they did each of the following:

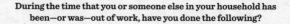

During the time that you or someone else in your household has been—or was—out of work, have you done the following?

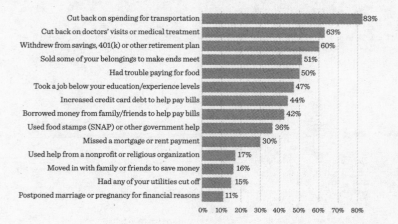

For many, being out of work, or living with someone who had been laid off, had emotional and interpersonal effects.

During the time that you or someone else in your household was out of work, did you notice these things happening to you?

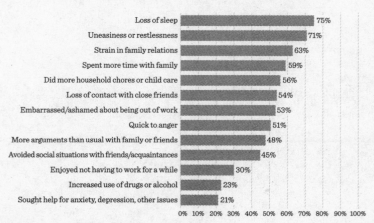

Appendix 2:

Explanation and Results of the Job-Retraining Analysis

E ven among people who disagree over almost everything else about the economy, the common wisdom is that workers who lose a job, without much likelihood of finding another in the same field, should go back to school to train for a different one. The federal government spends hundreds of millions of dollars each year for the retraining of such dislocated workers. However, research into whether this policy is useful is not extensive.

So, I decided to take a look at whether retraining was helping laid-off workers in southern Wisconsin during the first years after thousands of people lost jobs at GM's Janesville Assembly Plant and nearby.

The idea was to explore how factory-workers-turned-students fared in school and then at finding work. I focused on Blackhawk Technical College, a public, two-year school in Janesville that specializes in vocational programs. Just after the Great Recession, so many dislocated workers arrived at Blackhawk that the small school had the biggest enrollment surge in the Wisconsin Technical College System's century-long history.

The findings were surprising: Job retraining, it turned out, was not a path to more work or better pay in and around Janesville, at least not during this time when jobs were so scarce.

The analysis was patterned after a few older studies elsewhere, which had used similar methods to identify laid-off people who went back to school, examine how much they were working and earning afterward, and then compare them with dislocated workers who had not retrained. I collaborated with Kevin Hollenbeck, a senior economist at the W. E. Upjohn Institute for Employment Research in Kalamazoo, Michigan, and labor economist Laura Dresser, associate director of the Center on Wisconsin Strategy at the University of Wisconsin–Madison.

Several kinds of data went into the analysis. The Wisconsin Department of Workforce Development provided two data sets. To identify people who had lost a job, we used the department's records of unemployment claims from summer of 2008 to fall of 2011 for residents of Rock County and neighboring Green County—the parts of southern Wisconsin where most of Blackhawk's students lived. We also used the department's unemployment insurance wage records, a type of information that all states collect—and that all employers are required to report—of each employee's wages. The wage records for Rock and Green counties showed quarterly earnings—that is, what the employee was paid over three months. Blackhawk Tech also provided records of all students who enrolled in its credit programs between summer of 2008, when a large number of jobs began to disappear from Janesville, and summer of 2010. These records contained basic demographics, such as age, sex, race, and ethnicity, as well as academic information, including whether the students needed remedial work, what they studied, and whether they graduated.

The records did not contain names. To link the data sets, Matías Scaglione, a labor economist in the Department of Workforce Development's Office of Economic Advisers at the time, used Social Security numbers, and then removed the numbers so that our data were anonymous. We identified Blackhawk's dislocated workers mainly by finding the students who had received unemployment benefits at some point during the period we examined. We also relied on Blackhawk's new-student questionnaire, which asked about employment status. Students who answered that they were unemployed or dislocated were included in the analysis. We made certain that no one was counted more than once.

For the analysis, we created a "before" (pre-recession and pre-layoff) period from 2007 and an "after" period of the final year for which we had information—through mid-2011. In this way, we could look at how many dislocated workers were working for pay before and after they retrained. We could not identify whether people had full-time or part-time jobs, so we divided them into "steady workers" with earnings each quarter of the year; "intermittent workers," who had at least one quarter with earnings and one with no earnings; and people with no reported earnings. The data contained earnings only from Wisconsin, not from any other state, but other information suggested that relatively few people in the area had jobs elsewhere. We compared their earnings before and after retraining. Then we compared their work and income with those of others who got unemployment benefits in Rock and Green counties—and with those of other students on campus at the time.

Overall, we found that one third of the laid-off workers who went to Blackhawk completed their program of study within the expected time, a little more than other students on campus with them.

Here are some of our other main findings:

Laid-off workers who went back to school were less likely to have a job after they retrained than those who had not gone to school.

Who Had a Job?

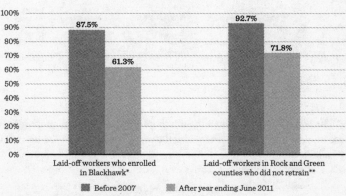

* 1,740 people, Summer 2008 to Summer 2010

** 30,777 people who collected unemployment benefits, 2007 to Summer 2011

Retraining did not translate into greater success at finding a job. Among those who went back to school, the proportion who ended up with steady work was smaller than among the laid-off workers who did not. Worse still, more of those who retrained were not earning any money at all.

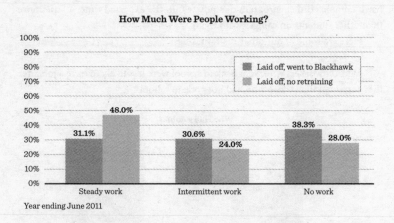

How Much Were People Working?

Year ending June 2011

The laid-off workers who went to school were earning less afterward than those who did not. Before the recession, the two groups' incomes had been about the same.

Did Retraining Pay Off?			
	Laid-off workers who enrolled at Blackhawk	Laid-off workers who did not retrain	Other Blackhawk students
Average quarterly earnings, 2007	$7,294	$7,239	$1,636
Average quarterly earnings, year ending June 2011	$3,348	$6,210	$2,788
Average change	–$1,935	–$534	$985
Average percent change	–35.5%	–7.5%	47%

The dislocated workers who found steady employment after retraining had started out with relatively high earnings before the recession. Afterward, their wages were a little higher than those of others who retrained—but much lower than those of steady workers who had not gone to school.

Even for people who found steady work, did retraining pay off?		
	Laid-off workers who enrolled at Blackhawk	Laid-off workers who did not retrain
Before Average quarterly earnings, 2007	$9,675	$8,390
After Average quarterly earnings, year ending June 2011	$4,821	$7,637
Average change	−$2,269	−$279
Average percent change	−28.5%	−3.5%

The laid-off workers who graduated from their Blackhawk programs were earning more money than those who did not finish. But because they'd had higher incomes beforehand, these completers ended up with a bigger drop in pay than the noncompleters.

Did finishing school help?		
	Completers	Non-Completers
Before Average quarterly earnings, 2007	$10,174	$5,833
After Average quarterly earnings, year ending June 2011	$4,275	$2,926
Average change	−$4,974	−$1,105
Average percent change	−49.0%	−25.9%

One group of dislocated workers received extra help through a special Career and Technical Education (CATE) program. Based on the predictions of Blackhawk staff and local business leaders about which fields of study would be the most promising paths to available jobs, some of these students were channeled into associate's degree programs in information technology and clinical laboratory technicians work. And others were enrolled in shorter certificate programs in certified nursing assistance, welding, and business. We looked at whether all the laid-off students who selected these promising programs fared better at finding work than those studying in other programs. They did not.

Did promising fields help?		
	Before	After
Promising	81%	62%
All Other Programs	89%	61%

Percent working for pay

Many of the laid-off workers who went to Blackhawk were older than typical college students. The older the students, the bigger the drop in their earnings from before the recession to after.

Which age group was hurt the most?					
	18–24	25–34	35–44	45–54	55+
Average quarterly earnings, 2007	$1,173	$4,316	$11,761	$11,747	$10,760
Average quarterly earnings, year ending June 2011	$2,519	$3,178	$4,128	$4,540	$3,387
Average change	$1,307	−$883	−$5,755	−$6,175	−$6,944
Average percent change	98.9%	−23%	−53%	−59%	−67%

Notes and Sources

T his book was researched primarily through interviews with the people in the story and others in Janesville, plus firsthand observation of some of the events described. The names are real. For events for which I was not present, descriptions of people's actions, statements, thoughts, and feelings are based on their memories and those of others who were there, as best they could relate them, buttressed in spots by written accounts and other sources.

A list of books and articles for further reading follows the notes.

Source Notes to Chapters

Prologue

2   *As the twentieth century opened:* Mike DuPré, *Century of Stories: A 100 Year Reflection of Janesville and Surrounding Communities (Janesville Gazette,* 2000), 17.

4   *Its innards:* Rick Romell, "Janesville GM Plant's Remains Go to Auction," *Milwaukee Journal Sentinel,* May 20, 2009.

Part One: 2008

Chapter 1: A Ringing Phone

9   *A dozen days ago, he issued a plan:* Rep. Paul Ryan, H.R. 6110 (110th): "A Roadmap for America's Future Act of 2008," introduced May 21, 2008.

10 *Where he was elected junior class president:* Prom '87, George S. Parker High School yearbook, 1987.

Chapter 2: The Carp Swimming on Main Street

16 *The first step is a protocol:* Jeffrey Salzman, Melissa Mack, Sandra Harvey, and Wally Abrazaldo, "Rapid Response Under the Workforce Investment Act: An Evaluation of Management, Services and Financing," U.S. Department of Labor, Employment and Training Administration, Office of Policy Development and Research, August 2012.

17 *By Wednesday, June 11:* Ann Marie Ames, "Rock River Flooding Could Threaten City's Downtown," *Janesville Gazette,* June 11, 2008.

17 *Volunteers and jail inmates fill:* Gina Duwe, "Rock River Rising," *Janesville Gazette,* June 15, 2008; The *Gazette* staff, "The Janesville Gazette's Top Stories of 2008," *Janesville Gazette,* Dec. 31, 2008.

17 *At the measuring station closest to Janesville:* Robert R. Holmes, Jr., Todd A. Koenig, and Krista A. Karstensen, "Flooding in the United States Midwest, 2008," U.S. Geological Survey professional paper no. 1775, U.S. Department of the Interior.

18 *Near the street's northern end:* Catherine W. Idzerda, "Carp Gathering to Mate in United Way Parking Lot," *Janesville Gazette,* June 21, 2008.

Chapter 3: Craig

19 *Within a decade, the company was the largest:* Carol Lohry Cartwright, Scott Shaffer, and Randal Waller, *City on the Rock River: Chapters in Janesville's History* (Janesville Historic Commission, 1998), 61.

19 *In 1909, the earliest automobile manufacturer in town:* DuPré, *Century of Stories,* 2.

20 *This was when Craig executed his ingenious maneuver:* Ibid., 32.

20 *GM turned out its first tractors:* Ibid.

20 *"In my entire experience I have never seen":* Letter from W. C. Durant, Rock County Historical Society, Feb. 26, 1919.

21 *Nevertheless, when Chicago's "Century of Progress" World's Fair opened:* Austin Weber, "GM Centennial: Show and Tell," *Assembly Magazine,* July 1, 2008.

21 *"Of all the brilliant spectacles"*: "The Making of a Motor Car," Souvenir Guide Book to the Chevrolet-Fisher Manufacturing Exhibit, General Motors Building, A Century of Progress International Exposition, Chicago, 1933.

21 *On December 5, 1933, the Janesville plant reopened:* "Janesville a Plant City for 40 of GM's 50 Years," *Janesville Daily Gazette*, March 6, 1958, 24.

21 *In Flint, Michigan, the strike lasted forty-four days:* Neil Leighton, "Remembering the Flint Sit-Down Strike oral histories," Labor History Project, University of Michigan–Flint; "The Sit Down Strike of 1936–37," United Auto Workers, Local 659.

21 *In Janesville, by contrast, the sit-down lasted:* DuPré, *Century of Stories*, 58–59; Gillian King, "The Cogs Fight the Machine: The Great GM Sit-down Strike," *Wisconsin Hometown Stories*, Wisconsin Public Television; Oral history of strike, Janesville Room, Hedberg Public Library.

22 *At 9 p.m. that night:* "Shifting Gears: Janesville after GM" (GM history timeline), http://gazetteextra.com/gmtimeline/, *Janesville Gazette*, Dec. 15, 2013.

22 *And for the next five weeks:* Irving Bernstein, Chapter 5, "Americans in Depression and War," *Bicentennial History of the American Worker*, U.S. Department of Labor, 1976.

22 *"Keep 'em firing" was their motto:* Letter from War Department to the Men and Women of the Janesville Plant, Dec. 11, 1943.

22 *In 1967, General Motors bestowed:* Mike Hockett, "Today in Manufacturing History, GM Celebrates 100 Millionth Car Made in US," *Industrial Maintenance and Plant Operation Magazine*, April 2016.

23 *In 1986, General Motors transferred:* DuPré, *Century of Stories*, 197.

Chapter 4: A Retirement Party

26 *As he approached the south entrance:* Gina Duwe, "Obama Visit Came Off 'Without a Hitch,' " *Janesville Gazette*, Feb. 14, 2008.

26 *Marv is a Democrat:* Stacy Vogel, "GM Workers Caught Up in Obamamania," *Janesville Gazette*, Feb. 14, 2008.

27 *Just the day before, General Motors had announced:* Nick Bunkley, "GM Posts Record Loss of $38.7 Billion for 2007," *New York Times*, Feb. 12, 2008.

27 *"Prosperity hasn't always come easily":* Transcript, Barack Obama, remarks in Janesville, Wisconsin: "Keeping America's Promise," Feb. 13, 2008, American Presidency Project.

Chapter 6: To the Renaissance Center

37   *The posse includes the two men:* Press release, Office of Wisconsin Governor
     Jim Doyle, June 23, 2008.

38   *Finally, the governor sums up the case:* Press release on meeting with General
     Motors, Office of Wisconsin Governor Jim Doyle, Sept. 12, 2008.

Chapter 7: Mom, What Are You Going to Do?

40   *Four Mondays ago, she watched as Lehman Brothers:* Heather Landy and
     Neil Irwin, "Massive Shifts on Wall St.," *Washington Post*, Sept. 15, 2008.

40   *By Friday, the Dow Jones Industrial Average:* Vikas Bajaj, "Whiplash Ends a
     Roller Coaster Week," *New York Times*, Oct. 11, 2008.

40   *On Saturday, at a meeting in Washington:* Adam Plowright, "World Powers
     Look to Solve Crisis with Collective Efforts," Agence France-Presse, Oct. 11,
     2008; "Financial Stress, Downturns and Recoveries," World Economic Out-
     look, International Monetary Fund, October 2008.

Chapter 8: "When One Door of Happiness Closes, Another Opens"

43   *He felt a take-charge satisfaction:* Rock County Community Resource Guide,
     Southwest Wisconsin Workforce Development Board.

44   *So on page A8 of the guide:* Ibid.

45   *So, late on the afternoon of December 10:* Meeting minutes, Southwest Wis-
     consin Workforce Development Board, Dec. 10, 2008.

Chapter 9: The Parker Closet

48   *Deri kept in her mind and spirit:* Adapted from Loren Eiseley, "The Star
     Thrower," in *The Unexpected Universe* (New York: Harcourt, Brace & World,
     1969).

Part Two: 2009

Chapter 10: Rock County 5.0

54   *The Beloit Corporation began as an iron foundry:* "From Beloit Iron Works
     to Beloit Corporation," Beloit Historical Society.

55   *A fall from industrial glory:* Superfund Program profile: Beloit Corp., U.S.
     Environmental Protection Agency.

55   *One of nine daughters:* As told to Amy Zipkin, "The Business Must Go On,"
     "The Boss" column, *New York Times*, Nov. 21, 2009.

55 *In 2006,* Inc. *magazine named Ken:* Leigh Buchanan, "Create Jobs, Eliminate Waste, Preserve Value," *Inc.,* Dec. 1, 2006.

55 *They built a fortune:* "The Forbes 400," *Forbes,* Sept. 20, 2007.

55 *The sixty-six-year-old roofer fell:* James P. Leute, "Billionaire Hendricks Dies After Fall," *Janesville Gazette,* Dec. 21, 2007; Krista Brown, "Reports Detail Fatal Fall," *Beloit Daily News,* Dec. 22, 1007.

Chapter 11: The Fourth Last Day

59 *He helped to prepare an application:* TAA Program Benefits and Services under the 2002 Benefits, Employment and Training Administration, U.S. Department of Labor.

60 *Two days before Christmas, the day that GM and Lear stopped production:* Reports of mass layoffs and plant closings, Wisconsin Department of Workforce Development, 2008 and 2009.

61 *No, it wasn't only GM and Lear:* Unemployment rate, Local Area Unemployment Statistics, Janesville-Beloit, Wisconsin, metropolitan statistical area, Bureau of Labor Statistics, U.S. Department of Labor.

Chapter 12: Bidding War

62 *In his booming voice:* Proceedings of the Rock County Board of Supervisors, June 11, 2009.

63 *It is the first time the supervisors have met:* Transcript, press conference by Fritz Henderson, president and chief executive of General Motors, June 1, 2009; Statement from General Motors, "GM Pulls Ahead U.S. Plant Closures; Reaffirms Intent to Build Future Small Car in U.S," June 1, 2009; Statement on General Motors and Chrysler, Office of Wisconsin Governor Jim Doyle, June 1, 2009.

63 *Rick Wagoner is not around:* GM Statement on Officer and Board Announcements, March 30, 2009; Peter Whoriskey, "GM Chief to Resign at White House's Behest," *Washington Post,* March 30, 2009.

64 *By the time Marv finishes and the votes are tallied:* Thomas Content, "State Bid $195 Million to Land GM Auto Line," *Milwaukee Journal Sentinel,* July 8, 2009.

Chapter 13: Sonic Speed

65 *The package adds up to $195 million:* Thomas Content, "State Bid $195 Million to Land GM Auto Line," *Milwaukee Journal Sentinel,* July 8, 2009.

66 *At 7 a.m. on June 26:* "Michigan Gets Small Car GM Plant; Doyle 'Deeply Disappointed,' " Madison.com/Associated Press, June 26, 2009.

66 *The company had merely used Wisconsin's offer:* Statement regarding GM decision, Office of Wisconsin Governor Jim Doyle, June 26, 2009.

66 *Home to the U.S. auto industry and a 15 percent unemployment rate:* Regional and state employment and unemployment monthly news release, Bureau of Labor Statistics, U.S. Department of Labor, July 17, 2009.

66 *Of more than a dozen factories that General Motors intends to close:* Statement from General Motors, "GM Pulls Ahead U.S. Plant Closures; Reaffirms Intent to Build Future Small Car in U.S.," June 1, 2009.

66 *"We would do everything possible":* Katherine Yung, "Creative Tax Plan Key to GM Triumph," *Detroit Free Press*, June 28, 2009.

67 *Everything possible included setting up a war room:* Ibid.

67 *Originally, it was to have been manufactured in China:* Statement from General Motors, "GM Announces Plan to Build Small Car in U.S.," May 29, 2009; Steven Mufson, "After Many Tuneups, A Historic Overhaul; A Global Industry Is Transformed in Race to Reinvent U.S. Automakers," *Washington Post*, May 31, 2009.

68 *Then, while the Orion assembly plant was shut down:* Tom Krisher and Dee-Ann Durbin, "Tiny Chevrolet Sonic Helps Detroit Shake Off Rust," Associated Press, Jan. 11, 2013.

68 *While waiting for the plant to reopen:* Chrissie Thompson, "Goal: All 2nd-Tier Pay at Orion," *Detroit Free Press*, Oct. 16, 2010.

68 *Scores of Orion workers picketed:* Kevin Krolicki, "GM Workers Protest Low-Wage Small-Car Plant," Reuters, Oct. 16, 2010.

68 *Another filed a complaint with the National Labor Relations Board:* Brent Snavely, "Laid-off GM Worker Files Complaint Against UAW," *Detroit Free Press*, Oct. 27, 2010.

69 *The NLRB dismissed:* Denial Letter, Case 07-CB-017085, International Union UAW and its local 5960 (General Motors LLC), National Labor Relations Board, Feb. 2, 2011.

69 *So at 6 a.m. on August 1, 2011:* David Barkholz, "GM begins Chevrolet Sonic Production at Suburban Detroit Plant," *Autoweek*, Aug. 1, 2011.

69 *Paul Ryan issues a joint statement:* Press release, "Reaction of Wisconsin Congressional Delegation Members to GM's Decision on the Location of its New Auto Line," June 26, 2009.

69 *Paul believes it is pointless to wait around:* James P. Leute, "So What Does 'Product-ready' Mean?," *Janesville Gazette*, June 27, 2009.

Chapter 14: What Does a Union Man Do?

71 *It goes back to the lead mines:* Carol March McLernon, *Lead-mining Towns of Southwest Wisconsin* (Charleston, S.C.: Acadia Publishing, 2008), 20, 28.

Chapter 15: Blackhawk

77 *Blackhawk Tech is named for a famed Sauk Native American warrior:* Michael J. Goc, "Origins," *Wisconsin Hometown Stories*, Wisconsin Public Television.

77 *In 1911, they became the first system:* Video, "100 Years of Making Futures," Wisconsin Technical College System, 2011.

Chapter 16: Ahead of the Class

82 ONE ROSE CAN BE MY GARDEN: Based on quote by Leo Buscaglia.

Chapter 17: A Plan and Distress Signals

86 *The next day, on October 29, stories announcing:* James P. Leute, "Public-Private Economic Development Initiative Is a First for Rock County," *Janesville Gazette,* Oct. 29, 2009; Hillary Gavan, "Rock County 5.0 Launched with Cooperative Effort," *Beloit Daily News,* Oct. 29, 2009.

86 *"It's a great idea":* Editorial, "Joining Forces for the Future," *Beloit Daily News,* Oct. 30, 2009.

86 *But now, signs of people's financial collapse:* Records, U.S. Bankruptcy Court, Western District of Wisconsin.

86 *Some aren't finding an escape plan:* Foreclosure records, Office of the Treasurer, Rock County, Wisconsin.

87 *Or because, with unemployment in Rock County:* Local Area Unemployment Statistics, Janesville-Beloit, Wisconsin, metropolitan statistical area, Bureau of Labor Statistics, U.S. Department of Labor, Sept., Oct., Nov., Dec. 2009.

Chapter 18: The Holiday Food Drive

90 *Last year, for the food drive of 2008:* Stacy Vogel, "Hundreds Turn Out for Food Drive," *Janesville Gazette,* Dec. 20, 2008.

90 *The food drive, he told a* Gazette *reporter:* Stacy Vogel, "UAW/GM Food Drive Is About Helping, Not Mourning," *Janesville Gazette,* Dec. 21, 2008.

90 *This year, ECHO is giving away:* Records from ECHO.

91 *So when Marv is quoted again in the* Gazette: Rochelle B. Birkelo, "Food Drive Comes to End," *Janesville Gazette,* Nov. 21, 2009.

Part Three: 2010

Chapter 19: Last Days of Parker Pen

96 *George Safford Parker was born:* Obituary, "George W. Parker Dies in Chicago. Famous Pen Manufacturer Stricken at 73. Was Most Widely Known Janesville Citizen," *Janesville Gazette,* July 19, 1937.

96 *He was a lanky nineteen-year-old when he arrived in Janesville:* Len Provisor and Geoffrey S. Parker, "History of the Parker Pen Co., Part III, Janesville," *The Pennant* (publication of the Pen Collectors of America), Winter 2006, 5.

96 *Run by two brothers of that name:* Ibid., 4.

96 *When he graduated, he was pleased to be hired:* Ibid., 7.

96 *So when Richard Valentine asked Parker:* Ibid.

97 *The John Holland Co. pens tended to leak:* Len Provisor and Geoffrey S. Parker, "George S. Parker, Part IV, The Early Years, Return to Janesville c. 1884," *The Pennant,* Spring 2007, 7.

97 *"It will always be possible to make a better pen":* Website for the Heritage House/Parker Pen Museum, London, U.K.

97 *The following year, he secured his first pen patent:* Len Provisor and Geoffrey S. Parker, "George S. Parker, Part IV, The Early Years, Return to Janesville c. 1884," *The Pennant,* Spring 2007, 8, 10.

97 *Camp Cheerio on the grounds:* Len Provisor and Geoffrey S. Parker, "The Early Years, George S. Parker, Part V, George Parker Travels the World," *The Pennant,* Summer 2007, 12.

97 *A housing development, Parkwood:* "Parkwood Addition to Janesville Wisconsin was laid out and platted by the Parker Pen Company by Geo S. Parker, president and W. F Palmer, Secretary on June 17, 1916 upon the following described parcel of land," Janesville city document, Rock County Historical Society archives.

97 *He instructed the personnel in charge:* Philip Hull, *Memories of Forty-nine Years with the Parker Pen Company,* 2001, 17.

97 *When, after his death, the Arrow Park factory opened:* Len Provisor and Geoffrey S. Parker, "The Early Years, George S. Parker, Part V, George Parker Travels the World," *The Pennant,* Summer 2007, 12.

97 *During World War I:* "Parker Pen Writing Instruments: A Chronology," Parker Pen Co.

98 *In May of 1945, the treaty of German surrender:* Timeline on website for the Heritage House/Parker Pen museum.

98 *At the 1964 World's Fair in New York:* brochure: "Peace Through Understanding Through Writing, the Parker International Pen Friend Program," New York World's Fair, 1964.

98 *Two years later, the year that Linda was hired:* Mike DuPré, obituary for George S. Parker II, *Janesville Gazette*, Nov. 7, 2004.

98 *In 1986, he sold the company:* Ibid.

98 *Then, in 1993, the Gillette Corporation bought out:* "Company News: Gillette Completes Acquisition of Parker Pen," *New York Times*, May 8, 1993.

98 *Six years later, the pen business was bought out again:* Jim Leute, "Writing Is on Wall at Sanford," *Janesville Gazette*, Aug. 19, 2009.

98 *So the final 153 workers:* David Schuyler, "Newell to Close Janesville Plant," *Milwaukee Business Journal*, Aug. 18, 2009.

99 *Late every Friday afternoon:* Lyrics to song, "May the Good Lord Bless and Keep You," Meredith Wilson, 1950.

100 *And there were elaborate Parker Pen floats:* Timeline on website for the Heritage House/Parker Pen museum.

101 *Then, on this August day, a corporate public relations manager:* Jim Leute, "Writing Is on Wall at Sanford," *Janesville Gazette*, Aug. 19, 2009.

Chapter 20: Becoming a Gypsy

105 *By this winter, hundreds of Janesville GM'ers:* Jim Leute, "It's Been a Year. How Are We Doing? Where Are We going?," based on General Motors figures, *Janesville Gazette*, Dec. 20, 2009.

105 *So far, fifty-five have transferred:* Jim Leute, "More Janesville GM Workers Get Jobs in Fort Wayne," *Janesville Gazette*, Jan. 28, 2010.

Chapter 21: Family Is More Important than GM

110 *They understand that their father:* "On This Date . . . ," *Beloit Daily News*, Dec. 22, 2011.

112 *Wisconsin allows teenagers as young as fourteen:* Guide to Wisconsin's Child Labor Laws, Wisconsin Department of Workforce Development.

113 *In March, 2006, a few months after the major cutbacks:* Statement, Rick Wagoner, chairman and CEO, General Motors, March 22, 2006.

113 *Nearly 35,000 took the offer:* "More than 900 Take Buyout at Janesville GM Plant," Associated Press, June 27, 2006.

113 *In February, 2008, the day before Obama arrived:* Bill Vlasic, "G.M. Offers Buyouts to 74,000," *New York Times*, Feb. 13, 2008.

114 *In May, the company will give:* Jim Leute, "Former GMers Face Transfer
     Deadlines," *Janesville Gazette*, May 11, 2010.

Chapter 22: Honor Cords

115 *The 268 students, to be handed their diplomas:* Ted Sullivan, "Blackhawk Tech
     Graduates Include Displaced Workers," *Janesville Gazette*, May 16, 2010.

116 *When she takes center stage at the Dream Center:* Video excerpts, Blackhawk
     Technical College graduation, May 15, 2010.

117 *Not long ago, she drove up to Madison:* Sharon Kennedy, testimony before
     Wisconsin Assembly Committee on Workforce Development, Feb. 12,
     2009.

119 *"Kristi Beyer Turns Hardship into Victories":* Newsletter, CORD, Southwest
     Wisconsin Workforce Development Board, June 1, 2010.

120 *Kristi will be profiled again:* Neil Johnson, "Hard Work Turns into Second
     Careers," *Janesville Gazette*, June 15, 2010.

Chapter 23: The Day the White House Comes to Town

121 *So it did not escape his notice:* "Remarks by the President on the American
     Automotive Industry," The White House, March 30, 2009.

122 *As a sign of the changes at GM:* Ibid.

122 *The White House had pushed him out:* Bree Fowler, "Wagoner Leaving GM
     with Compensation Worth $23M," Associated Press Financial Wire, March
     30, 2009.

122 *The specific form of this caring attention:* "Remarks by the President on the
     American Automotive Industry," The White House, March 30, 2009.

123 *By the time that the executive director of the White House:* Annual Report of
     the White House Council on Automotive Communities and Workers, The
     White House, May 2010, 25.

123 *More than one hundred people are waiting there:* Attendee List, Southwest
     Wisconsin Workforce Development Board, June 11, 2010.

124 *This morning he is in Washington:* Paul Ryan on the *Scott Hennen Show*,
     YouTube, June 11, 2010.

124 *Montgomery is seated at a small skirted table:* Photograph with story by
     Bob Shaper, "White House Official to Janesville: 'Don't Wait,' " WKOW 27,
     June 11, 2010.

124 *This is a listening tour, so Montgomery listens:* Materials for presentations
     during Montgomery visit, Southwest Wisconsin Workforce Development
     Board, June 11, 2010.

124 *A version of this very idea:* "Bridge to Work," Fact Sheet and Overview, American Jobs Act, The White House, September 8, 2011.

125 *During his wrap-up, Bob begins:* Text of remarks by Bob Borremans during Montgomery visit, June 11, 2010.

125 *On the day before he is in town:* News release, "Georgetown Appoints Edward Montgomery Dean of Public Policy," Georgetown University, June 10, 2010.

125 *Three days after Montgomery's visit, President Obama says:* "Statement by President Obama on Dr. Ed Montgomery," The White House, June 14, 2010.

125 *Another year will go by:* News release, "Secretary of Labor Hilda L. Solis announces new director for administration's Office of Recovery for Auto Communities and Workers," U.S. Department of Labor, July 6, 2011.

126 *The federal Government Accountability Office will say:* "Treasury's Exit from GM and Chrysler Highlights Competing Goals, and Results of Support to Auto Communities Are Unclear," U.S. Government Accountability Office, May, 2011, 32–41.

Chapter 24: Labor Fest 2010

128 *It comes late in the afternoon:* Catherine W. Idzerda, "Weekend's LaborFest Has Something for All," *Janesville Gazette*, Sept. 3, 2010.

128 *This "Jobs Now!" rally:* Krissah Thompson and Spencer Hsu, "Tens of Thousands Attend Progressive 'One Nation Working Together' Rally in Washington," *Washington Post*, Oct. 2, 2010.

128 *The Midwest Territory of the Machinists Union:* News release, "Janesville, Wisconsin, Laborfest 'JOBS NOW' rally draws statewide attention," International Association of Machinists, Sept. 1, 2010.

128 *When it is his turn, Milwaukee's mayor, Tom Barrett:* Video posted on Facebook, "Barrett for Wisconsin, Janesville Jobs NOW! Rally," Sept. 5, 2010.

129 *The president's shirtsleeves are rolled up:* Video, "Presidential Remarks on the Economy, Laborfest in Milwaukee," C-SPAN, Sept. 6, 2010.

129 *"The cornerstones of middle-class security":* "Remarks by the President at Laborfest in Milwaukee, Wisconsin," The White House, Sept. 6, 2010.

129 *Since this is an election year, political candidates:* Candidates at the Janesville LaborFest Parade 2010, YouTube, Sept. 6, 2010, https://www.youtube.com/watch?v=Xy03uejOAH4.

129 *His campaign issues a statement:* News release, "Walker: Obama Admits $1 Trillion Stimulus Bill Failure, Continues to Call for End to Boondoggle Train," Scott Walker campaign, Sept. 6, 2010.

130 *He tells a* Gazette *reporter today:* Ann Marie Ames, "Rock County Close to Home for Walker," *Janesville Gazette*, Sept. 7, 2010.

130 *He is wearing a white polo shirt and khakis:* Candidates at the Janesville LaborFest Parade 2010, YouTube, Sept. 6, 2010, https://www.youtube.com /watch?v=Xy03uejOAH4.

Chapter 25: Project 16:49

132 *The school system has more than four hundred:* Homeless data, School District of Janesville Demographic and Student Membership Report, 2016, 8.

133 *Kayla Brown, Cory Winters, and Brandon Lucian are Rock County teenagers:* R. E. Burgos, director, *Sixteen Forty-Nine*, 2010.

134 *Finally, one woman in the audience:* Ann Marie Ames, "Movie Showing Highlights Plight of Janesville's Homeless Kids," *Janesville Gazette*, Sept. 18, 2010.

Part Four: 2011

Chapter 28: The Ambassador of Optimism

143 *This morning, the* Gazette *has published a guest column:* Mary Willmer, guest op-ed, "All Can Play Roles in Moving County Forward," *Janesville Gazette*, Jan. 4. 2011.

144 *The ball was at Monona Terrace:* Jason Stein, "First the Dance, Then the Work," *Milwaukee Journal Sentinel*, January 4, 2011.

144 *Mary had fun watching the state's new first couple:* Ibid.

144 *It was a splendid ceremony:* Video, "Inauguration of Governor Scott Walker," C-SPAN, Jan. 3, 2011.

144 *When the time came for the gubernatorial inaugural address:* Ibid; transcript of Governor Scott Walker's inaugural address, Jan. 3, 2011.

145 *Directly behind him, seated in a chair:* Video, "Inauguration of Governor Scott Walker," C-SPAN, Jan. 3, 2011.

145 *As Mary and Diane watched Walker:* Video of coverage of Scott Walker inaugural ball and protests, News 3 WISC-TV, Madison, Wisconsin, Jan. 3, 2011.

145 *The name was meant to draw attention:* Scott Foval, "Progressives Vow to Hold GOP Lawmakers Accountable," *Wisconsin Gazette*, Jan. 13. 2011.

145 *To show up Walker:* Post, Rock the Pantry Facebook page, Jan. 3, 2011.

146 *He is setting off this morning on a tour:* Photo gallery, "Wisconsin Open for

Business: Governor Scott Walker Unveils the New 'Wisconsin Welcomes You,'" Office of Governor Scott Walker, Jan. 18, 2011.

147 *Before that, his day's schedule begins:* "Wisconsin's Governor Comes After Illinois Business," WREX, Rockford, Illinois, Jan. 18, 2011.

147 *When he strides through ABC's sliding glass doors:* Brad Lichtenstein, 371 Productions, *As Goes Janesville* (Independent Lens, PBS), 2012.

147 *Diane stands close and looks him straight in the eye:* Ibid.

147 *"Oh yeah," Walker replies:* Ibid.

147 *"You're right on target":* Ibid.

147 *The leaders of Rock County 5.0 have decided:* James P. Leute, "Walker Backs Interstate Expansion; Touts State's Business Opportunities," *Janesville Gazette*, Jan. 19, 2011.

147 *"You've made our job a whole lot easier":* Ibid.

148 *From Beloit, Walker goes on today:* Ibid.

148 *Mary types on her BlackBerry:* Mary Willmer, post on Facebook, Jan. 18, 2011.

Chapter 30: This Is What Democracy Looks Like

151 *The next day, a Saturday, will bring out:* Joe Tarr, "Wisconsin Capitol Protests Massive for Second Consecutive Saturday," *Isthmus*, Feb. 26, 2011.

152 *In 1911, a dozen years before the assembly plant began turning out Chevrolets:* Ken Germanson, "Milestones in Wisconsin Labor History," Wisconsin Labor History Society.

152 *In 1932 . . . Wisconsin was the first state to establish:* Ibid.

152 *It was in Madison in 1932, too:* AFSCME History Timeline, website of the American Federation of State, County and Municipal Employees.

153 *And in 1959, Wisconsin became the first state:* Primer on Wisconsin Labor History, Wisconsin Labor History Society.

154 *The grad students have designated the rotunda:* "Uprising at the Capitol: Week 2," *Isthmus*, Feb. 25, 2011; Ben Jones, "As Protest in Madison Goes into Its Second Week, Many Camp Out in State Capitol," *Marshfield News*, Feb. 25, 2011; John Tarleton, "Inside the Wisconsin Uprising: Teaching Assistants Help Spark a New Movement in Labor," *Clarion*, newspaper of the Professional Staff Congress, City University of New York, April 2011.

154 *Ian's has been deluged with phone calls:* Steven Greenhouse, "Delivering Moral Support in a Steady Stream of Pizzas," *New York Times*, Feb. 25, 2011.

154 *At 1 a.m., the Republicans in the Wisconsin Assembly:* Jason Stein, Steve Schultze, and Bill Glauber, "After 61-Hour Debate, Assembly Approves

Budget-Repair Bill in Early-Morning Vote," *Milwaukee Journal Sentinel*, Feb. 25, 2011.

155 *The vote lasted ten seconds:* Mary Spicuzza and Clay Barbour, "Budget Bill: Lawmakers, Already Frustrated, Brace for Impending Battle over Budget," *Wisconsin State Journal*, Feb. 26, 2011.

155 *The groggy GOP legislators then filed out:* Photographs, "Anger in Orange," *Wall Street Journal*, Feb. 25, 2011.

155 *The capitol police are now saying:* Clay Barbour and Mary Spicuzza, "Camp-out: Huge Protest Inside the Capitol Will Break Sunday for Cleanup, Police Say," *Wisconsin State Journal*, Feb. 26, 2011.

156 *They are staying at a La Quinta Inn in Gurnee, Illinois:* Tim Cullen, *Ringside Seat: Wisconsin's Politics, the 1970s to Scott Walker* (Mineral Point, WI: Little Creek Press, 2015), 191–92.

156 *On the next Sunday, Day No. 13:* Ibid., 193–94.

156 *On March 6, Day No. 20:* Ibid., 195–97.

157 *On Day No. 23, the Senate Republicans employ a parliamentary trick:* Mary Spicuzza and Clay Barbour, "Budget Repair Bill Passes Senate, Thursday Vote Set in Assembly," *Wisconsin State Journal*, March 10, 2011.

157 *And, on Day No. 25 of what is:* Jason Stein, Don Walker, and Patrick Marley, "Walker Signs Budget Bill, Legal Challenges Mount," *Milwaukee Journal Sentinel*, March 11, 2011.

158 *The day that the Democratic senators left for Illinois, Paul gave an interview:* Video from interview with Paul Ryan, *Morning Joe*, MSNBC, Feb. 17, 2011.

158 *The timing of this swelling resentment against public workers:* Frank J. Schultz, "Janesville School Board Votes to Cut Teachers," *Janesville Gazette*, April 7, 2011.

Chapter 31: On Janesville Time

163 *The imported workers came from:* Figures from human resources department, Fort Wayne Assembly Plant, General Motors.

Chapter 32: Pride and Fear

167 *He will tell a* Gazette *reporter:* Neil Johnson, "Blackhawk Technical College Graduates Pack Commencement," *Janesville Gazette*, May 14, 2011.

167 *Last year, when he started at Blackhawk:* TAA Statistics, Trade Activity Participant Report Data for FY 2010 for United States Total, Employment and Training Administration, U.S. Department of Labor; Trade Adjustment Assistance for Workers, Report to the Committee on Finance of the Senate and

Committee on Ways and Means of the House of Representatives, Employment and Training Administration, U.S. Department of Labor, December 2010.

167 *Nationally, nearly half the trainees:* FY2010 TAA Statistics; National TAA Program Statistics, Trade Activity Participant Report Data for FY 2011 for United States Total, Employment and Training Administration, U.S. Department of Labor.

Chapter 33: Labor Fest 2011

172 *The* Wisconsin State Journal *in Madison:* Clay Barbour, "Two Sides on One Mission; Dale Schultz, Tim Cullen Are Out to Show State Residents That Politicians Can Work Together, Bipartisan Barnstorming," *Wisconsin State Journal,* July 29, 2011; Frank J. Schultz, "Democratic, Republican Senators Work to Forge Relationship," *Janesville Gazette,* Aug. 19, 2011.

173 *The anger arrives in the form of a young man:* "Paul Ryan Labor Day Confrontation," YouTube, https://www.youtube.com/watch?v=YD0lh1Zj81I.

174 *Stoner does not mention that unemployment:* Unemployment rate and employment, Local Area Unemployment Statistics, Janesville-Beloit, Wisconsin, metropolitan statistical area, Bureau of Labor Statistics, U.S. Department of Labor.

176 *General Motors announces that the new contract:* Nick Bunkley, "G.M. Contract Approved, with Bonus for Workers," *New York Times,* Sept. 29, 2011.

177 *If Spring Hill is going to reopen, a newspaper article reasons:* Jim Leute, "Auto Recovery Would Bode Well for Janesville GM Facility," *Janesville Gazette,* Sept. 22, 2011.

Chapter 34: Discovering the Closet

182 *Since she started at Parker, she has been helping:* Figures from Parker High School.

Part Five: 2012

Chapter 37: SHINE

194 *But now, with the government encouraging them both:* Fact sheet, "NNSA Works to Establish a Reliable Supply of Mo-99 Produced Without Highly Enriched Uranium," National Nuclear Security Administration, U.S. Department of Energy, Oct. 29, 2014.

194   *Two years ago, a Madison business journal:* "2010's 40 Executives Under 40,"
       Business Madison, March 2010.

195   *Finally, not quite three weeks ago, Piefer announced:* News release, "SHINE
       Medical Technologies to Site New Manufacturing Plant in Janesville,"
       SHINE Medical Technologies, Inc., Jan. 24, 2012.

196   *A Janesville Gazette story, saying that SHINE had chosen Janesville:* James
       P. Leute, "Janesville Working with Medical Isotope Maker on Incentive
       Agreement," *Janesville Gazette*, Jan. 25, 2012.

197   *As part of its economic incentives to get SHINE:* Vic Grassman, Economic
       Development Director, Economic Development Department Memoran-
       dum to Janesville City Council, "Action on a Proposed Resolution Authoriz-
       ing the City Manager to Enter into a T.I.F. Agreement with SHINE Medical
       Technologies," Feb. 13, 2012.

197   *This future business park and a smaller site in Beloit:* Jim Leute, "Business
       Park Deemed Shovel-Ready," *Janesville Gazette*, July 25, 2012.

198   *But to put in perspective just how big:* 2012 annual budget, City of Janesville, 1.

198   *And this question of incentives:* Ibid., 13.

198   *For tonight's meeting, the city's economic development director has prepared:*
       Vic Grassman, Economic Development Director, Economic Development
       Department Memorandum to Janesville City Council, Action on a Pro-
       posed Resolution Authorizing the City Manager to Enter into a T.I.F. Agree-
       ment with SHINE Medical Technologies, Feb. 13, 2012.

199   *Still . . . as ten citizens take turns speaking:* Video, meeting of the Janesville
       City Council, Feb. 13, 2012.

199   *Nearly an hour into the meeting, Piefer moves:* Ibid.

200   *One speech is by Russ Steeber:* Ibid.

200   *He already was a Council member four years ago when a man in town was ar-
       rested:* Ted Sullivan, "Prison Time Ordered in Contract Killing Case," *Janes-
       ville Gazette*, April 19, 2009.

200   *The core of Yuri's soliloquy:* Video, meeting of the Janesville City Council,
       Feb. 13, 2012.

201   *By the time the Council members vote:* Ibid.

Chapter 39: A Charity Gap

205   *This is no longer the same Janesville in which Joseph A. Craig:* Obituary, "J.
       A. Craig Dies at 91, Leader in Many Fields," *Janesville Gazette*, Dec. 31,
       1958.

205   *Where is today's George S. Parker:* Obituary, "George W. Parker Dies in

Chicago. Famous Pen Manufacturer Stricken at 73. Was Most Widely Known Janesville Citizen," *Janesville Gazette*, July 19, 1937.

Chapter 41: Recall

211 *The recall fight is venomous, backed by twice as much campaign spending:* "Recall Race for Governor Cost $81 Million," Wisconsin Democracy Campaign, July 25, 2012.

212 *Last winter, a manufacturing association that supports him:* Frank J. Schultz, "Billboard Near Shuttered GM Plant Causes Stir," *Janesville Gazette*, Jan. 12, 2012.

213 *For decades, Rock County's Republicans:* "Recall Race for Governor Cost $81 Million," Wisconsin Democracy Campaign, July 25, 2012.

215 *As of a few weeks ago, Walker and Barrett were within one percentage point:* News releases, Marquette University Law School Poll, May 2, 2012, May 30, 2012.

216 *Rock County 5.0 is nonpartisan:* Tom Kertscher, "A Closer Look at Recall Donations," *Milwaukee Journal Sentinel*, May 17, 2012.

217 *On the stage of the Waukesha County Expo Center:* Governor Scott Walker victory speech, C-SPAN, June 5, 2012.

217 *Statewide, the governor may have won:* Statewide percentage results, 2012 Recall Election for Governor, Wisconsin Elections Commission.

217 *Rock is one of just twelve of Wisconsin's seventy-two counties:* County by county report, 2012 Recall Election for Governor, Wisconsin Elections Commission.

Chapter 43: The Candidate

220 *At 9:28 a.m., swelling, majestic music:* Mitt Romney VP announcement with Rep. Paul Ryan, C-SPAN, Aug. 11, 2012.

221 *"Paul Ryan works in Washington, but his beliefs":* Ibid.

221 *Paul was, in fact, home as recently as yesterday afternoon:* Rachel Streitfeld, "Ryan's Clandestine Journey to Romney's Ticket Went from 'Surreal to Real,' " CNN, Aug. 12, 2012.

223 *Less than a month ago, he quit the caucus:* Patrick Marley, "Cullen Returns to Caucus Fold; Senator Had Quit over Assignments," *Milwaukee Journal Sentinel*, July 29, 2012.

223 *After fourteen years as a congressman:* Mitt Romney VP announcement with Rep. Paul Ryan, C-SPAN, Aug. 11, 2012.

224 *It is an emotional scene:* Romney-Ryan bus tour rally in Waukesha, Wisconsin, Waukesha County Expo Center, C-SPAN, Aug. 12, 2012.

224 *Two weeks from now:* Paul Ryan send-off rally in Janesville, Wisconsin, JATV, Aug. 27, 2012.

Chapter 44: Labor Fest 2012

227 *Three years ago, the first Labor Fest:* Gina R. Heine, "Janesville Labor Fest Run by the Community, for the Community," *Janesville Gazette*, Sept. 4, 2009.

Chapter 45: Pill Bottles

231 *When he steps in, she is wearing:* Report of preliminary death investigation, Kristi Beyer, Rock County Coroner.

231 *She is on her left side:* Ibid. Ambulance report in records of Rock County Coroner on death of Kristi Beyer.

231 *That day, a sixty-year-old worker:* Sara Jerving, "Suicide Crisis Centers Report Increase in Calls. Is the Economy to Blame?," *Janesville Gazette*, Feb. 21, 2010.

231 *Since then, suicides in Rock County:* Data from Rock County Coroner.

231 *Across the United States, the suicide rate:* Aaron Reeves, David Stuckler, Martin McKee, David Gunnell, Shu-Sen Chang, and Sanjay Basu, "Increase in State Suicide Rates in the USA During Economic Recession," *The Lancet*, Nov. 6, 2012.

232 *A medical team tries to revive:* Mercy Hospital report in records of Rock County Coroner on death of Kristi Beyer.

232 *At 6:32 a.m., the team:* Ibid.

232 *The coroner's autopsy finds that Kristi died:* Autopsy report on death of Kristi Beyer, Rock County Coroner.

Chapter 46: Circle of Women

236 *Four weekends ago, the signs on all of M&I's banks:* Jim Leute, "Bank Makes Name Change Official," *Janesville Gazette*, Oct. 6, 2012.

236 *Last year, BMO took over M&I:* Paul Gores, "M&I Absorbed into Harris Bank; Former 'Crown Jewel' of Banks Had Been Slumping for Years," *Milwaukee Journal Sentinel*, July 6, 2011.

236 *When BMO took it over, M&I still owed:* John McCrank, "Canada's BMO Buying U.S. M&I Bank for $4.1 Billion," Reuters, Dec. 17, 2010.

Chapter 47: First Vote

240 *He is heading to Cleveland:* "On the Trail: November 6, 2012," "Political Ticker" blog, CNN.

240 *Still, Wisconsin is one of nine swing states:* Chris Cilizza, "The 9 Swing States of 2012," *Washington Post,* April 16, 2012; Attendance figure from a White House pool report, Nov. 5, 2012.

241 *Six out of ten have voted:* County by county report, 2012 Fall General Election, Wisconsin Elections Commission.

241 *Even in his own ward:* Precinct details, 2012 General Election, Rock County Clerk.

Chapter 48: HealthNet

246 *Except that BadgerCare Plus Core opened in July 2009:* Thomas DeLeire et al., "Evaluation of Wisconsin's BadgerCare Plus Core Plan for Adults Without Dependent Children," Report #1, University of Wisconsin Population Health Institute, 1.

Chapter 49: Out of a Job Again

252 *It's down to one, even though nearly half of the 1,400 kids:* "Percent of Children Living in Low-Income Household," School District of Janesville Demographic and Student Membership Report, 2016, 7.

253 *The school system has exceeded its target:* Blog post by Karen Schulte, superintendent of schools, "What's Right in the School District of Janesville: Delivering Bags of Hope," Dec. 27, 2012.

Part Six: 2013

Chapter 50: Two Janesvilles

261 *Premier banking is offered to BMO Harris customers:* Marketing material, BMO Harris bank.

262 *Leaving aside GM's 4.8 million square feet:* Jim Leute, "Marketing Tightening for Industrial Real Estate," *Janesville Gazette,* Jan. 28, 2013.

262 *Toward the end of January, Mary attends:* Posted on Facebook, Mary Willmer, Jan. 24, 2013.

262 *"Couldn't be happier":* Posted on Facebook, Mary Willmer, May 19, 2013.

263 *This year, 41,000 families in Rock County:* FoodShare Wisconsin caseload data, Wisconsin Department of Health, 2007, 2013.

Chapter 51: Night Drive

269 *Now its population of 78,000:* Indiana City/Town Census Counts, 1900 to
      2010, and Population Estimates for Indiana's Incorporated Places, U.S. Cen-
      sus Bureau data compiled by STATS Indiana, Indiana Business Research
      Center, Indiana University.

269 *Four in ten of the people:* Gary, Indiana, QuickFacts, U.S. Census Bureau.

269 *The Dan Ryan is easy to cruise along tonight:* Carl Sandburg, "Chicago."

Chapter 52: The Ebb and Flow of Work

272 *The 1.1-million-square-foot processing plant:* Jim Leute, "Janesville Plant Is
      Key for Seneca Foods, Company Says," *Janesville Gazette*, June 20, 2013.

Chapter 54: Glass More than Half Full

278 *Nearly two thousand new jobs are not trivial:* Employment statistics, Local
      Area Unemployment Statistics, Janesville-Beloit, Wisconsin, metropolitan
      statistical area, Bureau of Labor Statistics, U.S. Department of Labor, June
      2008 and April 2013.

Chapter 55: Graduation Weekend

286 *The school choir sings:* Garth Brooks, "The River."

286 *The stadium has stood since 1931:* Carol Lohry Cartwright, Scott Shaffer,
      and Randal Waller, *City on the Rock River: Chapters in Janesville's History*
      (Janesville Historic Commission, 1998), 186.

287 *All very nice as far as it goes:* Average cost, Wisconsin resident, 2013–14 cost
      chart, University of Wisconsin–Platteville.

Epilogue

291 *"It's Over":* Elliot Hughes and Neil Johnson, " 'It's over': Janesville GM Plant
      Identified in UAW Contract as Closing," *Janesville Gazette*, Oct. 28, 2015.

292 *Fifty-two percent of Rock County's voters:* 2016 Fall General Election Results,
      Wisconsin Elections Commission.

292 *That was nearly 10 percentage points:* Ibid.

292 *By the most recent count, unemployment in Rock County:* Local Area Un-
      employment Statistics, Janesville-Beloit, Wisconsin, metropolitan statistical
      area, Bureau of Labor Statistics, U.S. Department of Labor, October 2016.

292 *As many people are working now:* State and Area Employment Statistics,
      Janesville-Beloit, Wisconsin, metropolitan statistical area, Bureau of Labor
      Statistics, U.S. Department of Labor, October 2016.

292 *Beloit plants such as ones for Frito-Lay:* Job listings and job fair announcements, Rock County Job Center.

292 *And while factory jobs have been appearing:* Ted Mellnik and Chris Alcantara, "Manufacturing Jobs Are Returning to Some Places. But These Jobs Are Different," *Washington Post*, Dec. 14, 2016, based on analysis of Bureau of Labor Statistics quarterly employment and wages data.

293 *As for the results of Janesville's vigorous economic development efforts:* Memorandum and order (authorizing issuance of construction permit) in the matter of SHINE Medical Technologies Inc., U.S. Nuclear Regulatory Commission, Feb. 25, 2016.

293 *Yet in a tangible step, SHINE:* Neil Johnson, "SHINE Confirms Move to Downtown Janesville," *Janesville Gazette*, Sept. 21, 2016.

293 *In a sign of a lingering hunger for work:* Catherine W. Idzerda, "Thousands Attend Dollar General Job Fair," *Janesville Gazette*, Sept. 18, 2016.

293 *The next year, it was canceled:* Dave Delozier, "Labor Fest Likely Victim of GM Closure in Janesville," WISC-TV News 3, Sept. 7, 2015.

294 *Early in 2016, Janesville's city manager:* Elliot Hughes, "Janesville Asks GM to Create $25 Million 'Legacy Fund,'" *Janesville Gazette*, March 8, 2016.

294 *GM has identified as potential buyers:* Elliot Hughes, "Four 'Qualified Parties' Identified for GM Property Sale," *Janesville Gazette*, June 20, 2016.

294 *He was reelected in 2014:* James B. Nelson, "Economists Say Time Has Run Out on Top Campaign Promise," *PolitiFact*, Sept. 18, 2014.

295 *She gave $1.9 million:* Federal Election Commission data; Reform America Fund, contributors 2016 cycle, OpenSecrets.org

Further Reading

Beyond the sources mentioned above, here are some other books that helped shape my thinking, as well as articles and reports that helped ground me in recent research into recession effects.

Books

Bartlett, Donald L., and James B. Steele. *The Betrayal of the American Dream.* New York: PublicAffairs, 2012.

Ehrenreich, Barbara. *Nickel and Dimed: On (Not) Getting By in America.* New York: Henry Holt, 2001.

Garson, Barbara. *Down the Up Escalator: American Lives in the Great Recession.* New York: Doubleday, 2013.

Greenhouse, Steven. *The Big Squeeze: Tough Times for the American Worker.* New York: Alfred A. Knopf, 2008.

Grunwald, Michael. *The New New Deal: The Hidden Story of Change in the Obama Era.* New York: Simon & Schuster, 2012.

Grusky, David B., Bruce Western, and Christopher Wimer, eds. *The Great Recession.* New York: Russell Sage Foundation, 2011.

Kennedy, Sharon A. *Classroom at the End of the "Line": Assembly Line Workers at Midwest Community and Technical Colleges.* North Charleston, SC: CreateSpace Independent Publishing Platform, 2013.

Linkon, Sherry Lee, and John Russo. *Steeltown U.S.A.: Work and Memory in Youngstown.* Lawrence: University Press of Kansas, 2002.

Milkman, Ruth. *Farewell to the Factory: Auto Workers in the Late Twentieth Century.* Berkeley: University of California Press, 1997.

Osterman, Paul, and Beth Shulman. *Good Jobs America: Making Work Better for Everyone.* New York: Russell Sage Foundation, 2011.

Packer, George. *The Unwinding: An Inner History of the New America.* New York: Farrar, Straus & Giroux, 2013.

Peck, Don. *Pinched: How the Great Recession Has Narrowed Our Futures and What We Can Do About It.* New York: Crown, 2011.

Putnam, Robert D. *Our Kids: The American Dream in Crisis.* New York: Simon & Schuster, 2015.

Smith, Hedrick. *Who Stole the American Dream?* New York: Random House, 2012.

Van Horn, Carl E. *Working Scared (or Not at All): The Lost Decade, Great Recession, and Restoring the Shattered American Dream.* Lanham, MD: Rowman & Littlefield, 2013.

Articles and Reports

Brooks, Clem, and Jeff Manza. "Broken Public? Americans' Responses to the Great Recession." *American Sociological Review* 78 (2013): 727–48.

Burgard, Sarah A., Jennie E. Brand, and James S. House. "Causation and Selection in the Relationship of Job Loss to Health in the United States." Working paper, University of Michigan, August 2005.

Davis, Steven J., and Till von Wachter. "Recessions and the Costs of Job Loss." Brookings paper on Economic Activity, Brookings Institution, Fall 2011.

Farber, Henry S. "Job Loss in the Great Recession: Historical Perspective from the Displaced Worker Survey, 1984–2010." Working paper 17040, National Bureau of Economic Research, May 2011.

Goldsmith, Arthur, and Timothy Diette. "Exploring the Line Between Unemployment and Mental Health Outcomes." *The SES Indicator*, e-newsletter of the Public Interest Directorate Office of Socioeconomic Status, American Psychological Association, April 2012.

Heinrich, Carolyn, and Harry J. Holzer. "Improving Education and Employment for Disadvantaged Young Men: Proven and Promising Strategies." *Annals of the American Academy of Political and Social Science* 635 (May 2011): 163–91.

Heinrich, Carolyn J., Peter R. Mueser, and Kenneth R. Troske. "Workforce Investment Act Non-Experimental Net Impact Evaluation." IMPAC International, LLC, December 2008.

Heinrich, Carolyn J., Peter R. Mueser, Kenneth R. Troske, Kyung-Seong Jeon, and Daver C. Kahvecioglu. "A Nonexperimental Evaluation of WIA Programs." In *The Workforce Investment Act: Implementation Experiences and Evaluation Findings*, edited by Douglas J. Besharov and Phoebe H. Cottingham (Kalamazoo, MI: W. E. Upjohn Institute for Employment Research, 2011), 371–404.

Hollenbeck, Kevin, Daniel Schroeder, Christopher T. King, and Wei-Jang Huang. "Net Impact Estimates for Services Provided Through the Workforce Investment Act." Paper for Office of Policy and Research, Employment and Training Administration, U.S. Department of Labor, 2005.

Hurd, Michael D., and Susann Rohwedder. "Effects of the Financial Crisis and Great Recession on American Households." Working Paper 16407, National Bureau of Economic Research, September 2010.

Jacobson, Louis S. "Strengthening One-Stop Career Centers: Helping More Unemployed Workers Find Jobs and Build Skills." Discussion paper, The Hamilton Project, Brookings Institution, April 2009.

Jacobson, Louis, Lauren Focarazzo, Morgan Sacchetti, and Jacob Benus. "Improving America's Workforce Through Enhanced Collaboration Between the Public Workforce System and Community Colleges." IMPAQ International LLC, submitted to U.S. Department of Labor, Dec. 10, 2010.

Jacobson, Louis, Robert J. LaLonde, and Daniel Sullivan. "The Impact of Community College Retraining on Older Displaced Workers: Should We Teach Old Dogs New Tricks?" *Industrial & Labor Relations Review* 58, no. 3 (2005): 398–415.

Kalil, Arial, Kathleen M. Ziol-Guest, and Jodie Levin Epstein. "Non-standard

Work and Marital Instability: Evidence from the National Longitudinal Survey of Youth." *Journal of Marriage and Family* 72 (2010): 1289–1300.

Kalil, Arial, and Patrick Wightman. "Parental Job Loss and Children's Educational Attainment in Black and White Middle Class Families." *Social Science Quarterly* 92 (2011): 56–77.

Katz, Lawrence. "Long-Term Unemployment in the Great Recession." Testimony for the Joint Economic Committee, U.S. Congress, April 29, 2010.

Kessler, Ronald C., Blake Turner, and James S. House. "Effects of Unemployment on Health in a Community Survey: Main, Modifying and Mediating Effects." *Journal of Social Issues* 44, no. 4 (1988): 69–85.

Kochhar, Rakesh. "A Recovery No Better than the Recession: Median Household Income, 2007 to 2011." Pew Social & Demographic Trends, Pew Research Center, June 2014.

Stanley, Marcus, Lawrence Katz, and Alan Krueger. "Developing Skills: What We Know About the Impact of American Employment and Training Programs on Employment, Earnings and Educational Outcomes." G8 Economic Summit, 1998.

Stucker, David, Sanjay Basu, and David McDaid. "Depression Amidst Depression: Mental Health Effects of the Ongoing Recession," background paper to *Impact of Economic Crises on Mental Health*, World Health Organization Regional Office for Europe, 2010.

Sullivan, Daniel, and Till von Wachter. "Job Displacement and Mortality: An Analysis Using Administrative Data." *The Quarterly Journal of Economics* 3 (2009): 1265–1306.

Van Horn, Carl, and Cliff Zukin. "Shattered American Dream: Unemployed Workers Lose Ground, Hope, and Faith in Their Futures." Part of series of Work Trends surveys, John J. Heldrich Center for Workforce Development, Bloustein School of Planning and Public Policy, Rutgers University, December 2010.

Van Horn, Carl, Cliff Zukin, and Allison Kopicki. "Left Behind: The Long-term Unemployed Struggle in an Improving Economy." Part of series of Work Trends surveys, John J. Heldrich Center for Workforce Development, Bloustein School of Planning and Public Policy, Rutgers University, September 2014.

Von Wachter, Till, Jae Song, and Joyce Manchester. "Long-Term Earnings Losses Due to Mass Layoffs in the 1982 Recession: An Analysis of U.S. Administrative Data from 1974 to 2004." Working paper, Columbia University, April 2009.

Zukin, Cliff, Carl Van Horn, and Charley Stone. "Out of Work and Losing Hope: The Misery and Bleak Expectations of American Workers." Part of series of Work Trends surveys, John J. Heldrich Center for Workforce Development, Bloustein School of Planning and Public Policy, Rutgers University, September 2011.

Index

About the Author

AMY GOLDSTEIN has been a staff writer for thirty years at *The Washington Post*, where much of her work has focused on social policy. Among her awards, she shared the 2002 Pulitzer Prize for national reporting. She has been a fellow at Harvard University at the Nieman Foundation for Journalism and the Radcliffe Institute for Advanced Study. *Janesville: An American Story* is her first book. She lives in Washington, D.C.